PORTAL OF LIGHT

An Extensive Study of Wicca and Magick
from an African American Prospective

Jeanine DeOya

Spiritual She Inspirationals Publishing

AUTHOR'S PAGE

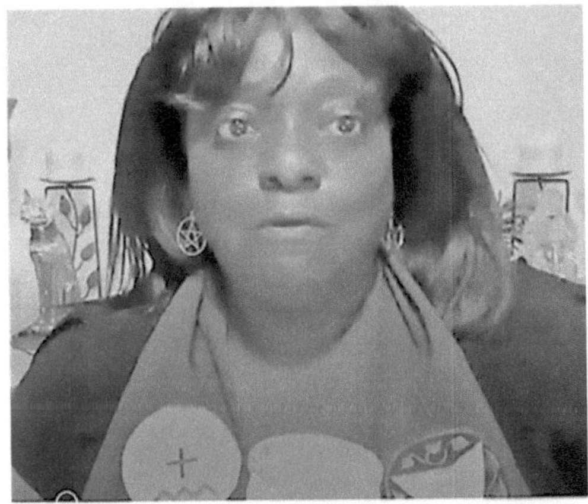

Rev. Ser Jeanine DeOya, HP

Priestess Jeanine DeOya has been writing professionally for over 25 years in the Pagan community. She has done telephonic prison ministry for 14 years, assisting those who have heard the call of the *Goddess and Lord*. Jeanine has had an online presence for African American Wiccans both with websites and as an administrator of forum since 1999. She has been practicing Wicca for 30 years, participated in many Pagan circles, and became a Priestess of the Correllian tradition in April of 2001. Because of her work in the African American Pagan community, she was bestowed the title of *Knight of the Order of the Round Table* from the Correllian tradition, and participates as a *Notable* in their Witan Advisory Council. Jeanine also works with a group called the *Order of the Ebony Knights,* which comes together to discuss how Pagans of color can effect positive change towards equality. She now teaches and mentors an online written course for African Americans and Pagans of color. Jeanine is a mother, grandmother and spiritual warrior, and she is proud to take the title of *Crone*. Jeanine has received a Master's in Social Work and has felt the call to help others in the Pagan community, as well as in the over-all society at large.

MY DEDICATION SPELL

I dedicate this to the Universe,
promise kept, and alone.
I dedicate this to the dragonflies,
who showed me, as a light body, I was their own.
I dedicate this to my spiritual maternal Great-Grandmother,
who I have never known.
I dedicate this to my only granddaughter,
may you find this spirituality your home.

CONTENTS

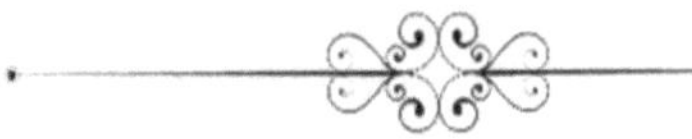

PREFACE

This is not my first rodeo. A few of you may know I have written before. While a few people have told me how much they really enjoyed the book, the reviews from my entrenched inner voices hurled flurries of rotten tomatoes. I would hear them say, *is this really it?* Or I would hear, *try, try again.* And worst of all I'd hear them say, *your ears were just too green to write this, so what were you thinking?*

Yet my Guardian Spirits whispered in my ear, "You have done what was required of you. Take what you have learned, in this first writing venture, and journey to a higher ascension."

I have come to realize that all of my inner voices were straight-up with me. I just didn't want to hear the truth. It was just that the need for black Americans and people of color to have an alternative voice in Wicca, witchcraft or any alternative or metaphysical spirituality, outside of *African Traditional Religions,* was so very great. Many of us of color don't feel the calling that some other practitioners feel we should about ATRs. While we love the *Orisha* and other African magickal lore, the initiation into ATRs is not for everyone. So, I was passionate about being that voice in the wilderness that many Wiccans and Witches of color were eagerly poised to hear. There was also, of course, the need to give assurances to people of color who wanted to leave the Christian church to seek other spiritual pursuits.

Since then, I have followed the paths that my Spirit Guides have laid out before me, with goals and challenges. I have engaged in circles with black people. I have engaged in other diverse circles. I have studied my craft and the crafts of others. I have devoted my life to the Goddess and the Universe as a Priestess to learning their mysteries. I do telephonic Wicca prison ministry. I attended institutions of higher learning. I continued as an admin to online forums for African American Wicca, and in these recent years, I have developed an online school for African American Wiccans. Amazingly, I heard the voice of my Spirit Guides speaking to me through my students and mentee saying, *"This course is really good. Don't you think it is time now to write it in a book?"*

So now, as the Universe would have it, twenty-one years later from my first book, I present this offering that is more than just a Wicca book for beginners. In its initial form it was an online study of Wicca from an African American perspective. This book offers a comprehensive study of magick that some other basic Wicca/ witchcraft books don't offer. This book not only teaches about Wicca, but it touches on other traditions of magick. It not only talks about magick but it explains how it works in theory. This offering not only gives some examples of different types of magick, but it also gives an editorial perspective on the magick—from the author's point of view. This book also has short stories and anecdotes throughout its pages. This is what distinguishes this book from others and makes it a true study guide. Because this book is chock full of theory, history, and information, it is my view that it offers something for everyone who wishes to study or practice in Wicca, witchcraft, the metaphysical, and not just people of color. It is for anyone who is an overall student in the magickal mysteries, and who is interested in learning from a diversity of perspectives.

INTRODUCTION

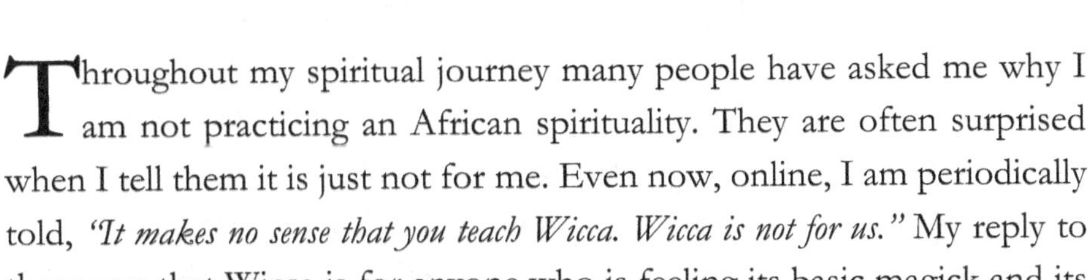

Throughout my spiritual journey many people have asked me why I am not practicing an African spirituality. They are often surprised when I tell them it is just not for me. Even now, online, I am periodically told, *"It makes no sense that you teach Wicca. Wicca is not for us."* My reply to them was that Wicca is for anyone who is feeling its basic magick and its call, and that *African Traditional Religions* are not for everyone. So, there is a definite need to address this question of why I or anyone else of color practice it.

Thirty years ago, in 1992, I stumbled upon the wonders of metaphysical life. Approximately 2 years after that I began practicing Wicca. Wicca is now my home, but between 1992 and 1994, before I found a home in Wicca, I set out to search for any African Traditional Religious practitioner who would be willing to teach me the ancestral mysteries. This was difficult in those days. I didn't live in spiritual diverse areas like New Orleans or in South Carolina on the barrier islands where many *Geechee* or *Gullah* people call home. I lived in Philadelphia where Christians, Catholics and Islam rules the multitudes and owns the parishes. Those who practice anything other than those were not easily found, and it was not for the lack of me trying. When I moved to North Carolina, it was even worse in the Bible belt. Asking too many questions on the subject was a risk. In those days in order to be initiated you would have to have a practicing relative or one would have to know someone who practices. It was not any easy find. This was before the Internet and the wonders of searching online.

Eventually I did find Witches at a Unitarian Church. They were open, and they invited me to their circles, and they taught me the ways of witchcraft and *Goddess worship*. I went to their free workshops and learned as much as I could. If I had found African Traditional teachers, in those days, I believe I would have gladly started my studies under them. But the question is, for how long would I have studied? Now that I have learned a little more about ATRs, I doubt it would have been for me. In ATRs you study under a *Babalawo* (male Priest) or *Iyanifa* (female Priest) or Elder. This is nice. This happens in Pagan circles with Priests and Priestesses too. However, with ATRs like *Ifa* it is required that you go through them for every step in your spiritual journey. You must go to them to be *read* or to find out who is your *head* or main deity. You must be advised by them on what ritual you should perform and how. In many cases each time you go through them it is a cost for their readings. Even your final initiation is a high cost which can be in the thousands. For many this is the way of the African traditions, and they wouldn't do it any other way. However, for my spirit personally, I feel it is not for me. While I love the fact that people are continuing the ways of the Ancestors, I personally would feel a restriction. I am not one who can be told how to pray or when to pray and who is my head (one's main or guardian Orisha). I feel I would be less restricted if I had stayed in the Christian church. I love the option of being my own Priestess or being initiated under a Priest. I love the ability to hold my own rituals and spells, and not be told how to and when. Respecting the Elders, and those who are our teachers is a most valuable tradition. But, I myself need to have my own autonomy, or else, quite frankly, my soul would just wither and die.

I find that I am not alone. Many people of color feel that African Traditional Religions are not for them. Many go to *Hoodoo* or *Kemetism* since there is no necessary initiation involved. But many have come to witchcraft and Wicca. A few of my students told me that they were initiated in an ATR or attempted to do so. But they came back to Wicca because it is less restrictive, along with its other attributes.

The other thing about Wicca is that while its practitioners, commonly used *pantheons* and other symbols that are European, the ceremonies of Wicca actually have its roots from the Kemetic Mystery schools that were appropriated by Greek philosophers, and used by Hermetic organizations like the *Golden Dawn* and *The Theosophical Society*. These Hermetic traditions, theories and rituals were practiced by European Witches, and the rest is history. So, while others feel there is a disconnection from the Ancestors, I feel there is a connection to the Ancestors that very few have connected the dots to.

So, for those on all sides of the spectrum who believe this book should never be written, I say it is time. Right or wrong it has been an ongoing debate if black people should practice Wicca. I say black people should never limit themselves in anything based on their own ethnicity or culture. Much less spirituality. People of all races throughout the Americas are practicing African Traditional Diasporic Religions. So why not I or any other person of color with Wicca? I feel that I was led to this path for a reason. *Oya* called me long before I knew who She was. She confirmed to me many times that my path is true, and I believe *Her.*

Regardless of its roots, I have never looked back because Wicca is a highly fulfilling spirituality for me. It connects me to Nature in a way that no other spirituality can. It gives the balance for me between Nature, the Ancestors and the *All,* and it ties and presents them into a delightful spiritual package. Wicca has opened Universal doors for me, and sacred channels that I never before thought possible, and it leads to the realm for connecting to the Divine. Wicca may not have given me all that I want, but it has most definitely given me all that I need. It helps me to work in conjunction with the spiritual realm and gives me confirmations through synchronicities.

It is the intention of this study to show you not only the basics of practicing Wicca but also some intermediate practices. Wicca may not be for everyone. It is a calling because it is not a religion of hexing or cursing, but a religion that is mostly of light working. It is also a religion that helps one to reconcile with the seasons. Before I became Wiccan, I had a mild to moderate case of *Seasonal Affective Disorder* (SAD). This disorder usually comes during the Autumn and Winter months. After I began to engage in the sabbats of Wicca (The Wheel of the Year) things began to change for me. I looked forward to the festivals of the Autumn and Winter months. This is because Wicca helps one embrace the seasons like very few religions do. So, I encourage the readers of this study to come with an open mind and an open heart and explore the lessons that are offered. You may find that Wicca is not for you, but the Universe brought you here to this door for a reason. It is up to you to turn the knob and determine why.

Much Love, Light and ASe!

LESSON ONE

How Did I Get Here?
My Journey into Wicca and Witchcraft

How Did I Get Here?

I didn't set out to be different. I AM what Eye AM.

Like most black Americans, Christianity goes back to the hard roots of my Ancestry. I grew up in a lower middle-class family. My father was a butcher for a meat processing manufacturer. My mother was an old school *"hair-dresser"*. A hairdresser, for those who are too young to know the term, is what hairstylists used to be called back-in-the-day. You know, the kind of hairstylist who would take a smoking-hot straightening comb or a fire-hot curling iron off the stove, and make your natural hair look like Lena Horne's hair without burning a strand. In that, my mother had a talent and a Witch's power to *transmute*. She did it without burning your ears too. Even though she had retired to be a full-time mom, some women would still come by her kitchen to get their "heads done". To this day I never met anyone who could match her in that old school stuff. She would even give the Dominicans a run for their money. That practice is slowly going away since many people, and notably many Witches, have gone back to the natural ways of loving our hair in its most beautiful and natural state.

From as far back as I could remember we went to church every Sunday morning. My mother started Sundays by making the best breakfast of eggs, steak with gravy, and homemade biscuits. Each biscuit was oblong, wide, fluffy, and shaped like a rectangle, and they were served with your choice of corn syrup and or butter. I personally did both. My father, an ex-Catholic who practiced in his youth, said a prayer over the breakfast before we ate. That was the extent of his religious activities. Well, that, and the other was dropping us off to church, and then driving himself back home like something out of hell was chasing him.

Dad was an atheist. He never said that word, because he probably wouldn't know what it meant in those days, but he always told my mom, *"When you're dead you're gone"* and there is nothing after that. My mother, my younger brother, my younger sister and I attended a small church in Philadelphia. It was a *Holiness* church and later renamed itself as a *Pentecostal* church. Yeah, that's right, religion by fire. Holiness, in my view, meant strict. It meant no pants for women or girls, no makeup, no smoking, no cursing, no card playing and most of all—no life. The pastor of the church had three children, two girls and the youngest was a boy. She and her husband adopted them after fostering them for a period. My siblings and I, and the pastor's children, formed a choir. The pastor's younger daughter played the piano and we traveled from church to church singing the old gospel songs. We were good enough to make a good reputation for ourselves on certain *fried chicken circuits* in Philadelphia and New Jersey, and many came to see us. I called it the "fried chicken circuit" because after each church service we would go to their church kitchen and get a fried chicken dinner or sandwich. I am sure those of you who go to black churches know what I mean. I led a few of the songs. I had a good voice in those days. I was about thirteen years old when we hit the height of our popularity, and the oldest singer was seventeen. We would stay in church most of the day on Sundays. On holidays, like New Year's Eve, we would stay overnight. It was during those times that I had agonizing psychological struggles. On the one hand, there was my mother and pastor telling me that this was all that there was for salvation, and any contentment in life was only with the bible, the Christian church, the trinity of God, Jesus and the Holy Spirit. But, in truth, I was not at all content. Even at a very young age. I questioned the validity of the bible. The stories made absolutely no sense to me, especially when everyone took the stories literally. Why would a loving God we *serve* be so vengeful and jealous? How did we all come from Adam and Eve and their three sons? How did we come from Noah and his family? Did they all practice incest? Why are we making Eve the scapegoat? Didn't Adam eat the fruit too? Why are just 5 to 8 percent of the bible stories about women? And, of that percentage why are most of the stories about women derogatory? Were most all women prostitutes, harlots, treacherous, devious and concubines in those days? Should we be thankful to the men for keeping women in line back then? If Satan is so bad and God is so supreme, why can't he just eradicate Satan and keep it moving? I was left with thousands of questions unanswered, because to be quite candid, no one could answer any of it. I just heard, *"God said it, I believe it, and that settles it!"* But it was not settled for me. In fact, I felt that it was all too unsettling. It all sounded like a cult to me. My question was how did they really know God said it? Where was the proof? Even if it was just parables, why did church people take it all so literally?

What was even more disturbing to me, in those days, was going into the tiny church every Sunday and seeing a large portrait of a blue eyed, and blonde hair Jesus centering the pulpit. Sure, a God could be white, but why can't there also be a God who is black, and one who is female, or one who is female and black like me? Is not *God* within me?

The internal psychological and spiritual conflict inside me continued, and going to church, listening to pastors, and staying all day left an awful void in my spiritual being. Even at a young age I sought out spiritual gratification. I went through the motions of becoming *saved* as a Christian, and I proclaimed to myself and to others that I was. But discontent ruled as victor and I found myself leaving that church, against my mother's wishes, when I was fifteen years of age, never to return to that church again. This was the hardest thing for me to do. Not because I had second thoughts about the theology, but because I had spent my young life being taught the ways of the Christian church, and I felt guilty for the lack of desire in wanting to practice it. Even when I declared myself fully emancipated, privately it took a long time for me to feel that I made the appropriate decision to cut it off cold turkey. I would ask myself, "How did I get here and where am I supposed to be?" I was born spiritual, and I somehow felt that leaving the church was my last chance of finding a spiritual outlet and solace. Like most people I thought Christianity was it.

Decades later, I came to realize that what I was going through was a *calling*. I was being called to a different spiritual path that was truly meant for me. Something that was a match for my spiritual wiring. Despite my upbringing, and all the cultural religious conditioning, the *mystical Universe*, in its divine wisdom, managed to break through and steer me towards a different path. A light was beamed, and it kept me woke. People around me found this difficult to understand. It was not easy for me. While I understood that Christianity was completely right for other people, and I acknowledged that it helped black people through difficult times like *Reconstruction, Jim Crow* and the *Civil Rights Movement*, I felt assured it wasn't for me. I tried the giving of my life to Christ thing. I tried the getting *saved* thing, but it only felt forced and artificial to me.

My true-life narrative is not an uncommon story for many people. It may even sound familiar to you. Wanting to find one's own way spiritually is difficult, especially when one was raised staunchly in a family with religious ties and traditions. The pressure to remain within the status quo and in one's family's traditional religious observance is real. For people of color, in the U.S., however, be it African Americans, Asians or Latin Americans, there is a particular social stigma when not conforming to family spiritual traditions. It makes one feel a bit of a misfit, an oddity and downright disrespectful. When you think about the history of black Americans, it is quite understandable. Africans were brought to the Americans and given a religion. The Africans practiced this religion. It is not very often that you find a large group of people with no real spiritual diversity. In the continent of Africa itself there are thousands of tribal religions. Today, in the United States, Christianity is the one hugely effectual juggernaut religion that rules the psyche of black people, and it continues to be passed down from generation to generation, with only a minor percentage in Islam and in Buddhism as its rivals. Many of its members are only reluctant to leave because of a fear of burning in hell or being chastised. It is this dread of leaving the religion that gives it such a spiritual monopoly of power over the people who admits to "serve" its god.

Within my journey as, what I call, an advocate for African American Wiccans, and Pagans, it is apparent to me that my story is not unique. My story is the story of multitudes. I have spoken with many people who felt that they were living the lives of *spiritual zombies*, and since their spiritual awakenings, they are now living to their best spiritual benefit and their highest good. They feel that they were trapped in a religion that was never of their own choice. Hundreds of people a year find my website or social media, and they write me to say things like, *"Thank goodness! I thought I was the only one!"* Or they would say, *"My family thinks I am going to hell and that I am the devil."* But most people would declare that since they left Christianity, they felt a weight lifted. I received lots of correspondences telling me that they stumbled upon my website looking for a theology that felt more like what they were looking for, and many believe that *paganism* is it. Furthermore, here is some good news for those who also feel like they are misfits. Newspapers like the *New York Post* and *USA Today* recently published articles online about a *Pew Research Center Study* (Fearnow, 2018) showing that "there are more Wiccans than Presbyterians in America."

According to these newspapers online there are approximately *1.4 million Presbyterians,* but they also estimated that there are *1.5 million Wiccans.* However, this does not account for the Witches and Pagans who do not recognize themselves as Wiccans, and that is a lot. This means that Witches and Pagans are not included in the research. I would also go out on a limb to guess that there are Witches and Pagans who would be hesitant to identify themselves for the fear of a backlash, and refused to participate or may have even denied being Witches altogether. This would put their numbers even higher. The difference between Wiccans and Witches will be explained in a later lesson. When you calculate that African traditional spirituality was not even considered in the research the numbers could be phenomenal. This means the population of Witches, Spiritualists and Pagans are growing, and the average person knowing people who are Witches will eventually become even more common.

So, what is the point I am trying to make here? Let me simply put it this way. Despite family and friends' assertions, in my view, no entire ethnic or cultural group of human beings should practice just one religion simply because they are of the same ethnic group, the same race or just because grandma practiced it and passed down the religion. If someone is in love with their family's faith, that is a wonderful gift.

However, if someone feels the need to seek, then they should. We are not a monolithic mass of African-descended humanoids. Spirituality is deeply personal, and we are each hardwired differently. We think differently. We all have different multiple bloodlines. We are attracted to different thoughts, different careers and different lifestyles. What makes one person want to dance in church does not make others want to dance in church. For example, even as a child, I hated going to church, because I never felt that God was inside the church. I always felt that God was outside of church, and in Nature. So, essentially, my thoughts were that going inside a church took me away from God. I always felt as though God was in the river, the Sun and the Moon. Being in church at night while the Moon was out seemed all types of wrong to me, and antithetical to what true worship was. Even though I liked gospel music I would have much rather danced with the Holy Spirit outside to the music of the crickets and birds.

I was once stunned to have stumbled upon a famous, and easy to access, quote by *Alice Walker*, writer of <u>*The Color Purple*</u> and a myriad of others in <u>*The New York Times*</u> top-selling books. Apparently, Ms. Walker was at a book signing. During that book signing she discussed her experiences in church as a child. Walker said, *"As a child I loved the singing, but the sermons were unintelligible. I understood at a very early age that in nature, I felt everything I should feel in church but never did. Walking in the woods, I felt in touch with the universe and with the spirit of the universe (MABE, 1989)."* It was so unbelievable that she was quoting my feelings syllable by syllable.

Forgive me for using the line that writer and producer *Rod Serling* often used in <u>*The Twilight Zone*</u>, but, *"imagine, if you will"* a world where everyone is in touch with Spirit through the medium of a religion or a spirituality of their choice. Imagine everyone being connected the way they are meant to connect or in the way they were hard-wired to connect. Can you imagine how nice our world would be if we were all connected to our Higher Selves? I think of religion as merely a language used to speak to the *God-head* or the Universe. Imagine this language is not passed to you by family, necessarily, but is given to one based on what is divinely written to one's own heart and soul. Imagine what type of world this would be like. It would mean we would all be in touch with our own *spirit, chi, life force* or *ASe'*. It would mean that we would all find our own peace.

Disclaimers

So, before readers label me as a hater, please let me place some cards on the table. Here are some thoughts you may or may not have, but need to be aired:

1) You didn't try hard enough with reading the "Word," if you read the bible, you would have never left.

Answer: Actually, the truth is, that was the trouble for me, the more I read the bible the more I disagreed with the overall philosophy. While the theology suits others it never suited me.

2) You are trying to sway people away from Christ.

Answer: No, and definitely not. That would be counter to my purpose with these lessons. My purpose is to be a beacon for those who have already been seeking mentally or physically, and are being called as I was to another path. These lessons are for seekers. While paganism may not be their path it may be a stop along their journey. To sway people away from what is right for them would be totally antithetical to my cause.

To be clear my intentions are not to bash any religion. For many people Christianity is a very rewarding and fulfilling religion that has brought happiness and solace to millions of people around the world for approximately 2 millennia. But, in this study, I do have to confront the obstacles and serious issues that many people, and especially people of color face when coming to a crossroad of spiritual transitioning, or why else write this book? If that were the case then people of color could just as well learn about Wicca and paganism in any other basic 101 witchcraft book. Based on my online correspondences, African American seekers are not just looking for lessons on Wicca or paganism. They are looking for consolation and affirmation that their journey is not malevolent, misguided, demonic or just off the mark. They are also looking for different ways to look at Wicca from their own cultural perspective. People want to know that there are others like themselves on the same journey, and that this spirituality is positive. The intention of these lessons is to inform that Pagan spirituality can be integrated into their Ancestral pursuits and worship. My wish is to present this study as an affirmation that seekers are not alone, and that most of us come from Christian or Abrahamic backgrounds. There is trauma and difficulty in separating what is in one's heart and what has been conditioned in us from the moment of birth. Such spiritual self-care and transitioning will not be easy. But if you are being called to your tradition as I was, the healing will eventually happen and the journey will become fulfilling.

My goal in this study is to tell bits of my own personal journey while giving information and education on paganism, witchcraft and Wicca. I feel that this is a story that I must convey. Spirit has led me to this path for a reason. There is nothing wrong with helping others identify what works for them and what doesn't work for them. As an ex-behavioral health professional, I know that finding what works for one is the way to recovery for good health and a better life. Religion and spirituality are not modes that should be forced on everyone. A religion should not be practiced just because one is in a particular culture. And, it should not be a one size fits all, and it shouldn't be a practice that is coerced by societal measures. It should flow naturally. And, it is only then, when one can begin a spiritual awakening, no matter what that practice is.

My Magickal Beginnings

Let me start here by explaining that you will find the word *magick* is spelled with a "*k*" in the Pagan world. This is to distinguish between stage or entertainment magic and the magick in the mystical/spiritual world. My magickal beginnings didn't start when I walked away from my Christian practices. Unbeknownst to me then, Spirit was with me as a child. Spirit taught me through comic books, TV shows and movies. I now know this because, in hindsight, there were only specific genres that I passionately cared about. Genres that I equate now with metaphysical philosophies in some way. I read every comic book I could put my hands on. It didn't matter. I would read *G.I. Joe*, *The Archies*, and one of my aunts used to give me her used graphic love comic books. These comics were okay, but I especially loved the *Marvel* and *D.C.* superheroes. To me they were godlike – and especially *Thor*, *Black Panther*, *Red Sonja*, and *Wonder Woman*. But, my most favorites of all were the *mystery* comics. You know, the *CreepShow*, the *Haunted House*, and the *Tales from the Crypt*. Give me anything that was vampires, ghosts and Witches. Th e TV shows and movies were no different for me. Although I was not drawn to the serial-killer-type slasher horror movies, I did enjoy the pure science fiction or the esoteric or unseen mysteries and the metaphysical viewpoint of the human and superhuman conditions. Shows like *Bewitched*, *The Twilight Zone*, *The Outer*

Limits, _Lost in Space_, _Star Trek_, _One Step Beyond_, _The Addams Family_ and _Thriller_ with _Boris Karloff_. I loved _Bewitched_ the most because _Samantha_ did things I would have loved to have done. She performed magick even though her husband wished that she wouldn't. I loved _The Twilight Zone_, because, in my view, _Rod Sterling_ was a High Priest. Okay, I didn't really know what a High Priest was in those days, but I intuitively knew that he was a teacher who taught moral lessons in the subliminal and the mystical, and he took me on a magickal experience every week. I loved _Star Trek_ because _The Enterprise_ took me places, I felt a familiarity with through space and universal travel. I always felt that the stars were my home in other past lives. Shows in those days gave morals to stories that are seldom conveyed today on television.

While others, of my young age, looked for a variety of basic entertainment in those days, I looked to TV shows for the teachings of morals, purpose, alternative universes and the challenges of the road ahead of me. They demonstrated life's lessons in which I personally couldn't get from a pastor. _Rod Serling_ was my _spirit guide_, _Samantha Stevens_ was my _mentor_, and _Spock_ was my _logical mystical host_ who led me through multiple planes of existences. It was unclear to me then why I felt a connection to these types of genres. But clarity is 20/20 in hindsight. I had an intuitive obsession towards otherworldly fantasies, because the Universe teaches, and it teaches those who are open to hear, and receive from it directly, and or indirectly. When I speak with others who practice the esoteric sciences, they tell me that they too were driven to connect as children to the same types of genres.

The interesting part about esoteric seekers is that we continue our studies through the same genres into adulthood. I know I still do. We are the ones who created the demand for the _Star Trek_ movies and TV shows to return. We are the ones who made the demand for the return of _Tales_ _from the Crypt_ movies and TV shows. We help increase demand for more _Harry Potter_ movies and other witchcraft movies. We kept box office returns high with movies like _Practical Magic_, _Doctor Strange_, _Avatar_, _The Black Panther_, all the _Star Wars_ sagas, and many Disney fantasy movies like _Pocahontas_, _Moana_, and _The Princess and the Frog_. Even, _The Lion King_ has a theme song that is very Pagan — _"The Circle of Life"._

So why would spiritual seekers have an interest in movies and novels like these? There is a theory that seekers instinctively seek adventure, fantasy or sci-fi genres. This is because they intuitively follow what is called, _"The Hero's Journey"._ The Hero's Journey is a very popular subject for many Pagans today. The theory of _The Hero's Journey_ was introduced and diagrammed in a book written by _Joseph Campbell_ called, _The Hero with a Thousand Faces_ (2008). This book explains how all successful adventure books, and movies are made with a recurring theme and formula. The recurring theme is of a reluctant hero meeting up with some type of adversity, and being forced into an adventure, and meeting a wise sage who teaches the hero the meaning of life while also teaching or directing the hero on how to conquer their opposition or trials. Through her/his journey the hero runs into multiple archetypes such as a _trickster, a strong aide or ally, a shapeshifter_ and _a guardian_. These archetypes either teach the hero valuable lessons or help the hero with their goals of overcoming challenges and or hardships. In this the hero will then slay the enemy and will eventually return to their home realm victorious. They then become adept in the once problematic aspects of their lives, and they make their home a better place for all.

Campbell's book explains that most successful adventure movies, books and plays take on this same format, although with different themes. In these common adventures the hero is learning about herself or himself by being pushed through a journey of challenges and adversities, seeking out other worlds, using newly received or realized mystical powers and abilities and foiling their enemy. At the same time the protagonist is also learning life's lessons by learning the types of people they will meet in their day-to-day life's journey. These types of stories speak directly to our higher sensibilities, higher minds and higher ideals to evolve the spirit which is called the *Higher Self*. Because of this many Pagans use *The Hero's Journey* parables and stories as lessons to help overcome adversities in their mundane and magickal journeys. And while we are not likely to slay an actual dragon or run into *Darth Vader* himself, we often have similar challenges and encounters within our everyday lives, and with the same various archetypes and circumstances.

What's Love Got to Do with It? Everything

As a young adult, I continued to instinctively wander through life. A long-term relationship had ended, and my baby daughter and I returned to live with my parents. One day, while waiting at an auto repair shop to have some repairs done to my car, and I don't remember what, I began speaking with a beautiful minded sistar and she was also waiting for her car to get repaired. We somehow got into a conversation about theology (of course because of me being an eternal seeker), and I mentioned to her that I was, at the time, an agnostic— still not finding the right fuel for my spirit. I expected her to be like most black women, unapproving, but caring enough to say the same old lines as, *well, maybe you just never went to the right church. Come to mine.* Surprisingly she didn't. She said, *"Yeah I definitely understand where you are coming from."*

I replied to her, *"Really! Are you an Agnostic too?"* I was ecstatically happy to have found someone who didn't drink the Christian Kool-Aid. She said, *"No. but I am a Buddhist and we often think along those lines."*

I had heard about Buddhists before. A good friend in high school became a Buddhist on one of her short ventures to something new. I went to one meeting with her, and they even gave her a *Gohonzon* (a sacred scroll object of devotion) to chant by, but it never piqued my interest to pursue it myself. This time was different. I was open to receiving. I asked her as much as I could about it. She had a peace about her, so I was ready to have a little of what she was having.

When I began to study *Nichiren Buddhism*, I was fascinated by how open the Buddhists were and how they constantly encouraged their members to read and be informed of other forms of spirituality and philosophies as well as their own. Buddhists believe that education is the key to enlightenment. To Buddhists, enlightenment is the path to *nirvana*, and nirvana is a place of peace. This was foreign for me. When I was a Christian, I was taught that learning something outside their biblical canons was just a path leading to Satan himself. This was ingrained in me, and I thought other religions were exclusive to learning from their own teachings too. I loved the open philosophy of the Buddhists. But it was when I first began to chant with them in unison, that I first felt the true vibrations of the Universe. It was like the singing of gospel in church, yet somehow different. It was different for me because it was not directed towards any particular god, but from my voice into the Universe, and beyond. It was also different because the chanting was with people of a more kindred spirit. It felt much more receptive and open.

During this period of time the movie, *What's Love Got to Do with It?* came out in the theaters. Black Buddhists were excited. It was like an affirmation to them. For me I thought it was a sign that I was on the right track. To find out that, the singer, *Tina Turner*, was a practicing Buddhist for many years was encouraging to me. Yet, disappointingly, Buddhism did not set a true sizable fire to my heart as I had hoped. It was like looking for the right mate or lover and just settling with the one you're with. I didn't want to settle, but at the time I felt I had no choice, because it felt close to what I had been seeking. As time went by, I realized that the void was still there and Buddhism was just not close enough. I was going through the dark night of the soul. Yet, I couldn't kick that feeling that somewhere something was waiting for me to discover it. But I also had a sense that I was getting closer to what I was looking for.

One Summer afternoon, while driving home from a shopping trip with my mother, I felt an impulse to turn on the car radio. There, playing on *National Public Radio* (NPR) I caught the ending of an interview. It was a local interview. The interviewer was a female commentator interviewing a Priestess who was an owner at a local Pagan store. I often think about that moment, and cringe, because if I had waited a few minutes more to turn it on, I would have missed it entirely. She spoke about *Nature*. She spoke about the *Goddess*. She spoke about the Moon, and all its wonders. She also spoke about the beauty of the *craft* (witchcraft). I was enamored. Finally, I found someone who stimulated me with the poetic language that defined what life was all about. It was like finding a lost soul mate. The gaping void within was replaced with sudden passion. In just a few words she answered a variety of questions I had about Deity and being connected to the Universe. For the first time, I didn't feel women and Nature were excluded from the inner workings of God. When she expounded about the Goddess, she gave a confirmation to the voice that spoke to me in my youth. The voice that took me, nightly, to a dream world, where *SHE* was comforting, worshiped, venerated and celebrated. It was that moment that I finally found out who I was. It was that moment I found out my spiritual identity. It was SHE, and SHE was me and the Universe. It was SHE to whom I chanted with the Buddhists. It was SHE whom I searched for in church and could not find. SHE was the *mother* to my lost inner child, and my inner child was no longer an orphan.

Synchronicity had happened for me again. I had become addicted to NPR for a while, because I always felt it would inform me on something in which I had been searching for, and that day it didn't disappoint. It was Spirit that directed me to turn on that show before it was too late. As the old saying goes, *"When the student is ready the teacher will appear."*

When they began to take calls during the interview, from the radio audience, I felt badly for the Priestess because the callers began to recite lines from the bible to her. They told her that she should be ashamed, and that God would forgive her if she was a believer. I was surprised because the *National Public Radio's* listening audience was normally very open, sophisticated, and liberal-minded. Regardless, she was a threat to the callers, but the Priestess was resolute. Without reprisal towards their bigotry, she stood her spiritual ground and expressed the fundamentals of her belief in what she called *"Wicca"*. I thought it was a beautiful word, and it all fitted together for me, like the missing pieces to an old puzzle that I refused to ever give up looking for. She spoke about celebrations of the seasons, and the oneness with the Universe. It was the last 5 to 8 minutes of the program, but I learned so much. Wicca was described to be harmonious with the ideas in which I thought of as wholesomeness. Her inspiring words propelled me to what I learned later to be a *spiritual awakening*. For the first time, I understood what the word *holy* really meant, because at that moment I felt in tune with mind, body, soul and spirit.

A short time afterwards I found myself in this Witch's store. She introduced me to books on witchcraft, and there I purchased my first *Aku-Aba* (African Goddess of Fertility.) It was a small turquoise colored cast iron icon. Lore has it that the *Ghanaian Aku-Aba* is a figurine that helps one overcome being barren, but it is also a true symbol for success, fertility, prosperity and happiness. Symbolically, it was a true expression of my rebirth and my new beginnings into a new *metaphysical* life. And, in that, love has everything to do with it.

Magickal Blood Line

A Rendition of an Aku-Aba Shown

Spirit convinced me to move out from the home of my parents again. I knew I couldn't be free to be me there. I knew that they wouldn't want me to practice witchcraft in their home, and you know what, I really wouldn't want to even if they would have. I was not sure what I was embarking on, but I knew I had to do it alone. I left Philly and moved to my mother's home state, North Carolina. We used to go there every summer when I was a child and played at my aunt and uncle's farm between the tobacco and corn fields. Summers on the farm were spiritual to me. I didn't have to go to church on Sundays and we could play in the fresh country air as opposed to the harsh inner-city streets. I always wanted to get back to that beautiful state of my Ancestors. I found out much later, by my mother's oldest sister, aunt *Lula Mae*, that my great-grandmother was considered a Witch where my Ancestral family lived in the eastern part of that state. She was a Midwife between the late 1800's and the early 1900s. It is said that she, and another black woman named Nancy, ushered in most of the county's babies for both black and white folks. My aunt Lula Mae told me that she hated seeing pregnant women come to the house, because she knew that, *"they were there to take Maw away"*. As a child my aunt loved being around her grandmother. According to my aunt Lula Mae, *Maw* (my great-grandmother) was also a healer. They called her *Venus*, like the Roman goddess, even though they said her other nickname was *Jensey*. My great-grandmother practiced the *old ways* with healing through herbs and roots. On her deathbed, my aunt Lula Mae felt the need to tell me that kids used to tease her first cousins that their grandmother was a Witch. It was never clear, but it was as if aunt Lula Mae found out I was a Witch, and she, needed to let me know that it was in my bloodline before she left this plane. It was almost as if she gave me her blessings, to which this was an absolute comfort to me.

Purple Haze

I am here to tell you that, *in many cases*, when a true seeker becomes *spiritually awakened* something that was dormant in the brain opensup or turns on. It is very hard to describe, but it is a type of euphoria. You feel like you are in a fog or mist. People and things get distorted as though the seeker is on a natural high. The symptoms are an insatiable desire to read and consume all information about conjuring, witchcraft or paganism. You also tend to question reality and its total existence. You are in constant contemplation and question why others don't see the new reality you see. There is also a desire to reach out and search for others of like minds. I do know. I have not only experienced this myself, but others have described it to me. It may last for a week. It may last for a month. It may last for a year. It is a wonderful sensation, and I always envy people who are new and going through it, because it is a very pleasant but strange feeling. While others may think of it as being in the grips of a *spiritual awakening*, I call it the *purple haze*, because purple is the color of the spiritual, and haze, because, well, you are in a haze. Ironically, though, I discovered I wasn't being unique at all in this name. Later I found out that the late *Jimi Hendrix* coined the phrased himself, and was thorough in describing the condition in his 1970 song *"Purple Haze."* Below are the mysterious lyrics to the song:

"Purple haze, all in my brain
Lately things they don't seem the same
Actin' funny, but I don't know why
Excuse me while I kiss the sky
Purple haze, all around
Don't know if I'm comin' up or down
Am I happy or in misery?
Whatever it is, that girl put a spell on me."

Of course, his purple haze may have been about a love jones, witchy woman or about a drug-induced haze gone awry, but it is uncanny how well it describes an awakening haze. When I first started seriously practicing witchcraft, I never understood why new seekers went through this type of transition. I now suspect that it is possibly because of the *pineal gland* (pronounced *pine-kneel*) or *The Third-Eye*. When one has a *spiritual awakening* the pineal may activate causing a chemical called *dimethyltryptamine* or *DMT* to activate. The pineal gland is considered *"The Seat of the Soul,"* or the area where our *spirit* resides. Located in the central part of the brain it was once considered a recessive organ and no longer useful to human beings. The Ancient Egyptians knew better. They noticed that the pineal gland looked like an eye and had mystical powers. The gland also looks like the *Eye of Ra* when it is seated in the brain. DMT is said to be a chemical like LSD, but it facilitates connection between humans, the spiritual worlds, other dimensions and *Source* (Divine Spirit). DMT is also called the *"Spirit Molecule."* Mind blowing huh? No pun was intended.

My Wiccan Practice

Finding information on Wicca when I first started out was a lonely journey. I read many books on the subject, but meeting someone who practiced the craft was impossible. Personal computers were new, and somewhat available in those days, but the Internet was not. Meetups may have been found by word of mouth, magazines, in flyers at metaphysical stores and at Unitarian Universal churches. Here in the bible belt of North Carolina, Pagans were elusive. At that time *African Traditional Religions* would only initiate you if you were a relative or if they knew you. ATRs hid deeper in the shadows than the European Pagan religions. One Universalist Church with their CUUPS (Pagan) organization took me into a few of their circles and I learned a lot from them within rituals of dancing under the Moon, circling around the bonfires and calling to the spiritual *Watchtowers* (spirits of north, south, east and west). Eventually, I created a group of four black women. We circled together every sabbat (Pagan religious holiday) for 4 years. We would also circle with an *Asatru* (Norse Ancestral tradition) group. The group circled near a private river. They were, without a doubt, the best dope sabbat rituals I had ever attended, and the natural high that one receives after a good ritual is indescribable. Never really partied like that again, unfortunately.

Eventually the Internet developed, and I was able to learn more about Wicca online. I spent much of my free time on Witch and Pagan websites, learning about how the other half lived, and how they worked their magickal practices. *Yahoo!* had newly created *"Groups"* (a type of Facebook in its day), so I joined as many Pagan groups that I could find. However, I couldn't find any that were African American. I joined one with the name *"The Black Goddess"* thinking it was about the melanated sacred Feminine, but later found out it was more of an ethnocentric support group. Not long after, in 1999, I decided to create my own group. I called it *African American Wiccans.* It was a scary thing to embark on, because I didn't know how it would be received. While I ran into a few people online who said that they practiced *Voodou* or *Hoodoo*, and even then, this was rare, I've never met anyone who practiced Wicca who was melanated.

I feared that maybe people would join my group just to see the freak show. Eventually people began to join. People gradually began to hold discussions, but oddly enough the discussions weren't about witchcraft or magick or paganism. It was about the weather, TV shows, and basic conversation on anything but Wicca.

I began posting information about Wicca and witchcraft. I suspected that Wicca was a new subject to people of color, and perhaps they just didn't know anything about it. My post continued to be unanswered, and at some point, I thought I actually heard crickets chirping. It was almost as if they were afraid to comment and ignored it all together. It wasn't until after almost a year that people finally began to post about witchcraft and gave discussions. At that point I had almost given up. But it finally began to happen. More people started entering the group all saying, *"Oh thank goodness! I thought I was the only one."* The collective unconscious of black folks had finally begun to kick in. Later we found out another black Pagan group had existed. They were called *Sistas of the Moon*. They were just as surprised to find us, as we were to find them. They came into the group and introduced themselves and we somehow linked the two groups together.

My Mentor

Approximately, in the year 2000, I met the *Honorable Reverend Don Lewis*, online, who was the High Priest of the *Correllian Wiccan Tradition*, and he agreed to mentor me in his tradition. We corresponded via email, and I studied his correspondence training format. Approximately a year later I was initiated as a *Correllian* Priestess with direct lineage from *Lord Reverend Don Lewis HP*. A few years later I created a website called, '*The African American Wiccan Society*' to correspond with the group I created in *Yahoo! Groups*. The group's members gave me ideas of what they wanted to see on the website, and some aided with the materials I posted. *The African American Wiccan group* eventually moved to Facebook in 2011. Today the Facebook group has a membership of approximately 17,000 members. Today "*The African American Wiccan Society*" website (now called *The African American Wiccan Society Online School*) continues to get many correspondences a year. And, its *Facebook* page has over 27,000 followers.

The Basics: Metaphysical Practices, Paganism and Witchcraft

The Metaphysical

The word *metaphysical* is derived from the Greek *meta ta physika,* meaning, *after the things of nature* (Wyard, 2011). It is difficult to get a clear consensus of the definition for the word metaphysical. When I was doing research, each source described it differently and it was rather confusing. Here I cite from the *PBS* (Public Broadcasting) website, which was pretty much on-point: *"Metaphysics is a type of philosophy or study that uses broad concepts to help define reality and our understanding of it. Metaphysical studies generally seek to explain inherent or universal elements of reality which are not easily discovered or experienced in our everyday life. As such, it is concerned with explaining the features of reality that exist beyond the physical world and our immediate senses."*

So, essentially, metaphysical studies often look beyond the explanations in the physical world, and what we see and feel day to day. It takes the studies of the physical sciences many worlds and dimensions beyond, and sees with the heart and soul for that which can't be seen merely with the human eye. It is with the human senses that we are limited, and cannot look past the Earthly veil. Metaphysical thinking and practices allow us to expand past our five senses and extend our hand and third-eye into that which is spiritual or unseen.

Metaphysical practices were universal, from the beginning of human origins. It was just like eating and sex, everybody did it. But, if I am persuaded to give an estimate of an area to where it all began, I would have to say Africa would have to be the place I'd point to, because scientific evidence revealed that the oldest human-like *bipedal hominin* was found in Ethiopia. The archeologists called her *"Lucy."* It is said that her remains are over 3.2 million years old (Lewis, 2015). So, if magick began from the beginning of human consciousness, then it is only logical to believe that it began with the African Ancestors. After all—we all came out of Africa, so it is logical to deduce that they were the first to practice.

Imagine if you will the first real ancient Ancestors living under the open sky. Day by day, and month by month, and year by year they see the changes in the seasons, planets, the constellations and the trajectory of asteroids and comets. They had no television, video games, radio or Internet, so the sky was their entertainment. The sky was their way of detecting possible weather changes and season changes. The sky told them when to go to sleep, when to eat and when to find shelter. To our Ancestors, the sky sent messages from the Universe directly to them, so it would make sense that they would believe that the stars, Moon and the Sun were their gods. It would make sense that on good harvests they would have celebrations. It would make sense that they would dance under the Moon and give thanks to the Moon god, the Sun god or the gods of the planets. While there may not have been a god that materialized in front of our Ancestors to make themselves known, they saw beyond the symbols of sky and felt in their hearts that they were nurtured by the Universe and beyond the ether. This was the beginning of metaphysical thought. Not only did they see beyond the physical, but the metaphysical was a part of their reality.

Some Evidence-based Proof of Earlier African Pagan Practices

The late *Dr. John Hope Franklin* earned his Ph.D. from Harvard University before embarking on a career as one of the most renowned historians of his time. Franklin released his groundbreaking book, <u>*From Slavery to Freedom: A History of African Americans,*</u> first published in 1947. In his book he wrote about the religions of Africans before slavery. He wrote, *"The religion of many African communities combined animism with the belief in what historian Graham Connah has described as 'whole pantheons of deities' and venerations of ancestors. Although the details of these practices were complex and varied widely, many scholars agree with historian Basil Davidson that most Africans awarded supreme power to an idea of God as controlling everything and everyone but doing this indirectly through subordinated spiritual powers."*

Franklin also wrote, "Africans believed that the spirits of their ancestors had great powers over their lives," (Franklin & Moss, 2000, pp. 24 –25).

Franklin's book also mentions that the observed ancient sites, in which the ancient Africans practiced, on the African continent, contained holy objects and icons like pieces of wood; bones of the deceased; rocks, bits of metal, bells and rattles. So, to extrapolate, our Ancestors performed magickal workings with the use of Nature and magickal tools. Our Ancestors believed in *polytheism* (the belief in multiple gods or lower gods.) They believed in *animism* (the belief that all things in Nature, animate and inanimate have souls.) They believed in Ancestor veneration or worship, which is the belief that there is a spiritual connection between ourselves and the Ancestors who came before us.

Paganism

So, based on Dr. Franklin's writings, an inference could be made that, our Ancestors practiced *paganism*. So, when you first hear the word paganism what do you think? What has our culture taught you to think? Do you picture "ungodly" people dancing around the fire like cannibals eating other people? Do you picture a group of people worshiping the devil and sacrificing babies and children? If you do, don't feel alone. We are all products of our environment and our society. Even though Jesus is said to have lived in the Middle East, when I hear his name, it still evokes, to me, the picture of that white man with blonde hair and blue eyes hanging in the middle of the church I used to go to. I was conditioned by the picture I saw in church every Sunday. Even though I resisted it then, and I try to resist it now, the dye has been cast. My brain has been programmed by those who have been programmed and so on. Although very few of us can totally stop the programming in us we can offset it with knowing the facts.

I remember once telling a very good friend of mine that I was Pagan and she, thinking I was just joking, gave such a hearty laugh that I decided not to out myself with her that day for the fear that she, or myself, would be embarrassed. I, for the stare that she would have surely given me, and she for laughing so hard at what she thought was a self-deprecating joke. We now have come to an understanding. She too has moved to a greater awakening. She has moved to a more New-Age way of looking at things, and she knows I am Wiccan. But I can't help but reflect on how the word "Pagan" has been so demonized that the very mention of the word conjures the vision of mindless savages and immoral people.

First let's discuss the origins of the word *Pagan*. The true meaning was sadly muddled through the ages. The average person does not know the real meaning unless they are in the Pagan life or connected with Pagans in some way. So, let's take *Glinda the Good Witch's* advice, from the movie, <u>*The Wizard of Oz*</u>, when Dorothy asked her where to start on the yellow brick road. Glinda said, *"It's always best to start at the beginning."* So, let's start from the beginning.

While black Americans, in most cases, believe in the biblical *Adam* and *Eve,* most Pagans believe in *evolution.* As previously mentioned, from the dawn of human time we were Pagan, or what we now call *Earth-based.* Science has a consensus that we first crawled out of our primordial soup, the ocean, and onto land somewhere in the continent of Africa. We crawled up, and then back down trees. But it was when we were first able to walk upright, and look up to the Sun, Moon, and stars, around 200,000 years ago, in East Africa, that we became what is now called *Pagans.* We developed consciousness and became self-aware, and we were Pagan-like because we were one with Nature, and we hunted and gathered as needed. We lived a nomadic life and would follow the seasons by sky and the constellations.

We later became an agrarian culture, so we depended on the sky to tell us when to plant, when it would rain, and when we needed shelter. Our Ancestors learned various herbs for healing themselves and each other. Fresh herbs, berries, and vegetation were available depending on the season, and according to the stars. Our Ancestors also had a relationship with animals. Some they ate, of course, some they befriended, like wolves. With many animals they depended on survival. They followed the herds to find watering holes and drinking water. When animals went to higher grounds humans knew a flood was coming or bad weather was ahead, and the sound of crickets told them how hot or cool it was going to be that day. People began to pay homage to the Moon and the Sun, and eventually the Moon and Sun became symbols of their deities. They thought, understandably, that one bestows adulation directly to that which is contributing to their quality of life, so the Moon and Stars were their gods. Good weather, good harvest and good hunting meant celebrations and rituals, because they were grateful that their *Being Supreme* was smiling upon them. Our Ancestors were in tune with the rhythms of the Universe and Nature.

In the beginning ancient humans were nomadic, but eventually they settled in tribes and villages, and followed the seasons as agrarians. Spring was for planting, Summer was for growing, Autumn was for harvest, and Winter (in colder climates) was for eating the storages and for hunting. To humans, all over the world, these times were sacred days or holy days (*holidays*). Although types of seasons vary with the geographic area, all people in history have celebrated some type of holy day for a given season. Any good harvest meant another year of survival, and this meant following the patterns of Nature regardless of what hemisphere the culture lived in.

Since Wicca is *Neo-Paganism* and uses mostly old European verbiage and language, let's discuss old Europe as history. In old Europe those who celebrated the seasons, or believed that the seasons were the reason to celebrate holy days, were called *Pagans*. Other countries may have called it other things, but here in America we use the word Pagan because, hey, "when in Rome…" If one is ethnocentric in their practice they may want to find out what it is called in their Ancestors homeland. They may call it what it is…their religious or spiritual beliefs.

The word **Pagan** originated from the Latin word "*paganus*"; meaning "*rural*", and or "*dwelling in country life*". The word *Pagan* originated from old Europe. People who lived in the cities were of course *city dwellers*. The people who lived in the country, or who were farmers, were called Pagans. It is much like the term urban versus suburban or rural today. Of the three terms, the word urban has also been demonized, although for totally different reasons.

The word Pagan was pretty much benign back then. It didn't get its sinister reputation until after the Roman Church took dominance in the cities of Europe. The Pagans, or *country dwellers*, were slower to catch on to that newfangled Christian stuff. They felt, *why break what is fixed? We will stick with the old ways* (the old religion). I am also sure they thought, *does Christianity help with the harvest or the planting? What about the holy days?* They loved their Harvest gods. They loved their natural holidays. They loved their old gods' festivals. The Christians in the cities began to demonize Pagans for their resistance to change, and the word Pagan became derogatory and synonymous with something evil.

Today we Pagans embrace the name. We *reclaim* it. We are what the word originally meant. We are close to the Earth and Nature. We believe that our healthiest life-forces come with being close to Nature. We follow the rhythms of the Universe. We believe that holidays are about the seasons, and that Nature knows best. And, most of all, we believe that the *Universal Powers* speak, and communicate to those who are willing to listen to Nature.

Paganism, in general, is not always a religion. It is a spirituality. It is instinctive, intuitive and primal, so, in its purest form, it is not human-made or human-organized. In this I mean it is what anyone would practice if they were born on a deserted island with no knowledge of religion. It is simply one's unadulterated love for the environment that one inhabits, and one's veneration of Nature. The caveat is that Pagans believe that there is magick in the natural world, the Universe and beyond. What each of us does with that magick is totally up to the individual Pagan. Some practice magick and some don't. Many just celebrate the seasons, the sabbats and the holy days. Some just love to hug trees. ☺

Paganism, like Christianity, is an umbrella term for certain spiritual affiliations. For example, a Christian could be either a Protestant, Methodist, Catholic, Baptist or etc. A Pagan could be a Wiccan, Shaman, Witch, Conjurer, Mage, Taoist, Hermetic, Ifa, Alchemist, Kemetic etc. To make it simpler, any religion, or spirituality that is not of the *Abrahamic religions* (Christianity, Judaism, or Islam) is considered Pagan. Some people also include Buddhism as non-Pagan since it is so mainstream. There are some who may debate on if African Traditional Religions should use the term *Pagan*, but for the most part many people who practice ATRs celebrate sabbat holy days with Pagans, and more and more African American Spiritualists are embracing the word *Pagan* as harmless, and they are more accepting of it. As Pagans, we believe in *magick*. We believe that magick can happen through the power of *our own minds, the will*, the power of *natural elements*, and *through the forces of the Universe*. We believe that through magick the Universe bestows to us the powers to adapt, change, transmute and thrive. For the most part, most Pagans do practice some form of magickal arts, at least from time to time.

Paganism Today

The remnants of the old *Earth-based* spirituality is still celebrated, even though most of today's Pagans are not only farmers or living off the land. As a matter of fact, most Pagans live in cities, urban areas, small towns, and in suburbia. Today's Pagan practices are called *Neo-Paganism*. So, what are the Pagan basic principles of today which make up their practice? In most cases it depends on the tradition and the person practicing, but some of the basic principles of Neo-Paganism are:

- Respecting and connecting with *Mother-Earth*, the whole of Nature and the Universe,

- The belief that, "We Are All Relations,"

- The belief in Veneration and Reverence for Our Ancestors,

- The belief in the connection with the elements (*Earth, Water, Air, Fire, and Spirit*),

- Celebrating the Seasons, and or the *Wheel of the Year,*

- Sabbats and Esbats.

In addition, many Neo Pagans also practice *polytheism* and celebrate the *divine Feminine* and the *divine Masculine.* For many black Americans, Pagan principles fit into their everyday lives, and their spiritual desires and pursuits.

Now there are other basic characteristics of paganism that I may be missing here, and if you are already a Pagan, I am sure you have one or more that you would love to add. These are just the beginning basics and I will be elaborating other attributes and definitions in further details in other sections of this study. Please note that some practitioners may practice all the above, and a few more. Some may practice only part of these. What makes paganism special is that each practice is as different as a snowflake. Each Pagan may have their own deity or deities, and everyone has their own idea of what works for them. Some Pagans may not even work with deities at all.

While African Traditional Religions do adhere to their own rules of Priesthood to various degrees, in most basic Pagan traditions anyone can think of themselves as their own Priestess or Priest in their own right, regardless if they are initiated in a circle or coven or not. What I mean is communication and magickal workings with their gods are direct and personal. To most Pagans it is not necessary to have a middle person like a pastor or minister or Priest to go through in order to make sure one's prayers are sanctioned, ordained, registered or answered. It is believed, by most Neo Pagans, that we all have an open channel to the *Most High* or the *"God of Our Understanding"*, and it is up to us to have the will to make the call or pick up the receiver—sort of speak.

Earth is My Mother – Universe My All

Most Pagans, in general, believe in science. We believe in science because, unlike a few religions, science does not clash with our beliefs. On the contrary, it only boosters our theories. For example, there is a theory by scientists that as the molten Earth developed, and the vast waters cooled; and its primordial soup became fertile with nutrients, huge asteroids entered the oceans carrying microbial substances. In these waters, the microbes developed, and through the millennia they evolved into beings with the ability to crawl out of the enormous earthly amniotic fluid. Many scientific theorists believe that this is how human and animal life began on Earth. This theory is called *panspermia*. Panspermia is the belief that micro-organisms or seeds can travel via interstellar means, like comets and meteorites, and survive to initiate life on a planet by contact with water or other means. So, as the way animals, humans and plant-life proliferate, so does the Universe. To many Pagans, the ocean is our Mother's *holy primordial womb,* and oceans were the means through which living beings on Earth began.

Another scientific belief that I love is that we are all made of star-stuff. The stars are our Mothers, Grand Mothers, and GreatGrandmothers and…well I guess you get the point. We came from them, just as categorically, as we came from our own mothers and fathers. Every bit of chemical, mineral, gas and even liquid in our bodies came from the stars. Very simply put, when certain stars begin to age, they begin to lose their fuel. This fuel is hydrogen, and hydrogen is the fuel that makes them burn bright. When the fuel is spent the star begins to have expansions and contractions, just like a pregnant female. As it goes through these contractions it gives off helium. Later it begins releasing nickel, silicon, magnesium, carbon, nitrogen and oxygen. It reduces itself very much like the peeling of an onion. When the star gets to its inner core it converts to iron and that is when it begins to collapse. The results are that all the layers of the star are propelled out into space, and into the Universe. From their gases they form "nebulae" clouds. These are nurseries for fledgling stars. My point to this narrative is when a star begins to die it is pregnant, and when it goes supernova, it gives birth to other stars and spreads its fertility throughout the Universe. We and our wet nurse star, the Sun, may have had the same mother that gave birth to us, perhaps hundreds of thousands of galaxies or lightycars away. We are connected to the Universe. We are a part of the Universe. We all are the Universe. The etymology is that the word Universe *is* like the word *union, united* or *unit*. It means *One*. We are *One* and *The All*. So, if we are alive, it makes sense to believe we came from that which is alive. This means that the stars and the planets are alive. They are just alive on a level that we have yet to comprehend.

Pagans are considered *Earth-based,* meaning, we are passionate about our living Mother Earth. Many Pagans believe that the Earth is a living breathing organism called Gaia. It regenerates, renews, repairs and creates. Pagans charge themselves by submerging in the spirit of the Earth's land, water, plant-life and soil. The Earth is magnetic. It has a geomagnetic field. This field extends from the Earth's interior and stretches out into space. So, it is hard to deny that we are affected or even charged by this field.

Most Pagans are unapologetically tree-huggers. Trees are our Ancestors. They were here before any animals. We share their DNA. Pagans dance in the rain. We often have little use for gloves when planting or working in the soil, because of our essential attraction to touch, and to bear witness to the soil. We *ground* ourselves with Nature. We walk barefoot and do *"Earthing."* What gives life to plants gives life to us.

Communing with Nature, climbing a mountain path, walking in the sand on a beach, or wading in a river is where the *Holy Spirit* lies for us. It is not necessarily within a temple or in a church, but looking up to the Sun in the morning, and the Moon and the stars at night. In my opinion, most human beings have lost their connection to Nature and animals. They think of Nature as—*it verses us*. Pagans believe that the Natural world is where our inner battery is charged and where spiritual healing begins. It is also where our spiritual substance resides. Thus, is the reason why many of our brothas and sistars appear so soulless. It is because we all lost touch with Mother Nature, and the understanding of how important it is to link with Her.

We Are All Relations

There are sayings within many Native Indian Nations. In the Lakota Sioux Nation, it is "Aho Mitakuye Oyasin". In the Cherokee Nation, it is "Ea Nigada Qusdi Idadadvhn". Roughly, they are translated as, "We are all related", or "All my relations in Creation", or "We are all relations". The people who are native to this country, for thousands of years, knew a very important secret of the Universe. It is not us versus them, because we are all relatives. We all have a common Ancestor in the clouds, the air, the soil, the trees, the rocks, the ocean, the animals and the planets. We are all made of the same atoms and our gene pools are only slightly different. Pagans acknowledge that understanding these facets is very spiritually powerful. We believe these facets to be important to understand before taking actions of clearing forest, trees and woods. We believe them to be important to understand before polluting oceans and waterways. We believe there should be more thought placed before doing things like building fossil fuel pipelines to pollute the waterways of Native People in North Dakota. We believe there should be more thought placed before shooting human beings in routine traffic stops just because an officer is too afraid to do the job of seeing another person's humanity. When knowing that we are all related there would be less desire to funnel inferior water to cities like Flint Michigan. There would be less desire to practice cruelty to animals in circuses, industrial farms and water parks. When we think of the Universe as one, or related to us, we understand that what we do to another we do to ourselves. We are all connected as one tribe. We are all connected within the circle of life. Vanessa Williams sang it best in Disney's Pocahontas song, "Colors of the Wind", when she sang, "We are all connected to each other, in a circle, in a hoop that never ends."

Earth, Water, Air, Fire and Spirit

One of my favorite Pagan songs or chants goes: *"Earth my body, water my blood, air my breath and fire my spirit. I am born of the elements."* This is so apropos to me because it is the epitome of what the sacred elements are, and they are the major tools of a Pagan. They are the literal and figurative fundamental building blocks of the Universe. My body came from the Earth, my blood flows like the river, my breath blows like the wind, and my healthy spirit burns like fire. These are also called elemental tools of magick, and they are often used contemporaneously in spells and rituals. If a spiritualist has no other tools the symbols of these will do just fine.

Pagans believe that the elements of earth, air, fire and water are the sacred keys to life. Pagans immerse themselves in the beauty and symbolism of the elements to receive positive results. We also turn to these elements for worship, ritual and celebrations. For example, there is nothing more exciting for a Pagan than to do spiritual workings near a river or a mountain top. Fabulous workings can be done with a colorful burning candle, an open fire pit and or working with incense. In these examples you will find water, earth, fire and air respectively. Other examples are herbs, spring water, bonfires, seashells, graveyard or garden dirt, eggs, fruit, tobacco, feathers (from a bird that had already passed on or has shed them naturally), drums, bells, homemade incense, myrrh etc. I will explain more about elemental tools in a later lesson.

Spirit is also a special element that is used in rituals or magickal workings. We often call them elemental spirits. They are very hard to explain, and it took some years for me to truly understand their concepts or nuance. These are ancient spirits who were here long before the coming of humans, and they will be here long after we are gone. In the Wiccan belief they are considered 'universal witnesses or watchers of…' You can fill in the blanks from there. We often call to the elemental spirits to bear witness, protect, serve, or even to give advice. Further in the nuance, it is believed that all things have a spirit, even inanimate objects. This theory is called *animism*. And, for that reason, spirits can be invoked. To add to further confusion, Pagans believe that Spirit is everywhere—above, below, surrounding and within. For Wiccans they are often called *"the Watchtowers"* or *"Elder spirits."* I call them the *Old Guard or Ancestors*. I will explain more about using elements in another section.

Devotion and Veneration of the Ancestors

With the belief that energy is reshaped and transmuted, and is never truly departed, so too are the spirits of our Ancestors. While they are not here with us in the physical form, their past lives have made an indelible imprint upon our own, either directly, indirectly, present generation or past generations. Regardless of the ethnicity of our Ancestors, many of their struggles have helped us to get where we are today. So is the reason many people, cultures and religions, throughout the world, celebrate and venerate their memories. They were our teachers, sheroes and heroes, trailblazers, protectors and inspirations. We bare the genomes of who they were and with the blueprint of who we can be. What they have taught us makes us who we are regardless if they were our parents, grandparents, great-great aunts or a well-remembered distant cousin.

In particular, black Americans have deeply held beliefs about our Ancestors. They were, after all, what many would call the ultimate heroes/sheroes. Not only did the African Ancestors survive the horrors and traumas of strenuous ocean voyages through the *Middle Passage,* and the 400 plus years of slavery, but they survived building America and Jim Crow. So, the old saying, *"that which does not kill you makes you stronger"* definitely applies here. As another old adage goes, "…*there was an attempt to bury their roots and they only grew deep and bore fruits"*, and we are the fruit of our Ancestors. Because of their sacrifices and resilience, present-day African Americans rise like the phoenix. Black Americans are strong because the Ancestors who gave us life, were strong, and our spirits and mental fortitude can also be strong if only we remember them. Remembering our Ancestors also helps us to know ourselves. This is why many revere, celebrate and give thanks to those who came before us.

The other aspect of Ancestor veneration or worship, is the belief that their spirits peep in, check on us and may even assist us in our everyday lives, just like that of the belief of Angels or *spirit guides.* Pagans believe that these spirits or energies are real. They believe in the knowing, that certain energies are assigned to many of us. Just as quoted previously in *John Hope Franklin's* book, the African Ancestors believed that the spirits of their Ancestors have a great amount of power over their lives, and African religions believe this today. Some spiritualists pay homage to their Ancestors by creating temporary and or permanent Ancestor altars, and paying homage on to them on special days like *Samhain,* and the Mexican holiday, *The Day of the Dead* (El Día de los Muertos.)

Celebrating the Seasons with the Wheel of the Year

 Wheels, spirals and circles are very special to Witches, Pagans and Earth-Based Spiritualists. T e wheel and circle are the paradigms of the Universe. We are literally surrounded by wheels and circles. Our planet Earth is a sphere, along with all the other planets in the Universe. The Sun and other stars are spheres. The solar systems, galaxies and constellations revolve and orbits in circular or spiral motions. It is even believed that our known Universe is shaped like a circle created by the explosion of the *Big Bang*. If you think about it, you are a being who is comprised of atoms and molecules, which have electrons dancing in spiral motions right now. You can't see it, but our entire existence depends on what Pagans call the *spiral dance*. The term "spiral dance" was used by the Pagan writer and feminist *Starhawk* in her book by the same name— <u>The Spiral Dance</u>.

The Pagan spiral dance is the magick that can be weaved and cast by dancing in a spiral motion—mimicking the various motions within the Universe. The Universal spiral dance is the engine that runs the Universe. It is what makes all things work. This spiral engine is the energy that keeps the Universe moving and alive. It is the movement in the weather systems, the planets, and it is the orbit of the Moon which controls the tides. Many Witches and Pagans dance in circles or spirals to conjure energy into a *cone-of-power*. They dance either in rituals, festivals or alone.

The Wheel of the Year

Seasons also turn as a spinning circle, year after year. Because of this calendar circle, Pagans call the ever-changing seasons *The Wheel of the Year*. The Wheel of the Year consists of chronological holy days within any given Year. If one could bend a year from beginning to end, and fashion it into a hoop or wheel, the Pagan holy dates would be evenly separated like 8 spokes on a wheel. Therefore, they call it the *Wheel of the Year.* The Wheel then turns around and around from one year into the next. The Wheel of the Year is celebrated annually, with eight holy days or what are called *sabbats.* The sabbats represent the relationship humans have with the seasons, and the agriculture during the seasons. Often these sabbats are celebrated with festivals, rituals and or individual devotion. The Wheel of the Year was inspired from European Pagan traditions. Here and in Europe it is practiced as a macro celebration that is representative of the four seasons and planetary changes.

From the time of antiquity, humans, in every culture, have celebrated some type of ever-turning wheel with seasonal offerings, holidays and annual traditions. However, in the United States we have disconnected ourselves from the seasons. We have detached and separated ourselves, our psyche, and our spirit from Mother Nature (our giver of life). We have forgotten the purpose for the festivals, and as a result the natural world is meaningless to many of us. We have become materialistic, dehumanized and consumer driven. At the ring of a calendar date, we have been conditioned to crowd into stores at the mention of sales and Santa Claus. It has been my observation that human beings in general, and black Americans, specifically, have substituted their ancestral history of being close to the good green Earth for the harshness and barrenness of the cement jungle, the desire for materialism, and the stimulation of social media. Nature is nothing more than a place to seek refuge away from. Even when vacationing on a mountain, or a river, or a beach, Nature is no more than a visual backdrop for a selfie, and there is no incentive to look within the substance of Nature.

As for myself, I have always enjoyed Nature. So, the Wheel of the Year is more of a home for me. Besides birthdays, they are the only holidays I ever celebrate. Well, except for one or two other meaningful secular holidays, because the mainstream holidays correspond with them, I can celebrate some of my sabbats with my family without too much conflict. I just integrate my ideals of Nature and the seasons into their traditions, so my extended family has no problem with going with that flow.

Pagans celebrate eight festivals that mark the important themes in the cycles of Nature. The two solstices and the two equinoxes are observed. These are called major *sabbats or quarter days.* In addition, there are four *cross-quarter* days, which are seated between the major sabbats. These Pagan festivals are commonly celebrated across many Western Pagan traditions, including the Druid, Wiccan, Celtic, Norse (Asatru) and other Pagan spiritualistic paths. Oddly enough, these holidays are also becoming somewhat popular amongst people who practice or follow the African Traditional Religions or ATRs in North America. This is because the sabbats accommodate the ATR practitioner's desire to celebrate with seasonal offerings without celebrating heavily commercialized secular holidays. So, the quarter days celebrate the solstices and the cross-quarter days are equally divided between the major sabbats. They all mark the seasonal directives for farmers in the times of sowing to the times of harvest. The following will discuss the different sabbats in The Wheel of the Year.

Pagan Sabbats (Holy Days)

1) YULE – December 21st. *Major quarter sabbat. Pronounced: *u-all*. Winter Solstice (you know it as Christmas).

2) IMBOLC – February 1st - 2nd. Cross-quarter day. Pronounced: *em-boke*. Considered the time of the returning light. Also, a time of the first plantings (You know it as Groundhog Day).

3) OSTARA – March 19th - 21st. *Major quarter sabbat. Pronounced: *o'star-ah*. The Spring Equinox (Many relate it with Easter).

4) BELTANE – May 1st. Cross-quarter day. Pronounced: *bell-tain*. Average time for planting (You know it as May Day).

5) LITHA – June 21st. *Major quarter sabbat. Pronounced: *lee-tha* (You know it as the Summer Solstice).

6) LUGHNASADH OR LAMMAS – August 1st. Cross-quarter day. Pronounced: *lou -nasa*. Considered the first of three harvests. (The Catholics call it Lammas).

7) MABON – September 21st. *Major quarter sabbat. Pronounced *may-bon*. This is the second harvest (You know it as the Autumn Equinox).

8) SAMHAIN – October 31st. Cross-quarter day. Pronounced: *sal-win or sow-win*. Considered the *Witches' New Year* and the last harvest (You know it as Halloween).

So, I am sure by now your question is *"Why are most of the Pagan holidays surrounding the secular holidays?"* That is a great question, and the answer to that question is Pagan holidays were not created around the same period as secular holidays. It was the secular holidays that were created around Pagan holidays. You see, the secular holidays were not always secular. They were Pagan holy days for the seasons and celebrated by Pagans. The Catholic Church put their own spin with their religion and designated new holidays around Pagan holy days. And, yes, even Christmas. The following are the Pagan sabbats of the Wheel explained, and their corresponding secular holidays:

Peg #1 You Call it Christmas and We Call it Yule (Between December 20th and 23rd)

Yule is the Pagan festival we celebrate today as a 'peg' in the *Wheel of the Year*. The name has Scandinavian origins, but our celebration of the *Winter Solstice* has always been universal—just like the Summer Solstice and the Equinoxes. This holy day came before Christmas. In ancient Rome there was an old Pagan holiday called *Saturnalia* (the celebration for the god *Saturn*), that was celebrated in conjunction with the Winter Solstice, and during the end of the planting seasons for farmers. In Rome the celebration lasted from December 17th until December 23rd.

The old Pagans of Europe celebrated Saturnalia with outdoor festivals, food, greenery, trees in the home and gifts. In circa 315 A.D., and after the *Emperor Constantine* converted to Christianity, the Roman Catholic church declared that the Saturnalia celebration would also celebrate the birth of Jesus, and the celebration of Saturnalia took on a different energy. Approximately in the mid-4th century A.D., it is said that the Roman Catholic Church officially declared December 25th as the date that Jesus was born. Not that there was any real proof of that, and his birth date is not recorded in the bible. Consequently, the festival of

Saturnalia, and Pagan customs surrounding the festival, were absorbed into the celebration of Christmas. But, to the Paganhearted, the old customs of Yule and the Winter Solstice continue to live on as what has always been called *"the return or the rebirth of the Sun"*. Doesn't that sound familiar?

Peg #2 What is Imbolc?
(Between February 1st and 2nd)

Imbolc is a major Pagan holiday that falls an equal distance between the Winter Solstice and the *Spring Equinox*. Although this festival has a European name and roots, like most of the other eight holidays, it is said that the ancient Egyptians, Babylonians, Sumerians and many indigenous groups have celebrated similar festivals for the return of the Sun as well. Pagans consider this day *"the return of the Light"*. It is the time when the Sun reveals itself to us. We celebrate with candles and lights. African American Pagans wear white clothes and head wraps to pay tribute and to welcome the light. In secular terms it is celebrated as *Groundhog Day*. Both holidays suggest the anticipation of Spring, but in Imbolc culture we show gratitude for the Sun's return by giving offerings of milk, fresh-baked bread and cakes to the land, and at our altars.

Peg #3 They Celebrate Easter and We Celebrate Ostara
(Between March 19th and 21st)

In around 325 A.D., Constantine organized the *Council of Nicaea* to fortify the Christian church by inviting almost 2000 bishops to a conference. The council also gathered to discuss the refinement of the binding of chosen gnostic cannons we now know as the bible. They also proposed that Easter would fall on the first Sunday after the first Full Moon after the *Spring Equinox*. This directive is the same calculation that the church uses today for Easter. Prior to this many old Pagans celebrated *Ostara*. In the days of old, Ostara was a festival for the celebration of the Spring Equinox. It was named after the *Teutonic* (Germanic) goddess of Spring named *Ostare, Oestre or Eastre*. Her name means "shining light." or "the dawn" or "the bright eastern star." The goddess Ostare had a pet rabbit who laid colorful eggs and gave them out to children in the Spring. Let's see now where did we hear that before? Ostara is the celebration of the rebirth of Nature's regrowth energy. It is the mating time for animals like birds and rabbits. It is also a time of giving thanks for the lactation of farm animals like goats, lambs and cows. This is the purpose of giving milk as an offering.

Peg #4 They Call It May Day and We Call It Beltane (May 1st)

Beltane is a major time for planting both physical and mental seeds. It is considered a season of fertility, a season of fire to represent new light and new ideas, and it is the season for seeking love. Because of this, people consider this a time of fiery magick. Beltane sits between the Spring Equinox and the Summer Solstice. When I was a child, we called it *May Day* even though I didn't understand it's meaning at the time. Even in the inner city, where I grew up, my elementary school had big *May Day Parades*, and we nominated a May Queen and King to march in the school parade. The scenario of the May Queen and May King comes from the ancient lore of the Universal goddess and god courting together during this time of year. Because many animals tend to mate and have offspring during Beltane it is considered a very fertile time. Pagans celebrate Beltane by dancing around a maypole, as they wrap ribbons around it. The maypole represents this time of the great phallus and yoni. It represents a time of fertility and virility.

Peg #5 Litha is the Summer Solstice (Between June 21st and 23rd)

Litha is the time we celebrate the *Summer Solstice*. It is believed that the word Litha is the Latin name for both June and July in ancient times. It is a period of mating, coupling and the *dyad*. This is because June was the ancient Pagan traditional wedding time when many couples got married. As a matter of fact, June was named after Juno, who was the Roman queen of the gods and patroness of love, weddings and marriage. Many people still believe in June weddings, even though most don't know where the tradition originated. In ancient times in Europe couples would get married during the Summer Solstice, and then the bride and groom would be locked in their wedding chamber, by family and friends, with a good supply of honey wine or mead. They were challenged not to come out for a month or until the next Full Moon or until the bride was pregnant. This is how the term "honeymoon" was conceived—no pun intended. The festival of Litha celebrates the Sun's energy or the masculine energy's and is the most potent solar day of the year.

Peg #6 Lughnasadh or Lammas – The First Harvest (August 1st)

As the year's wheel continues to turn, we get to the next peg, and first of the three harvests. *Lughnasadh,* (word of Gaelic Celtic origins) or *Lammas* (the Catholic name for this festival), celebrates the beginning of the end of the crops season. This holy day is observed on the 1st of August. Historically it was when the first grain was cut and the first loaves of bread were baked. Baked bread truly represents this time period. The power of the Sun god has hit His peak, and now His powers will begin to wane, and His energy will start its decline. Most Pagans think of this sabbat as the beginning of an evaluation period for their successes, or accomplishments. It is also an evaluation of what they could perfect for themselves in the next coming year.

Peg #7 Mabon – The Second Harvest (Between September 21st and 23rd)

This is the second of the harvest celebrations. It is also the time of the *Autumn Equinox*. As with the *Spring Equinox*, this is the time when night and day are equal in time duration. The date falls approximately between September 21st and the 23rd. This is also the time when everyone is celebrating harvest festivals. The *Harvest Moon* appears during this month and it often falls near or during the time of the Autumn Equinox. Harvest festivals are celebrated all over the world, and during the waning part of the year. In North America people decorate festivals and homes with dried samples of fall crops like pumpkins, apples, grapes, berries and squash. The symbolism, during this time period, engages the passion of many Pagans. Again, it is in Nature and in the changes of the seasons where Pagans find spiritualism. It is in the beauty of the harvest where we find sacrament. Some African American festivals demonstrate the spirit of the African harvest like the *Gullah Festival* in South Carolina, *Africa in April* in Memphis Tennessee, the *Odunde Festival* in Philadelphia, Pennsylvania, the *African World Festival* in Detroit Michigan (this festival is truly dedicated to the Ancestors), *IFE-ILE Afro-Cuban Dance Festival* in Miami, Florida, and the *Bimbé Cultural Arts Festival* in Durham, North Carolina—just to name a few.

Peg #8 They Call it Halloween and We Call it Samhain (October 31st)

The Pagan festival, *Samhain,* was a part of the ancient Celtic religion in the British Isles. At Summer's end the Celts believed that the veil or the barrier between our known world, and the spiritual realm, became thin.

On or around October 31st, the Celts believed that the souls of the dead were able to peer through, if not come through the thinning veil to roam the streets and villages. To appease these spirits, food and libations were left outside the doors at night. They may have also thought that if dearly departed Uncle Brewster had a few drinks outside he may forget about coming in and troubling folk. It was also believed that leaving offerings for the spirits would ensure the good outcome of crops the following year. Many people didn't believe it was a good time to come outside during that period, but when people did emerge from their homes they dressed up in costumes and masks, so as not to be recognized by unsavory Ancestors, and so that they would be mistaken for spirits themselves. I guess they thought spirits didn't talk to each other.

In approximately the 8th century the Catholic church again intervened. They changed the name of Samhain to *"All Hallows' Eve"*, meaning Holy Day's Eve, and later, in more contemporary times, it was changed to *Halloween* for short. The Catholic holiday on November 1st marks *All Saints' Day, or All Hallows' Day, or Hallowmas or the Feast of All Saints.* So Hallows' Eve is the night before their festival day. Pagans keep the traditional awareness of the thinning veil, and believe the thinning veil marks the time of a new year or *Witches' New Year.* Samhain is, without a doubt, the most favorite holy day among Witches and Pagans, because, be them in or out of the closet, we Pagans use this day to be who we are without fear of persecution. It is the one day we are free to look and be ourselves. I will explain in more detail about the *Wheel of the Year* when I discuss the Pagan lore in a following lesson.

Diagram of Wheel of the Year

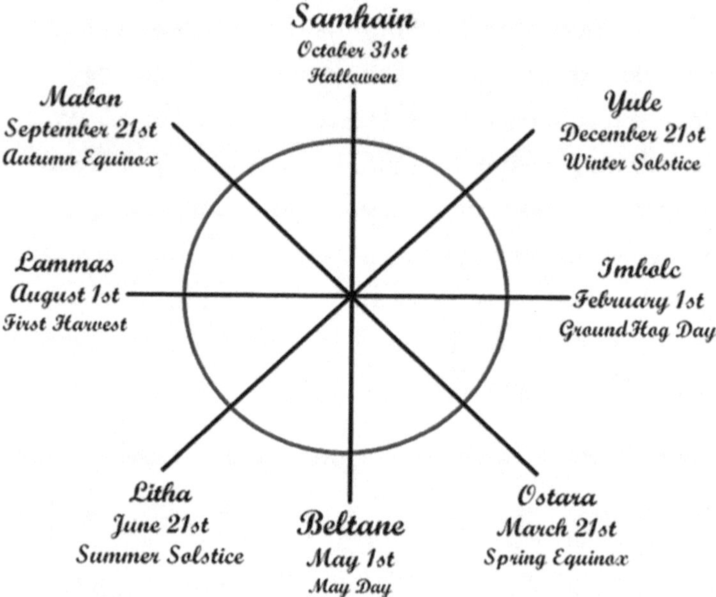

The 13 Esbats

While the sabbats represent *celebrations of the Sun* or *solar holy days*, the *esbats* represent the Pagans' *lunar holy days*. There are thirteen Full Moons per year. So, in essence, there are thirteen esbats total per year. This means there is one Full Moon per month, except for one month having two Full Moons. The second Moon in that month is called a *Blue Moon*. The Blue Moon is a rarer Moon and it is considered a very potent Moon, and it is used to get strong magickal ambitious work done.

The word esbat has origins from the Old French word *s'esbattre* or the modern French word *ébat*, meaning to frolic, dance and amuse oneself (Wigington, 2019). This is apropos because in many esbats rituals Witches dance, frolic and are festive. The Moon is the natural symbol of the Witch. We naturally feel its power and we use our connection with it in rites, reflections, spells, shadow work etc.

Esbats

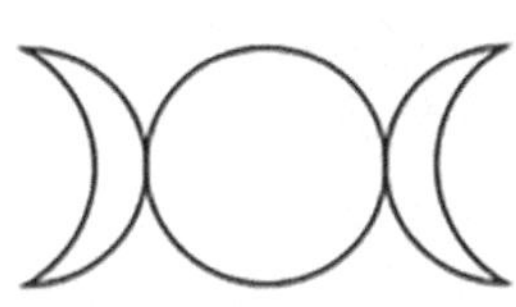

The Triple Goddess Moon is the witchy symbol of two crescent Moons, and the Full Moon in the center. It represents the *Maiden, Mother* and *Crone* aspects of the Goddess in which we celebrate. The Maiden is the left crescent (New Moon or Waxing Moon), the Mother is the Full Moon in the center, and the Crone is the crescent on the right (Waning Moon). This *holy trinity* symbol is used in many rituals and during the esbats, or at least it is a symbol we think of meditatively.

Most Pagan literature gives the definition of *esbats* as rituals an individual, or a coven, or a circle perform on a *Full Moon*. Or, you may have read that esbats are rites or spells performed by practitioners under a Full or *New Moon*. But, simply put, an esbat is a particular observance, of a moon-phase, on a particular month. That observance could be any appropriate ritual, meditation or gathering for practitioners. It could also be a prayer, chant or brief recognition or acknowledgement by an individual. My esbats as of late have been to simply smoke some mugwort in my favorite pipe, have a glass of wine, say a simple prayer or chant while watching the Full Moon. Full Moons are considered major esbats or holy days for Pagans. However, to many people, *New Moons* and *Dark Moons* are considered important esbats too. Especially when there are specific rituals or magickal workings needing to be done within the phase.

The Full Moon

The *"Full Moon"* is the most popular of Moon phases for Witches and is believed to be the most powerful phase of the lunar cycle. The Full Moon is a representation of the Mother goddess in Her most radiant form. It represents the feminine energy at its most potent. It is considered a magnetic energy that has the sensation of a pulling and or tugging at the heart strings, which is why it is a symbol for love and romance. This Moon is often used for the start of eliminating bad habits or it is often used to chime in the hours for devotion and meditation. Others may use it for divination, clairvoyant activity, and to obtain enlightenment since it is a wonderful period of free-flowing psychic energy. This is because the light that reflects from it is believed to bring some of the sharpest clarity. Placing a cauldron of water or mirror under its reflection creates an insightful tool for scrying. In old school terms this is called *drawing down the Moon.* For many people, the Full Moon provides a period of reflection and is a meditative time for purging and releasing that which no longer serves.

The Waning Moon Period

'The Waning Moon' is what I call the *'partial'* phase that actively fades immediately after the Full Moon. In this phase the Full Moon begins to diminish its girth or circumference, and its energy begins to wane with it, because of its position with the Sun blocking its power. This allows spiritualists to align their magick with the waning Moon to eliminate bad habits, bad relationships, road blocks, bad situations, bad jobs and to eliminate anything that blocks one from the success of their goals. The Crone goddesses rule here.

The Dark Moon

 As the Waning Moon completes its cycle and comes to an end, *"The Dark Moon"* phase begins. The Dark Moon is just before the New Moon, and the day when the Moon is not seen at all by the human eye or by a telescope. It is in this transitional phase where the Moon sits between its waning (decreasing in illumination) state, and waxing (gaining in illumination) state. This *in-between* state is why many people believe the Dark Moon to be so special since any *in-between* or transitional state is said to be extraordinarily magickal and or a type of *singularity power source*. When I was in my beginning stages, as a Witch, the Dark Moon was very important to me. I did workings during, and paid homage to, the Dark Moon monthly for over a year. I heard the call of the Crone goddesses *Hecate and Oya*, and the Dark Moon is a Crone's most beloved of the waning states. The other reason I may have been in such a Dark Moon period was because, in hindsight, my spirit may have instinctively felt the need to "clean house" before dedicating myself fully to the craft. While waning Moons are used to cast out or eliminate bad habits and things which no longer serve, and waxing Moons are used to gain assets in some way, the purpose of the Dark Moon is to disinfect, deep clean, lay a foundation for or to sterilize. It cleanses in order to promote a fresh start, or before setting a new tablecloth or a clean slate. It didn't occur to me then, but it was the Crone spirit that moved me to do Dark Moon rituals in order to clear the way for my new life as a Wiccan. The Crone spirit made me wash behind my green ears, in a manner of speaking, before coming to the magickal table.

The New Moon

 Although it may not be used as often as the Full Moon, the *"New Moon"* phase is well known to most Witches as the second favorite of Th e Triple Goddess Moon phases. Th e New Moon phase occurs when the Moon begins to become visible to the telescope and or the human eye. As a result, a vision of a small slither of a *Crescent Moon* appears as it grows back to a Full Moon state. Wonderful spells are cast by this Moon and can be used for any spell with intentions for new beginnings and new starts like a new job, starting a new business, magickal initiations or new relationships. Because of its emphasis on newness, freshness, and new beginnings this Moon is favored by Maiden goddesses like Oshun, and the Maiden aspects of the Universe.

Waxing Moon Periods

The Waxing Moon Periods are the periods after the Moon becomes new, and up until when the Moon is at its fullest. This period is considered the time of gaining attributes or assets, just as the New Moon is used for harnessing one's power. Use this Moon for starting a new relationship, new job, new business, buying a new home, car or taking on a new venture. The difference between this Moon and the New Moon state is that the Waxing Moon is considered as a period to work towards a goal. This time is favored by the Mother aspect. The tarot card of the Empress is thought of in this phase, because it is a period of feathering one's nest, nesting, feeling prosperous, increasing family, finding comfort and nurturing oneself.

SOME TRADITIONS PRACTICED BY AFRICAN AMERICAN PAGANS

It is true that many black Americans practice some type of spirituality outside of the Abrahamic religions, and the numbers are indeed growing. Although more African Americans identify as non-affiliated with any religion, some of these black non-affiliates (NAs), have a spirituality that ranges far beyond mainstream religions. Another *Pew Research*, which surveyed 8,660 Black adults between November 2019 and June 2020, reported that approximately 21% are non-affiliated with any particular religion. This survey reports that of the NAs, 12% say that they have an altar or shrine in their homes, and they pray to it at least monthly. They also stated that 40% of NAs meditate at least monthly, and that 40% of the NAs believe that if they pray to the Ancestors, they will protect them from harm. In addition, 30% of the total 8660 surveyed say they have a practice of burning sage and incense. And lastly, this Pew Research reported that 50% of NAs say that they believe in reincarnation (Cox, 2021).

In this section, I will be introducing some basic types of spiritual Pagan traditions that African American Pagans may also practice. While this study will primarily discuss Wicca, I thought it would also be appropriate to first add some information about other Pagan practices in case there is an interest in some other traditions. The black Pagan community often blends traditions so I felt it would be helpful to give some vignettes about some other traditions. As an online administrator for African American Spiritualist forums for 23 years, I have privy to some insights of African American Pagan practices. One forum, at this time, holds approximately 17 thousand members. I will present here just a few of their professed traditions. Again, please note that most people practice a few or even several of these traditions together. It can be done.

By its very nature much of paganism is *eclectic*, allowing one to integrate various techniques and spiritual pursuits. Pagan practices have been evolving by blending various disciplines. It is a freedom that big brother, and the commonly-known belief systems, cannot control which is why it is so very liberating. Just to restate from the introduction, paganism is an umbrella term for any religion that is not Abrahamic, such as Christian, Judaism, or Islam. However, all Pagans don't follow the Wheel of the Year or esbats. African Traditional Spiritualists do not follow the Wheel, officially, although many practitioners may celebrate in the spirit of comradery, or to just engage in the season with other Pagan communities. For example, many ATR practitioners enjoy a good Samhain festival.

African Traditional Religions

African Traditional Religions or *ATRs* are indigenous Spiritual Systems that originated from times of ancient Africa and are still practiced, and are unabridged no matter where they are practiced. According to the late *John S. Mbiti* in his book, *African Religions and Philosophy,* he says that within the continent, there "are three thousand African peoples (tribes), and each has its own religious system" (Mbiti, 1990, pp. 1). However, many of the African religions are practiced in the Americas and all over the world. Some examples of these religions are *Yoruba religion, Akan, Ifá and Vodun.*

African Diasporic Traditional Religions

African Diasporic Traditional Religions or *ADTRs* are religions that originated from the time of ancient Africa and were brought to the Americas and the islands by the slaves. However, aspects of each religion were altered as a hybrid in order to hide their practices from the slaveholders in the guise of Christian practices. So, while the slaveholders believed that their bondspersons were practicing a form of Christianity, the slaves were, in effect, integrating a Christian veneer over their own religion. These religions are still practiced today in the African Diaspora. Some examples of these religions are: *Santería, Haitian Vodou, Louisiana Voodoo, Candomblé, Palo, and Obeah.*

These are just a few names to introduce you. My intention here is to present the names of these religions to help to familiarize the reader. I will not go deeper into descriptions since I have not studied their disciplines extensively and since ATRs or ADTRs are not in my purview. There are books and online information available for these traditions and more. If you decide to study these religions, know that they are in-depth processes. Finding a reputable Priest may not be easy, and once you do you are required to eventually go through initiation processes that can be very expensive for most people. But many people have found great satisfaction and joy in the practice of ATRs and ADTRs.

Alchemists

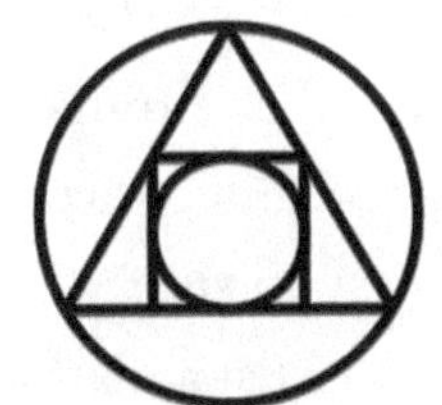

While some people may not think of *Alchemy* as Pagan, many Pagans are extremely interested in the subject of Alchemy, and they may in fact call themselves *Alchemists*. Alchemy is a subject of interest in black Pagan forums. A good book to introduce the theory is called <u>The Alchemist</u> by *Paulo Coelho* (Coelho, 2014), which is written in novel form. This is the same book that the Oscar-nominated and Golden Globe winner and actor *Will Smith,* announced on the <u>Tavis Smiley Show,</u> that it was his favorite book. He went on to say, *"I consider myself an Alchemist. An Alchemist is basically a mystical chemist."*

So, that about explains alchemy in a nutshell. Right? Close. But there are also some other factors too. Alchemy is a type of mentalism. Alchemy is the three-way junction between the mental, material and the spiritual world. This junction is considered the place where creation, manifestation and magick is formed. It is literally mind, consciousness and spirit over matter. When one has the intentional mind at its purest form, spirit at its purest form and matter at its purest form entangled, then magick happens. The word Alchemy has some origins in both Egypt, and in the Arabian countries. Its name even comes from the Arabic word, *al-kimiya*. It is "*Al*" meaning *"the"*, and *"kimiya"*, meaning *"black land"*. Although, it is said that the Arabs were among the first to practice Alchemy, the ancient Egyptians created profound mystical laws around its practice. Because of this, some people believed that Alchemy got its name from *Kemet,* the ancient name for Egypt. Kemet is translated as *"The Black Land".* Some say it is because of the black skin of the people who lived there. Some say it is because of the richness of the soil that developed because of the Nile River's seasonal floods. Some argue that Alchemy got its name because of the dark mystery the practice has always been shrouded in. Whatever the reason, Alchemy has never lost its popularity since its ancient days of practice.

The beginnings of Alchemy were also the beginnings of chemistry. It was the belief of early scientists that turning lead, and other ordinary metals into gold was a sure thing. They believed that if all things were made of the basic elements of air, fire and water it was easy to start with minor metals and build gold from there. They believed it was just a matter of scientifically adding and subtracting the Earth elements, plus a few other elements like mercury, sulfur and salts. This process of scientific manipulation is called *transmuting.* Today's Alchemists may have or may not have discovered the theory of transmuting to gold or finding the *Philosopher's Stone* (the miracle gold or the elixir of youth) which was called *"The Great Work".* However, they do believe that they have found a way of transmuting consciousness with the same metaphor of transmuting matter. That is, what can be used in chemistry can be used in the spiritual sense to forge an existential life, and to make things manifest. From this outlook comes the ancient adage *"As Above So Below."* Alchemists use symbols and elements to transmute, so as to bring consciousness, intuition, and energies for the higher vibration of the Soul.

Brujas, Brujos y Brujeria

These names, *Brujas and Brujos,* are becoming just as popular in the black community as the word *Witch.* The actual craft of *Brujeria* (witchcraft) is a practice of Spanish folk magick, and somewhat similar to *Hoodoo,* which is practiced in the American South. Those of many Spanish-speaking cultures refer to individuals, who are practitioners of Brujeria, as *Bruja*—a female Witch, or *Brujo*—a male Witch. Brujeria is practiced across the Afro-Latin diaspora. Magick from the Latin Americas is rooted and steeped in African magick, and is associated with many *African Diasporic Traditional Religions* like *Santeria* and *Candomble.* Like Hoodoo, Brujeria is often practiced with a fusion of both Pagan and Christian theologies, which can include charms, conjuring hexing, roots, herbal magick etc. Since the *African Diaspora* is so entrenched within Spanish culture, many non-Spanish black Witches, as well as Latinx Witches, have claimed the name for themselves.

Often, in this movement, there is a sense that many who claimed the Bruja (also called *Afrowitch*) or Brujo name have aligned themselves with the ever-growing *Womanist movement.* This movement is being ignited by many singers and actors who are *gangster,* so of speak, in the ideology of realizing their own power, regaining control of their own bodies, and finding the Goddess, Priestess and Bruja within. Sistars like *Princess Nokia, Beyoncé, Erykah Badu, Cardi B., Ida Divine, the duo OSHUN, Summer Walker, Azizaa, Rihanna,* and the duo *Ibeyi,* just to name a probable few. These performers are prominent in their Bruja type artforms. While they may keep us guessing on what their true artistic Bruja-like symbolisms are, or if they are even practitioners at all, they appear to demonstrate the spirit of inner Bruja.

Chaos Witch

"In all chaos there is a cosmos, in all disorder a secret order." ~ Carl Jung

Chaos magick refers to a type of magickal practice that is simple, ceremonial but yet unique. One would imagine that by the word's very definition it is something that anyone would want to steer clear from. When we think of the word we all think of mayhem, havoc and disorder. But, as the goddess *Khaos* might say, *there is order in disorder.* Chaos magick is more benign than it sounds. It is eclectic, drawing magickal technique from all forms of magick, and each practice is as unique as the individual who practices it. Chaos magick is a Neo-Pagan practice and draws techniques and tools from the Shaman, the Witch, the Pagan etc. Chaos magicians are free spirits having no love for rules or dogma. They are Agnostics to any organized rules or systems of magick or societal rules and believe that magick is effective just as long as the practitioner believes in their power and their craft.

Ethnocentric and Afrocentric Paganism and Witchcraft

"Know God" African Adinkra Symbol Shown

Simply put, *ethnocentric* paganism is the theory or practice of spiritual work or ritual work done with one's own cultural identity, garb or tools. It often involves the veneration of Ancestors and one's own bloodline. Ethnocentricity is practiced all over the world from the United States to Europe to Asia. So, *Celtic, Strega, Druid* and *Asatru* are examples of European Ancestral magickal practices. They observe their Ancestral pantheons. They practice the magick of their Ancestors, and that which is passed down to them. Many people of African descent practice ethnocentrically, or in this case what is called *Afrocentric* paganism. In this tradition, they may practice an indigenous religion of Africa, or an African diasporic religion or Kemetic religion. Some may perform basic Pagan practices, but will include African-based tools, African pantheons (family of patron gods), or they may decorate their personal spiritual space with the décor of their Ancestors or African homeland. Often, black people who practice ethnocentrically will dress in African garb, headdress, headwraps or ritual robes for sabbats or other cultural wear. They may also meditate with African music, vibrations and drums. The depth of an Afrocentric practice varies from person to person. It may range from minor adornments to a full African Traditional Religion initiation. What is often common is that the Afrocentric practitioner, more often than not, works with direct Ancestors and or African deities such as the *Orisha*, the *Loa (also spelled Lwa) or* the *Neteru*.

Goddess and or Wombmyn or Wombman or Womyn Centered

"The Divine Mother Earth" African Adinkra Shown

Goddess-centered paganism is the practice and/or study of journeying into the realm of the *divine Feminine* and engaging in Her mysteries. Practiced by both women and men, it is about seeking the divine Feminine within and without. This subject resonates deeply for me, because it is my feeling that we, as a human race, have allowed the excesses of *patriarchy* to run so rampant throughout the world, and so completely that we are entrenched in wars, divisions, racism, overpowering structuralism, authoritarianism, misogyny, tribalism, diminutive empathy, unrestricted capitalism, nationalism, oppression, sexual abuse, and low levels of compassion, school shootings, gun violence and we have a penal system that has gone absolutely amuck. Many spiritual theologians believe that the reason for this is the total disregard for the *Female aspect of the Universe*. This includes the total disdain for the aspects of the female side of the brain, and the disregard for the divine Feminine.

The Female aspect of the Universe imbues expression, creativity, sympathy and liberty. The *Male aspect* is rigid, logic-driven, disciplined and structured. The Female aspect allows negotiation while the Male aspect looks for conquest. The Female aspect calls for nuance while the Male aspect seeks the bottom line or that which is black or white. The Female aspect travels through that which is scenic, while the Male aspect is direct and straight in its route. The Female aspect is social, altruistic and nurturing, while the male aspect seeks autonomy, solitude and security. This is the *Yin-Yang* aspect of the Universe. The Universe needs all of these characteristics for harmony. But, if one side of the Universe is disregarded then societies become unbalanced, dysfunctional and chaotic.

Since before the societal peak and heyday of Mesopotamia, the Sumerian empire, and Ancient Kemet, all of the symbols, statues, icons, and hieroglyphics of the divine Feminine were abundant. The worship of the Goddess reigned all over the world. It was understood that it was *She* who was the Mother, and all came from *Her.* However, since the rise of the patriarchal religions of Christianity, Judaism, and Islam, the male aspect has had a thumb on the Universal scale leaving the world completely unbalanced for thousands of years. Subsequently this is resulting in humanity in a totally dysfunctional state. This virtual blackout of the Yin has over-shadowed and demonized the studies and practices of Goddess veneration, the divine Feminine, and witchcraft. Even many women, particularly contemporary women of African heritage, do not seek to find balance in the divine Feminine. To most people God is a male deity who gave birth to the world, and to the All. So, to them, the fact that the Female aspect, of the Universe, is the aspect that truly gives birth is a minor detail that is not worth contemplating.

The good news is there is a resurgence of what is called *Neo-Feminism or Womynism*. Neo-Feminism, despite detractor's persistence, is NOT a movement of women working to take over the world, or to develop a movement that believes women are superior to men. It is NOT a group of female Nazis working to destroy the autonomy of black men or to emasculate them (yes that is a real and widespread assertion, believe it or not). Neo-Feminism is the effort of women to find their own loss power, to seek EQUALITY with their male counterparts, and to add more of their voice in, or to, society and the world. In spiritual terms women are seeking to find the Goddess within themselves. As a child I searched for the Goddess within, and without. Years later I found that *She* had always been with me. I just needed to open my third-eye to see Her. It has been my witness, working in Pagan groups, that many black women have rejected the term feminism or neo-feminism, because of the misconceptions surrounding the term. For over 400 years African American women have bent a knee to a male God who they were told gave birth to the Universe. However, some black women are now calling themselves *Womynists, Womanists, or Wombminists*. The spelling changes with the person. The term *Womanist* refers to the consideration of women's issues and family causes, equality, seeking selfbalance, seeking knowledge of self, and the study and the exploration of the divine Feminine and *Her Mysteries*. Be it Womanist or Feminist, the Goddess is slowly returning to the consciousness of humanity. A new generation of women is now discovering that they are themselves goddesses, and it is the Female aspect that gives birth to creation in all things, and spiritual balance is only found in finding both the *Pagan Goddess*, as well as the *Pagan*

Lord within. Attention Spiritualists, we are being called to impart balance. One tradition that works to this cause is Dianic witchcraft or Wicca. Dianic Witchcraft came into its own starting from the 1970s. The writer *Starhawk* leads a movement of Dianic Wicca today.

Green Witch or Pagan

 A *Green Witch/Pagan* is a spiritualist who is either an *herbalist* or is *Earth-centered,* or is an *environmentalist.* It is not unheard of for a Green Witch or Pagan to be all three. The *herbalist* is into growing herbs and or collecting herbs for magickal uses or for healing. These Pagans are usually aficionados, of sorts, and can give advice about *tinctures, oils, potions* and *natural medicines.* They may also use their home-grown herbs for cooking or culinary pursuits.

A *Green Earth-centered Pagan* is someone who enjoys the surroundings of the outdoors. They often go camping, hiking, and on retreats. They perform rituals, spells or sabbats near fields, oceans, lakes or mountains. In short, they honor the Earth and Nature. These Pagans prefer the natural basics, and they may love living off the land or close to the land. They believe in aspects of healthy living, and they pay homage to *Great Mother Earth* to whom they may refer to as *Gaia.*

Many Green Pagans and Witches are *environmentalists* by heart, and may have deep concerns about the Earth, because of the human exploitation of the land, the destruction of natural resources, the increase in *climate change* and the pollution of our natural waterways. These Green Witches and Green Pagans are more often than not vegans or vegetarians, because of their consciousness for animal rights, their own *carbon footprint,* their own physical health or the over-all health of our environment. Green Pagans may consider themselves to be *humanists.*

Hedge Witch

I am interested in disclosing here that I have a heartfelt interest in this nature of witchcraft, because, among some other traditions, I fancy myself as a *Hedge Witch*. This form of witchcraft is becoming intensely popular, because its mysteries are very alluring, or may I say enchanting. There is some debate on where the word Hedge Witch originated from. Some say the name came from the spiritual, mystical, but non-physical act of jumping over or passing through hedges into other worlds or realms. Some subscribe to the belief that the name comes from old Europe in the time when spiritual practitioners practiced their craft just outside of the villages or just beyond the tree lines, which were then called hedges, thus the name *Hedge Witch*. The Hedge Witches of yesteryear lived and worked in seclusion, and people would travel through the hedges to these Spiritualists for medicine, potions, healing, midwifery or whatever their needs were. This, of course, was before doctors, or when doctors were not available.

Hedge Witches are characterized by a few attributes. The first attribute is that Hedge Witches spend most of their practice alone. While they are often married, and with children, they spend lots of alone time learning, studying and practicing their ancient arts in secret and away from prying eyes. Their second attribute is that they live a Shaman-like lifestyle. Hedge Witches are much like *Sorceresses* and *Sorcerers*, where they draw on their power from an inner and or ethereal Source. This means that much of their time is spent in meditation, *spiritual journeying* or in *trance-like states*. In addition, Hedge Witches are travelers between worlds, and they may spend even more time than the average Witch, with one foot in other worlds and communing with spirit(s). Lastly Hedge Witches have special relationships with plants. They are Green Witches, spiritually communing with their plants in order to aid them in creating salves, teas, tinctures and potions for healing and such. For example, some potions may be used for night traveling (out of body experiences), and journeys into other realms. They may create *flying salves* to aid them in astral projections through the stars and beyond.

Hoodoo/Conjurer/Root Worker

 *Hoodoo*, which is also known as *Conjuring or Conjurer magick, Mountain Magick, Root Worker or Root Doctor magick, is* a magickal practice that most likely originated from the mid- to the late-1700s, when the steady stream of Africans was transported to the southern parts of the United States. Its magickal workings began in the south and eventually spread to the mountains of North America. It is believed that Hoodoo was rooted from multiple African magickal practices from ethnic groups in West Africa and those in Central Africa.

Hoodoo developed when many in bondage lost knowledge of their homeland religions. This was because of all of the multiple cultural spiritualities in the African population. Many bondspeople were sent to areas isolated from those who would teach the homeland religions to others, which made it completely impossible to maintain cohesive religious or spiritual belief systems. According to *Katrina Hazzard-Donald,* in her book, *Mojo Workin',* the Africans turned to lots of Native American spiritual beliefs, "…*when encountering fragmented African spiritual belief disrupted by insufficiently concentrated numbers in the enslave African ethnic groups as well as by removal from the African homeland*" (Hazzard-Donald, 2012, pp. 36). Hoodooists also had the additional struggle of concealing their religious practices from slave traffickers. While it was easier for those in the Catholic regions to utilize saints and other artifacts, those in Protestant areas found great difficulty obscuring their religious beliefs.

Because of the lost religious knowledge, Native Americans contributed spiritual knowledge to the Africans, as well as botanical, root and animal knowledge, since many American plants, animals and roots were, at fi rst, unfamiliar to the Africans. But Hoodoo had other contributories to its practices too. Depending on the population of where it was practiced, Hoodoo had mixtures of diff erent European folk magick like *Stregheria* (Italian witchcraft) or *Celtic* folk magick or even *Jewish mysticism.* As time passed Hoodoo became more of a practical application of magick, than a religious one. Most of the practitioners became steeped within the black Christian church and their Hoodoo practices reflected it with the use of the bible, Christian icons and the use of bible passages as charms.

Hoodoo was first practiced by bondspeople as a work of protection against the slaveholders, and for forms of healing since doctors were not available to them. Hoodoo allowed the conjurers or practitioners to practice midwifery, defend themselves from harm, to cure their own ailments, and to gain personal control over hardships and bad luck. Today Hoodoo is practiced all over the United States by those who are Christians, those who practice ADTRs and some who are Witches or Pagans and enjoy the old or new practices of it.

Kemetism

 *Kemetics, Kemeticism or Kemetism* is an African Traditional Religion or ATR. I am giving a little more information about this tradition here, because, unlike other ATRs, people don't have to necessarily go through extensive initiation as they do with other ATR or ADTR training. This is because it is considered an *open* tradition and it is easier for readers to research and study on their own. There are many people who are *Kemetic, Kemetic Witches*

or even *Kemetic Wiccans*. Since it is said that Wiccan rituals were adapted from Ancient Kemet or *Hermetic* spiritual ceremonies, and its old Mystery Schools, it is entirely fitting that there would be Kemetic Wiccans.

Kemet (or spelled KMT) is the original name of ancient Egypt. The name Egypt was given by the ancient Greeks. Kemetic spirituality is considered a religious movement seeking to capture the heart of ancient Kemetic/Egyptian spiritual practices. Kemetism is practiced by many different types of people and races throughout the world, but is highly favored by people of African descent, because it provides a cultural and religious connection to a spirituality of African ancestry. Many Kemetic practitioners consider Kemetism *a way of life* since it is considered *a type of* systematic philosophy for higher living. Kemetics also teaches how to adhere to a type of *cosmic* and *moral* order. Its principles teach about the metaphysical connections between the Earth realm and the higher cosmic realms.

Kemetic practitioners follow the principles of the *Ntcheru* or *Netjeru* also spelled *Neteru* (Egyptian deities) energies. Some of these deities are *Ma'at, Ausar, Auset, Wadjet* and *Ra*. Each deity is a representative of a particular aspect or energy that has meaning to the human spirit. Kemeticism also incorporates magickal practices and rituals similar to practices of ancient Kemet, which are ceremonial in nature. While Kemetic practitioners recognize the *Feminine aspect of the Universe* many of their practitioners are more often orientated towards the *divine Masculine,* which is why some black American males, seeking the *black divine Masculine,* find the practice very attractive to them.

While Kemetism is considered an *open religion*, meaning one doesn't have to be initiated to learn or practice, there are *Kemetic Orthodox* traditions that require some training, in order to assure respect for and knowledge of the origins of its tradition. Th ere are Kemetic schools and teachers in the United States. Th ere are even online classes one can attend. One popular organization some Kemetic Pagans belong to is the *Ausar Auset Society*. I received good feedback about its studies. If you are interested in Kemetic studies do look around, ask questions, and compare the cost of the courses. One standard book for reading about Kemetism is called <u>*Metu Neter*</u>, written by *RA Un Nefer Amen*.

Kitchen Witch

A *Kitchen Witch* is a Pagan who prides themselves on their culinary, herbal and spell casting skills in the kitchen. They may do all or most of their spell casting there. They may do most of their spiritual work there. They may produce tinctures, oils, healing medicines, creative workings and potions in the kitchen. They may even have an altar near their stove. Pretty much, a Kitchen Witch's kitchen is her/his place of business. Often, they are the best cooks, or will seek to become one, and everyone really wants to be over when they hear they are making a meal. Kitchen Witches usually have a well-stocked cupboard, cabinet or pantry of herbs, spices and even homemade remedies. Most of the time they are also Green Herbal Witches and grow their own food and herbs.

Magi or Mage

The origins of the word *Magi* (pronounced Maa-jii) dates back to an old ancient Persian word *Magus,* rooted from *"Zoroastrian Priest"* or an experienced Persian religious teacher (Magi | Encyclopedia.Com, 2020). Today's word

Magi often refers to a *Magician* who dabbles in multiple disciplines like *astronomy, astrology, shamanism, witchery, sorcery, alchemy,* and/or *wizardry.* The word *Mage* appears to have other origins later in Latin, but with similar meanings. If the title of Magi rings a bell for you it could be because you heard the biblical story or myth about three Magi coming to see the baby Jesus. You may have thought the Magi were kings. Some people called them that. Actually, the term *"Wise Men"* is more correct because Magi are considered Wise Men. In those days Magi were people who studied the sciences like astrology and practiced spiritual mysticism. In the biblical story the three *Wise Men* followed a star that led them to baby Jesus. What makes the story interesting is that there was a common belief, among certain people, in those days, that certain star conjunctions, meteors or bright comets meant the birth or coming of a king. If these Magi were astronomers and practiced astrology, then they certainly followed their astrological predictions. But I digress.

I have witnessed a few African American men referring to themselves Magi or Mage. This could be because they were not really feeling the word Witch, Wiccan, Wizard or any other magickal name. It may be that they just love the sound of the name better. Or perhaps the tradition of Magi or Mage embodies the attributes and practices that they aspire to for themselves.

Shamanism

Shamanism is an ancient healing tradition, a spiritual practice, and a practice that walks between worlds. The actual word *Shaman* may have originated from the Russians who got the word from the *Tungus* tribe in Siberia, but the name is now adapted internationally by the Western world for similar indigenous traditions. It is said that its root word *sa-man* in the Tungus means "to know." We in the United States relate shamanism to the *Native American Indians* or other indigenous people in North America whose Shamans continue to practice the various

Ancestral traditions. However, various types of shamanism have been practiced by indigenous peoples all over the world, and from the beginning of human history. For example, in South Africa they are called *Sangoma* in the Nguni tribes. In Hawaii they are called *Kahuna or Huna* or *Kahuna Nui*. For the south tribes of Australian Aborigines, it is *Ngangkari*. For the Yoruba people of Nigeria in West Africa they are *Babalawo*. In Japan a female Shaman is called *Miko*, and the Bantu people of Central and Southern Africa call them *Nganga* (in the Kikongo language of the DRC). While each cultural practice is different there are common aspects to shamanism throughout the world.

The commonalities of shamanism connect at the primordial source of spiritualism. It connects with Nature and all of creation. It is a way of life and they live their mysticism every day of their lives. Most believe that we on Earth are all related and born of a common Ancestor. Shamans are the herbal healers. Shamans seek to honor the spirits to help promote harmony and balance. Shamans are the spiritual and solid leaders among their people. Shamans speak to spirits and some go into altered states in order to do so. Shamans walk between worlds to learn and sometimes to get answers. While shamanism is well practiced within indigenous cultures worldwide, a new generation of westernized people are seeking its practices through training with master indigenous Shamans.

While I've never met or chatted with any African American who claimed to be a Shaman, I have noticed that some have adapted some shamanic practices in their workings. Some of these practices are working with *spirit guides*, spiritual journeying, paying homage to Nature, using a *Medicine Wheel*, walking between the spirit worlds, interacting with spirit world, *channeling transcendental energies*, making use of sweat lodges and having *vision quests*. A vision quest is going into an altered state or using different mediums to venture into the spirit worlds on a particular mission for higher knowledge or *ascension*.

Spiritualists

The word *Spiritualist* was once just considered for people who were talented mediums, or those who were called to contact departed family members. However, today's term 'Spiritualists' is a more generalized one referring to anyone practicing Pagan traditions for spiritual attunement with their helpful spirits, spirit guides, deities, Ancestors etc. The term is often used by African American Pagans, of whom have not claimed an official path or have no desire to claim a name for their spiritual path. These practitioners may pay homage to the "Wheel of the Year" and or the esbats. They may participate in rituals, circles and acknowledge the Pagan *Lady* and *Lord*. Some may even practice witchcraft but prefer a more neutral title. At the same time someone who considers themselves as a Wiccan, Witch, ATR, Magi or Bruja may still refer to themselves as a Spiritualist.

Warlock

Just an honorable mention here. I have spoken with only a few black men, and white men, who call themselves *Warlocks*. In the common definition Warlock means a "male Witch". They said that they were reclaiming the name of Warlock just as Witches are reclaiming the title of "Witch." Like Magi and Mage, it could be that they just prefer the name instead of a Witch or any other Pagan name. It could be that they are avoiding the female connotations of the word Witch, so they are using names like Warlock or Wizard. In general Pagan circles, however, and not necessarily black Pagan circles, it is thought that being called a Warlock is a derogatory term, because it is said that the root meaning is "not trusted" or "oath breaker" or "outcast." However, my belief is if the vibrations of the name feels good to you then vibrate with it, or if you like the name go with it. Th e only name you really have to go by is the one your parents named you at birth, and even that can be changed. Just saying…

Witch and Witchcraft

 Last, but not at all least, we come to the definition of a *Witch*. I will give a general definition of a Witch and witchcraft here. The next lesson will begin the discussion of *Wicca*, which is a form of witchcraft, and what this study is really all about.

When *Phyllis Curott*, who is a Priestess and author of witchcraft books, was asked on video, what is witchcraft, she gave a reply that, I felt, was the best answer I have ever heard for the definition. She said that it was about, *"…taking off the blindfold to see the sacred. To see the world in the natural world…It is a way of discovering the presences of the Divine and making magick with it"* (What Is Witchcraft? | Wicca, 2013).

If I had heard that definition before I began my journey into witchcraft approximately 30 years ago, I probably wouldn't have quite understood her meaning. But now her statement rings clear as an altar bell because of my greater understanding of magick. *Magick* is more than wiggling of the nose or waving a wand. It is a feeling. You feel its vibration, and you feel the energy around you, surrounding you, conspiring to make your intentions happen. It is a way of life. While much of witchcraft is not considered a religion, but a practice, it is often referred to as *"the old religion"*. In fact, witchcraft should be called *"the oldest religion"*, because indeed, without a doubt, no other religion came before it. It is the sheer definition of primordial spirituality. We know for certain it is primordial and intuitive because every culture in the world has its own form(s), tradition, group or aspects of witchcraft, and no other religion or spirituality can claim such a history. And, because it is the old religion, there is a quaintness and spiritualism about witchcraft that stems from its world views of one *"living in the old ways"* and living the methods of our mothers, grandmothers and the spiritual practices of our grandfathers. I say spiritual because there is nothing more spiritual than the memories of the *fire cider* that grandma gave during the times of a cold. There is nothing quainter and more spiritual than a protection *poppet* a grandfather whittled to give to his grandson for a long voyage. These are the traditional ways that are passed down, remembered and valued like links on a spiritual chain fortifying our lives with their fond memories. These unique memories imbue qualities and ethics to our lives that in fact cast their own intricate and charmed spells.

Although the word *Witch* derived from the Anglo-Saxon word meaning *wise one,* the true magickal practices of witchcraft occurred tens of thousands of years before the European people even reached Europe, and definitely long before the advent of the *Abrahamic* religions. The origins of magick itself came out of Africa with the human exodus.

Afro-Witches use the word Witch since it is in the Western culture in which we live today. A West African term relating to the word Witch is *Aje* or *Aye.* Aje (pronounced "I – Jay") is a term of endearment for a mystical, magickal woman of African heritage with cosmic powers. The term *Iyami* (pronounced Eye-yum-mee) is a term of endearment meaning Mother. The two terms are often together as *Iyami Aje* (High Priestess or Spiritual Mother.) These terms are used by people who practice Ifa/Yoruba traditions.

Magick and witchcraft are instinctual and universal. Witchcraft is a practice of spirituality, and it is enjoyed by both men and women alike. There are some basics and natural laws that most Neo-Witches follow, but for the most part everyone practices witchcraft differently. Some practice as solitaries or alone, and some practice in circles or covens. For most Witches, Moon phases and esbats are very important. Some integrated practices of a Witch are *Oracles* or *Divinations, Potions, Meditation, Rituals, Medium Work, Herbalism, Healing, Conjuring, Astrology Reiki, Crystal Healing, Sacred Geometry, Spiritual Journeying, Talismans, Past Lives Research, Akashic Records and Out of Body Experiences,* just to name a few. This is one of the reasons why witchcraft is called the *craft of the Wise.* There are so many arts and disciplines that could be learned and incorporated into a practice that sometimes it feels like you are matriculating at your own university, selecting your own courses and developing your own degrees. How far you wish to go into your practice is totally up to you, be it an Associate's degree or PhD. Best of all there is often an inner drive, for most of us, to never stop learning new things to enhance our practices and understanding.

Of course, nothing says Witch, more than the casting of *spells.* And, to be real, that is why many people come into the *craft.* This is really quite unfortunate, because although spellcasting has its own apparent rewards, witchcraft has so much more to offer. Engaging in the various aspects and practices of Witchcraft can open one's mind to the universal mysteries and release the soul from the bonds of human mediocracy. Witchcraft offers the key for ascension and to an inner power or *Chi.* When one truly and earnestly takes on the practice of witchcraft, they immerse themselves with the frequencies and vibrations that only witchcraft can offer, because of its various disciplines. Depending on the goal of a Witch, one can become in tune with the Universe, at which point, spell work becomes merely a byproduct of the practice. Let me now pose some questions you may still be having about Witches and witchcraft.

Q1) Who Can Be a Witch?

Answer—While some people are born with the talent or were born into a family of Witches (hereditary Witches), anyone can study and learn the craft no matter who they are and no matter what ethnic background, ancestral history, sexual preference or gender (yes brothers, you too can be a Witch!) It is just a matter of studying and understanding their craft. You cannot learn or master the craft in a day or a week. It is actually a lifetime of study. The more you know the better you are at your craft.

Q2) Are Witches Evil?

Answer—Witches are just like anyone else regardless of what they practice. There are some really good people, and there are some really bad people, and there is a myriad of temperaments in between. Witches are teachers, doctors, mail carriers, church Mothers, corporate executives and business owners. Some practice Abrahamic religions along with their craft, and some are strictly Pagan. Many Witches call themselves *Lightworkers*. Lightworkers make it their charge to heal and make the world a better place for everyone, either through their magickal workings and or through their life's practice. These Witches never wish to curse or cause harm to anyone. There are others who believe in self-defense and may practice *baneful magick* (hexing). There are other Witches who, while they may stay away from baneful practices, will use it as a last resort, and only as a last resort.

As a Witch, one makes the choice based on their own temperament on what direction they cast, and how they wish to cast their spells into the Universe. As a Wiccan and Lightworker myself, I do have a dream that everyone in the world would practice with *perfect Love* and *perfect Trust*. But the reality is everyone is different, and extremes are all a part of the Universal design. When you think about it though, there are some

Christians who will use the bible as an amulet against others, and there are some Christians who will tell you that they will pray to their God that non-Christians will change their minds and think the way they want them to think. They do this not knowing that they are, in effect, casting baneful spells that will have others change their minds against their own wills and their own hearts. I just read about an Evangelical pastor who claimed that the reason why the Supreme Court Justice, *Ruth Bader Ginsburg*, died was because he prayed for her death. Now if that is not a practice of *dark baneful magick* I would like to know what is. But it has always been the Christian privilege of many to do what they don't want other religions to do.

Q3) Who Do Witches Worship?

Answer—In belief systems Witches are all over the map. Witches tend to be *pantheists*—that is they recognize the Divine in all things. Many Witches in various fashions venerate multiple deities (minor gods and goddesses), so they could be considered *polytheistic* as well. Some believe in *dualism*, which is the belief that there is only the Goddess and the God, and all other minor deities are only theoretical aspects of them. You may even run into someone who is *monotheistic*, believing in only one God or one Goddess. Many Witches practice *Ancestor Veneration,* with memorial to immediate relatives or veneration of cultural deities.

Depending upon their practices and traditions Witches will have different concepts of deity. For the most part though, Witches don't worship *God* as the Abrahamic religions do, or rather they don't think of God/dess as an entity outside of themselves. Some Witches are *deist,* believing that while God/dess may have created the Universe, God/dess is merely one of the cogs in the Universal engine, just kicking back and watching the Universe play itself out on automatic, with no intervention on their part. Most Pagans believe that as humans we are a part of

God/dess, *the divine Spirit, the ALL, the Source, the Most High,* and therefore when we cast spells, or are actively spiritual, we are activating the part of God/dess inside of us. So, in essence, when we speak to God/dess, we are speaking to ourselves. This is why you may hear practitioner Witches say: *"I AM What I AM."* That means *"I Am"* a part of the *ALL* and *"What I Am"* is Divine.

Q4) Heard Some Witches Worship the Devil. What's Up with That?

Answer—So, I am going to do a *Glinda the Good Witch* again and start from the beginning. Now let us get this out of the way first. Yes, there may very well be a handful of those who actually worship the *devil.* I personally have never met them in my groups or online. I am just guessing with the laws of averages there will be some people in the world who worship the devil and call themselves Witches. As the Universe goes, there are people who do just about anything. When you think you have seen it all—the all surprises you. With that said, it is not common or the norm. If they do exist, they are more geared to the Abrahamic belief systems since only Christians believe in the devil, or that the devil exists. So, in effect they would be more Christian than Pagan. Pagans as a rule do not believe in the devil as characterized in the biblical canons.

Now, there are *Satanists.* However, in general, Satanists are more *atheists* than anything else, so they are not true Satan worshippers per say. They don't believe in any gods whatsoever and consider themselves skeptics and pragmatics. I suspect that their title is more of an *in-your-face* jab at Christians. I have witnessed a couple Satanists in the online group, and they have discussed the theory of Satanism (Vernor, 2011).

Finally, I suspect that with the show, *The Chilling Adventures of Sabrina,* many may believe that pop culture is imitating life. Nothing could be further from the truth in this example. The latest Sabrina series is nothing more than entertainment. Good entertainment. I would even go as far as saying…the show is lit! I will definitely give them that, but NO true Pagan Witch would worship the devil. Why? Because, as stated before, the devil is an invention of Christian dogma. As shocking as it may be to some readers, very few religions, theologies or faiths have any belief, doctrine or information on the devil. Only Abrahamic belief systems have the "devil" as its fearful deity. So, it stands to reason that since Pagans, *in general*, don't believe in Christianity or the Christian devil, they wouldn't worship, have rituals for, have icons of, or say prayers to the devil. It would make as much sense as me saying that Christians worship *Thor* on Sundays, or it would be like me asking a Muslim if they worship *Zeus*. Not happening.

Q5) Can I Be a Witch and Still Practice Christianity?

Answer—Yes! Now that could be a little confusing after I just stated that Pagans don't follow Christian theories. Well, let me say that this is an exception to the rule. There are Pagans who refer to themselves as *Christian Wiccans* or *Christian Witches*. These are people who are attracted to the Pagan philosophy, but don't want to or are not ready to leave their Christian traditions. Christian Witches combine the two theologies together, to some extent, to create a practice that appeals to them. There are people who practice other faiths also and combine witchcraft. The best examples are *Buddhists Wiccans* and *Jewish Witches*. Just to note that Jewish Witches are often called *JeWitches*. I thought that was pretty cool!

What is Wicca?

Yeyyy! You made it through the first two lessons. Now that you know some of the basics of paganism and witchcraft, let's get to the basics of *Wicca*. Back in the day, if you would read most of the basic Wicca books, the first thing that you would read is something like, *"The word Wicca originated from the old Anglo-Saxon word wice, which means to twist and bend."* So that was pretty much drilled in our minds that Wicca means *to twist and bend.* While this is a quaint notion of Wicca as being an agent of change, I am no longer convinced that this is the total root of the word Wicca. Since I have been reading through the etymology of the word through the years, I am now more inclined to believe that it pretty much sprang from the same root words as the word *Witch.* I believe it could have origins from the Germanic root words, *wit or witz or wizzi,* which means to be *smart, clever* or *intelligent.* This would explain where the word *Wizard* comes from. Or it could have roots from the Old English word *witan,* meaning *to know* or *wise person.* These words could have been the root word for *Witch,* and subsequently Wicca. But since language is a living and ever evolving thing, it could very well be that all these root words, including wice, are the precursors of the name Wicca. Witchcraft after-all is the practice of the wise.

What I am about to tell you is of the old school Wicca. This is the *Scott Cunningham,* writer of <u>*Wicca: A Guide for The Solitary Practitioner,*</u> and the other old school Wiccan guides-type Wicca. And, in addition, this is the type of Wicca that I was taught approximately thirty years ago when I first started out, and before the lines between basic witchcraft and Wicca were blurred. This is my traditional home and what my various mentors of Wicca have taught me. This type of Wicca, that I am about to explain, is the Wicca that I have learned online from many old websites when the Internet was new, and when the old Crone Wiccans and Witches poured their knowledge onto, what was known then as, the *"World Wide Web."* While I have integrated some of the previously stated disciplines like Hedge Witch and Green Witch, Wicca is where my heart is. Why you may ask? Here are my thoughts:

1) Because I am a romantic at heart, and Wicca speaks to that part of my spirit with romantic theories, poetry and proses as part of its lore.

2) Wicca also integrates the *divine dualism* which is perfect for me since I have always been *Goddess-centered* and interested in the *divine Feminine* for as long as I can remember. While, in most Pagan practices the Goddess or divine Feminine is optional, the Goddess is an integral part of the Wiccan practice. Wiccan lore tells the story of the *Lady* and *Lord* from sabbat, to sabbat, from ritual to spiritual devotion. It is the embodiment of a romance that is the foundation of the *"Wheel of the Year".* This is important to me since I believe the Universe works on harmony, sexuality, sensuality and romance.

3) Wicca also appeals to me because it is a practice that favors *Lightworkers.* We subscribe to what is called the *"Wiccan Rede"* which has a final line stating, *"An Ye Harm None, Do What Ye Will."*

   This last passage of the *Wiccan Rede is* essentially saying: **enjoy yourself – just don't hurt anybody doing it.** But I take it as a deeper meaning also. To me it means: *leave things better than when you came, be the protector of your environment and pay it forward.* While others may not see that in the verse, I believe it is the way of the Lightworker to add meaningful value to a practice and the world around them.

4) The final point to why I love Wicca is that I can integrate any deity I wish to integrate into my practice. It allows for cultural diversity. So, if I wish to integrate *Afrocentricity* to my practice and add gods like *Orisha* (West African deities) I can. If I wish to add *Neteru* (Kemetic deities), or *Loas* (Haitian Vodou deities) I can. Alternatively, if I wish to add *Aesir* (Norse deities) I can do that also. As long as I follow the basic framework of Wicca, I can integrate any spiritual god/dess or pantheon I wish. So, while people may say that I am doing a disservice by my Ancestors in practicing Wicca, I say false. I say that if I choose to venerate my Ancestors in any way, I can do so in my practice with Wicca. Wicca is a basic framework that accommodates me and my eclectic, diverse and Afrocentric practices. And it can accommodate anyone's ethnocentric practices. There is no particular god one has to pay homage to. That decision is totally up to the practitioner. This can be done because Wicca accommodates eclectic ideas within its practice.

To understand how one can integrate African pantheons into Wicca is to understand how Wicca works. Wicca is practiced by, for example, many who are Norse or Asatru Wiccan practitioners. So, they pay hail to the *Aesir* or Viking pantheon. Wicca is also practiced by many who are Kemetic Wiccans, so they practice Wicca with the Neteru or Egyptian gods on their altars. Wicca is also practiced by Celtic practitioners, so they may use Welsh, British or Irish god/desses like *Morrigan* or *Cernunnos.* Jewish Wiccans may invoke goddesses like *Shekinah, Asherah* or *Astarte.* I even met a Native American woman, many years ago, who told me that she was considering practicing Wicca because its magick was so close to her Native spirituality.

In essence, Wicca can be integrated by all these traditions and more, because Wicca is a basic framework of ceremonial spirituality, wherein its style of ceremonies goes back to ancient Kemetic and Hermetic origins. These ancient sacred ceremonies were replicated by secret societies like the *Freemasons* and magical orders such as the *Golden Dawn* and *The Theosophical Society*.

Paschal Beverly Randolph
Multiracial medical doctor, occultist, spiritualist, trance medium, practitioner of sex magic and writer.

These practices were also practiced by prominent occultists like Aleister Crowley, and the nineteenth-century black American spiritualist, Rosicrucian and magician named Paschal Beverly Randolph. Randolph was the founder of the first Rosicrucian lodge of the Nation in San Francisco, California in 1858.

So, in summary, a Wiccan practice can be malleable for any tradition. Its rituals and ceremonies are basic enough to accommodate and integrate any cultural pantheon, spiritual tools or ethnocentric ritual practice.

Some History of Wicca

Wicca was brought to the consciousness of the mainstream by the British coven leader Gerald Gardner and his followers, between the 1940s and 1950s. He was initiated by the *New Forest Coven* in the late 1930s and became enamored by the spirituality of witchcraft. Contrary to popular belief, it is highly debatable if Gardner was the founder of Wicca, or *"Wica"*, as they called it in his day, but he did popularize it by writing a number of books about the craft, and received permission to do so from his coven leaders. Two of his most popular books, still in print, are *Witchcraft Today* and *The Meaning of Witchcraft*. Gardner eventually became leader of his own coven, and founded the *Gardnerian Tradition*. He is also given credit for being one of the contributors in developing the modern day *"Wheel of the Year"* with festivals Wiccans and Witches practice today.

Wicca Comes to America

Wicca became truly popularized in the United States by the *Feminist movement* between the 1960s and 1970s. There was a desire amongst the women in the movement to not only cancel the overbearing culture of patriarchy within the mundane world, but to free themselves from the patriarchal religions bound to solely express the male perspective and male deity. This need for spiritual autonomy led many feminists to discover Wicca and the practice of *Goddess worship*. Alternatively, many black women in the early Feminist movement looked to *African Traditional Religions* to find spirituality for the divine black Feminine.

Court Cases on Wicca

An inmate named *Herbert Dettmer*, who was studying Wicca in a correspondence course from the *Church of Wicca*, was awarded his right to practice, and the limited use of ritual objects for worship while incarcerated in 1986. The *Fourth Circuit Court of Appeals* ruled in Dettmer v. Landon that "…*Wicca was entitled to First Amendment protection like any other religion.*" (History.com Editors, 2018).

In another case, in Virginia, on April 23, 2007, and after two years of consideration, the Wiccan symbol of a pentacle was declared acceptable by the military and *Department of Veterans Affairs*, and they are now displayed on military service personnel's headstones, markers, and plaques at veteran's cemeteries (Hart, 2009). Prior to this it was denied to Pagan military families.

Further Facts About Wicca

Here is another important fact about practitioners of Wicca that is essential for understanding: ***Wiccans ARE Witches but NOT all Witches are Wiccans.*** This seems to be the confusion even among Witches since pop culture tends to call all Witches Wiccans now. The true Wiccan practice is a very distinctive tradition and it differs from freestyle or eclectic witchcraft, because ***Wicca is a religion*** and ***basic eclectic witchcraft is not technically or normally a religion.*** Eclectic witchcraft hails its freedom to practice as it chooses without restraints or any particular framework or dogma. Dogma is, by definition, what makes religion a religion. Below is an outline of what makes Wicca a religion and how it differs from all other witchcraft:

1) *Wiccans follow the Wheel of the Year.*
2) *Wiccans tend to be more Goddess-centered traditionally and follow the dualism of both the Lady and Lord.*
3) *Wiccans work with specific tools at their altars and arrange their altar in accordance to the divine Feminine and divine Masculine.*
4) *Wiccans follow or respectfully observe the Wiccan Rede.*
5) *Wiccans practice in the direction of Lightworkers.*
6) *Wiccans tend to follow and or respect different types of ethical codes.*

Please see **Exhibit 3.1** so as to help differentiate and clarify the dichotomy between the two practices of Wicca and Eclectic witchcraft. While the exhibit gives some clarity on what Wicca is about, it is not etched in granite. Every Witch is different so the chart may not be all inclusive. But again, it should give a good basic guideline. Wicca is not for everyone. It is a discipline, and like most religions it is a calling. While people who practice basic witchcraft/paganism may choose to integrate any of the above practices, it is the traditional old school Wiccans who follow at least 5 of the above.

Exhibit 3.1		
The Dichotomy between Old School Wicca and Eclectic Witchcraft		
The Practice	Wiccan	Eclectic Witch
1) Follows the Wiccan Rede	Always	Depends on the Witch
2) Light Worker	Almost always	Depends of the Witch
3) Follows the Wheel of the Year	Always	Depends on the Witch
4) Follows the Altar's Principle of Gender	Always	Depends on the Witch
5) Recognizes both the Goddess and the God	Always	Depends on the Witch
6) Practices magick, spells and rituals	Depends on the Wiccan	Almost Always
7) Feels the Craft is mainly about spells	Almost Never	Almost Always
8) Feels the Craft is about theory first.	Almost Always	Depends on the Witch
9) Hexing, cursing and crossing is okay	Almost Never	Depends on the Witch

10) Believes their practice is a religion	Always	Depends on the Witch
11) Follows spiritual affirmations and dogma in order to seek the Higher and Authentic Self	Almost Always	Depends on the Witch

Wheel of the Year

Wiccans follow the metaphorical journey of a love story *lore* between the *goddess* and *god*, we sometimes call them the *Lady and Lord*. Their love story makes up our yearly journey through *The Wheel of the Year*. As you recall, from the last lesson, *The Wheel of the Year* consists of 8 chronological holy days within any given year. These holy days are divided so evenly within the year that if one would bend the calendar from January to December and put them together end to end it would look like a perfect wheel with evenly divided 8 spokes. Thus, this is the reason they call it *The Wheel of the Year*. It is a forever revolving hoop, turning year after year. The last lesson gave the name of each sabbat, the date of the sabbat, and the corresponding secular holiday. The following gives an explanation for each holy day with its metaphorical story of the Lady and Lord in conjunction. The Lady and Lord here are the *female and male expressions of Divinity* itself. Again, this is the saga that I learned from old Witches on the Internet many years ago. While I seldom see this story anymore, I am very proud to present it to you now as follows:

Yule/Winter Solstice – December 21st (Major Sabbat)

Yule is considered the first holiday of the Pagan Wheel of the Year. It is also called *Yuletide* and *Winter Solstice*. For some Pagans this is celebrated between the dates of December 20th to January 1st, thus coining the phrase, *"The Twelve Days of Christmas"*. Approximately between December 20th and December 23rd, is the time when the Sun stops its trek away from our hemisphere and begins its trek back to us. The old Pagans called this *"the return of the light"*, and personified it in the spiritual story of the goddess giving birth to the *Sun god*, or *god of the Light*. The Winter Solstice was the time in which they celebrated His birth and return. Does this sound familiar to you? Okay, I'm just saying.

The birth of the Sun god is celebrated with candles and fire. The fireplace is lit with the *Yule log*. The Yule log is a piece of a log that was burnt from the previous year at Yule, but a piece of it was preserved for the next year. This represents the continuous spark of the Sun god's life. It symbolizes His return over and over again and bringing His light into a brand-new year. The Winter Solstice was a time of good cheer. It was the time of exchanging gifts and visiting family and old friends after being shut-in during the dark Winter months. The homes greeted their guests with Winter decorations and evergreens. All types of baked goods and cakes were made. Altars, fireplace mantles and tables were also decorated with wreaths, bayberries, candles and symbols of the Sun god. The symbols of the Sun god on Yule are candles, bonfires, pine, holly, and woodland creatures like reindeer, elk, and colorful birds like cardinals. Meanwhile the goddess celebrates the birth of Her newborn child.

Imbolc – February 1st (Cross-Quarter Day)

As the Wheel turns, the next holy day is called *Imbolc*. This sabbat represents the next lesson in the universal goddess and god's saga. February 1st represents the awakening of the young god of *Light*. His consciousness begins to develop, and He is getting stronger every day. More candles are being lit now to represent His return to vigor. The corresponding secular holiday for this is *Groundhog's Day*. Both holidays represent the anticipation for the coming of Spring. For the goddess, the *Maiden aspect* of the Universe begins Her rule here. This is the first of the Maiden's three favorite holidays. This is the time when Pagans begin to dust off the mental and physical cobwebs from their lives. It is the time to start thinking about the *Spring-cleaning* of one's home and the evaluation of one's life. In other words, starting things anew. This is the time to set goals and to prepare to implement them. Incense and herbs are usually burnt now in order to heighten the senses. This is a time of *Awakening*. More candles are lit and placed on the altar to bring back mental consciousness. This is a good time of year for meditation and to look towards the *Higher-Self* for answers.

Ostara, or the Spring Equinox – March 21st (Major Sabbat)

The god of Light continues to grow on this sabbat, and He is now beginning to reach the theoretical equal to the *Maiden goddess*. They begin to enjoy each other's company. This holiday is on March 21st. This celebration is called *Ostara* for the *Spring Equinox*. It is the time of equilibrium. It is the time when day and night are in equal balance. In old Europe, *Ostare* or *Eastre* was worshiped as a Germanic *fertility goddess* and *goddess of the Morning Sun*. She had a pet rabbit that would change eggs into different colors, and the rabbit would give them to children. From Her name came the holiday Ostara. From Ostara the Roman Christian church changed the name to Easter.

Ostara is a time that symbolizes rebirth, renewal and awakening. It is the time when grass begins to grow, and spring bulbs begin to bloom. It is the time when animals leave hibernation and begin to choose their mates. This is the time when energy begins surging throughout the Earth and its vibrations are increasingly more potent. The Roman Catholic

Church understood the magickal significance of this natural time of year, and used this season to symbolize the resurrection and ascension of Jesus.

The Maiden continues to rule on this second holy day. Her colors of pastels like yellow, pink, baby blue, and new grass green are seen all over the commercialized world. This is a good time to finish your meditations and your house cleaning. It is also a good time to pull out your seeds and place them on the altar for the blessings of the upcoming garden sowing. The symbols of the Ostara/Spring Equinox are eggs, baby birds and rabbits. These are the symbols of birth, rebirth, spiritual ascension and renewal.

Beltane – May 1st (Cross-Quarter Day)

Beltane could begin April 30th but generally starts May the 1st. This is the last holy day that represents the Maiden aspect of the universal goddess. The goddess (our Lady) begins to mature and is heading into the direction of flowering into full-fledged womanhood. She contemplates mating. The god (our Lord) is now a maturing young male at the pinnacle of young adulthood. His attentions are now veering towards the goddess and they fall in love. This is a symbolic representation of all things in the eternal circle of life. The Lady and Lord are now fertile during this time of the Wheel. This is a good time to start the general planting. On Imbolc we presented our thoughts and plans as we did our seeds. Now it is time to sow them. During the 1st of May, trees grow their green leaves, animals gather and frolic, flowers are blooming with their fragrant perfumes, fruits like strawberries are ripening, the rains have slowed, and the skies are clear. These are the similar settings to where Shakespeare wrote his best plays of love. The ancient Pagans of Europe celebrated these times by gathering early on the

1st of May. The children would make wreaths of flowers and all would gather in places like the center of town, and around what is called a *Maypole*. The Maypole is a tall pole with long, multicolored ribbons hanging down from the top of it. The pole represented the full phallus of Nature and our Lord's apex of fertility. The children and young adults would each grab a ribbon and circle around the pole decorating it with a woven pattern of the multicolored strips. In the old days the celebration of *May Day* would last for days on end.

My Elementary School May Days

I must admit I have fond memories of *May Day*. My elementary school, in Philly, used to have Mayday celebrations. A *May Queen* and *May King* were usually voted on by the school children. The school would dismiss us early so that we could watch the festivities. The May Queen and King would stand on a float while we cheered. There was dancing, singing, music, marching bands, and drill team and step performances. There was also a parade around the school. Confetti was thrown everywhere, and hot dogs and drinks were sold. I remember three years of this event, and then finally it stopped abruptly. I enjoyed the celebration tremendously, and I never understood why it stopped. Yet, I feel lucky that, even as a child, in the inner city, I had a taste of what the old country festivals were like. I do often wonder if the school officials knew the significance of pairing the May King and Queen together, and if they didn't, I often wonder if they would have still done it if they had found out. In the old countries of Europe, the May Queen and May King would parade through the streets of Spring festivals personifying the image of the divine Lady and Lord holding court.

Litha or Summer Solstice – June 21st (Major Sabbat)

This holiday is on the 21st of June and known as *Litha* or *the Summer Solstice*. This is when we celebrate the longest day of the year. This means the god of Light is at the peak point of His life cycle, and *the Green Man* becomes His other aspect. The Green Man is the *god of the Woodlands*, and He has domain over forests, green lands and animals. Male Witches often take advantage of this potent time for themselves by performing magickal workings. The *Mother* aspect of the Universe rules here also. The Maiden aspect has transformed into a full-fledged Mother and She is strong, highly fertile, and independent. The Mother aspect means the goddess is mature and ready to conceive. The goddess and god begin *hierogamy* (sacred mating rites).

Rituals are conducted during this time for the female aspect of the Universe around the Full Moon, which can be potent when performed during menstrual cycles. Bonfires are also made during this time, representing the burning passion between the mating couple. It is said that leaping over bonfires, for this season, brings prosperity, fertility and good health. The Earth is at its greenest now, and is thriving on the saturation of the Sun's solar rays. This is the time of the great Earth's bounty. The goddess *Gaia* (Earth Mother) is fat with contentment. Sunflowers and green corn stalks are the symbols used during this time of the year.

Lughnasadh or Lammas First Harvest – August 1st (Cross-Quarter Day)

As the Wheel continues to turn, we are arriving at the first of the three harvests. *Lughnasadh* (lou-nasa), also known as its Catholic name *Lammas*, celebrates the beginning of the end of summer. This is observed on the 1st of August. The god of the Sun begins to lose His strength now. He is older and weaker. The *Mother aspect of the Universe* becomes older too. This is considered the beginning of the waning part of the Wheel. During this season, in years past, our parents and great grandparents began to harvest fruits and vegetables to do the yearly canning. I would be willing to bet that almost everyone knows someone who does this or used to do this. Our memories of our grandmothers or our great-aunt's kitchen cupboard filled with canned peaches, homemade preserves, and pickled three-bean salad would most likely bring fond memories to most of us. I can even remember jars of candied watermelon rind in my Aunt Lily's cupboard. During this period, we are saying goodbye to the fresh fruits and vegetables with every spoonful we eat. Constant prayers and meditations of thanks are given to the Universe for the bounty of the Summer. Grapes and apples are the symbols of this holy day.

Mabon or Autumn Equinox – September 21st (Major Sabbat)

This is the second of the harvest celebrations, and it is the second time, during the Wheel of the Year, when the duration of night and day are equal. The date for *Mabon* falls between September 21st and the 23rd. This holy day of harvest is traditionally celebrated to give thanks to the *gods for the bounty,* and to give observance to the Autumn season. It also marks the near end of the hard and laborious work in the gardens and in the fields. In the past the people of the towns, tribes or regions came together and shared the wealth of the yield. Harvest festivals were very common and are still seriously celebrated in many places today both rural and urban.

On Mabon the *god of Light* is fading rapidly, and His life force has weakened. The goddess mourns over Her declining mate, yet She feels a spark of life growing inside of Her. His decline begins to affect the once bountiful vegetation all over the hemisphere. In the saga of the Universal deities our Lord rules over *Matter* (carbon) and our Lady rules over *Spirit.* All Matter dies, transmutes, deviates or changes at some point, but the

Spirit lives on. Now He is fading and so is the vigor of the vegetation. Most of the last of the wheat and grains are being harvested now, as well as the corn in the fields. The Mother aspect of the Universe is developing into a more mature and matronly aspect.

Energy is beginning to be absorbed back deep into the Earth so to be conserved for the Winter months ahead. This is also a time for us to reap the bounties we sowed on Beltane. We would also do well to prepare to draw into our spiritual selves, conserve energy and to reflect on our own lives of our past achievements, successes and failures during the year. It is the time of evaluating if any changes are needed for the coming year, for *self-development, self-improvement* and greater successes. Grape vines, squash and crows are the symbols of Mabon.

Samhain or Witches New Year – October 31st (Cross-Quarter Day)

This is undeniably the Witches' most favorite holiday on the Wheel. In fact, I looked forward to getting to this point of the study. The energy of this festival is incredible, and energy is what Witches thrive on. Many people are unaware of what Halloween is all about. They only know the fun and enjoyment of the time. They love the dressing up in costumes. They love seeing the sparkle in their children's eyes when they've collected bags full of treats. Adults also love the parties, harvest celebrations and the costumes for themselves. The workplace is usually festive during this time. I do enjoy all of this, but I also enjoy the generally unseen aspect of this holiday. But here is the back story. To Wiccans, and other Pagans the original name for Halloween is *Samhain*. In *Gaelic* it is pronounced *Sow-in* or *Sal-win.* Either one of the Gaelic pronunciations is acceptable. Pagans often think of it as *The Witches New Year.*

In the Pagan culture it is believed that this part of the year marks the *darker part of the Wheel.* The days become shorter, the nights become longer, and the air becomes colder. To Pagans this seasonal triquetra of sorts marks a pretty sacred time called *the thinning of the veil.* Pagans believe this to be the time when the veil between our Earthly world and the spiritual realm is so thin that spirits, Ancestors, ghosts, and other magickal beings can peer through and see us or even enter our Earthly plane. It is also believed that Pagan Spiritualists can peer through and or walk between worlds. Because of this some Spiritualists use this time to do oracle workings.

As stated in the previous lesson, the beginnings of the Samhain festivals started when the Celts believed that the souls of the dead roamed the streets and villages during the thinning veil. To appease these spirits, food and libations were left outside the doors at night. This was the so-called *treat.* When people were brave enough to venture out while the spirits roamed, they dressed up in disguises hoping that the ghost or spirits wouldn't recognize them. This was the so-called *trick.* Thus, is where we get the phrase, *"Trick or Treat?"* This ancient cultural tradition managed to find its way to the United States as *All Hallows' Eve* (name given by the Catholic church) as a type of seasonal festival, and it eventually caught on nationwide by the late 1700s or early 1800s as *Halloween* for short. Many Witches say that the reason they love Samhain is because it is the one time of year that they can dress up, let their hair down, be themselves, blend into secular society, and no one would be the wiser.

During this sacred time the goddess grieves over the passing of Her mate as He travels through the veils and into the *underworld.* There He becomes the aspects of the *Magician, Hermit, Oracle and Student.* But the goddess' womb holds the spark of life, which is His promise that He shall return again. His sacred journey into the underworld is said to have also contributed to the seasonal thinning of the veil.

Wiccans use this time for a variety of workings. While many believe that this time of the *uncloaking Universe* is too precarious and unstable to do anything else other than meditate, many still use this time for other workings. They may use it for seeking prophecy or oracle work, self-reflection or involution, communication with Ancestors or paying memorial to Ancestors, vision quests or some other benign magickal work or rituals. Wiccans may set a place at the dinner table as tribute to a beloved Ancestor or the Goddess and or God. It is said that back in the old days, on Samhain, metaphysically astute AfroAmerican women would cook food specially for the spirits to help bring themselves luck in the coming year, or to make company for an old family member who had passed on. It was normally cooked without salt, since salt offends spirits, and these offerings were given with a place setting made for each member in memorial. This is called a *dumb supper*. Dumb meaning presenting the dinner in silence.

Many years ago, I went to a Samhain ritual ceremony, in a garden called Gaia, where a long table was set with a place setting for the Goddess at its head. The seat was of course vacant in Her tribute, and a place setting was made there. We then all stood in 2 lines by order of our ages. The oldest were the first in line and the youngest was the last. I was somewhere in the middle of the line. I wasn't quite that old then. We were then seated with the oldest two people on both sides of the Goddess. The youngest was furthest from Her and seated at the very end of the table. We were then served a vegetarian or vegan meal of navy pea bean soup with spices, herbs and vegetables like mushrooms. Silence filled the table to give respect to the *Queen of the Universe*, the spirits, and the Ancestors we held dear. We spoke only when we were dismissed from the table. We ate dinner under the stars, and I had a great mystical sense that the Goddess and the *Holy Spirit* were among us. There was Power in the silence.

Samhain is truly a time of meditation since *second sight* is at its height of clarity, which makes it a perfect time to complete one's plans for the coming year. During this time Wiccans pay tribute to the *Crone aspect* of the Universe, because She is now of a full connection with the spiritual realm. This is why we see so many pictures of the old *Crone Witch* flying on Her broom on Samhain. It is the Crone aspect that guides us through the veil of communication with the Ancestors. The reason why Samhain is called the *Witches' New Year* is because it marks the last celebration of the wheel with the passing of the Sun god. It also represents the last of the harvests, because the final harvest in the fields is taken in for storage. Although we grieve for these things, we again celebrate the spark that the goddess holds inside of Her. This spark being the promise of the *light's return* in the upcoming year – *Yule* (Winter Solstice). Some symbols of this season are squash, haystacks, Full Moons, dried corn stalks and pumpkins. Witch *familiars* like owls, crows, bats, spiders and black cats are heavily seen during this season. Other symbols are archetypes of the *Crone* goddess Herself such as *the sacred Hag, Sorceress, old Sorcerer* or the *old Witch.*

Dualism: The Universe is Ruled by Gender

I have often seen some African American spiritualists remark online about Wicca, saying that it is a European concept. To be honest though, in the beginning, I believed that too. In the beginning of my practice my rebuttal with them was, "…and so what? Th e Christian church certainly is too!" However, as I continued my overall metaphysical studies, I realized that we were all dead wrong. Many of the esoteric techniques in Wicca were integrated with ancient Kemetic/Egyptian mysticism from the great schools of the teacher *Tehuti*. Some call him by the Greek name *Hermes* because the Greeks studied the philosophy and cultivated it for themselves. To the Western world the philosophy is called *Hermeticism*. One of the theories of Tehuti is called the universal *Law of Gender*. In this mystical rule it is believed that everything has its feminine (yin) and masculine (yang) principles. Th e Universe runs, and is created and functions on the laws of the female and male principles. Th is means in everything that exists, you, me, and everything in between, even rocks, there are both male and female aspects. In this principle, creation is possible. Without this dualism aspect, all life, manifestation and creation end. Therefore, because of this knowledge, Wiccans divide their *altars* in half. One side seats the female aspect or *Goddess' attributes*. The other side seats the male aspect or *Gods' attributes*. This is how Wiccans manifest after magickal workings. The symbolism of the Goddess and the God, combined with spell work or ritual, brings change.

So why would this *Rule of Gender* be so important in spell work? Okay, so, let's talk about balance in our lives. We all seek balance and if you think about it right now you may be able to think about something important for you to have balance. You may want a balanced meal every day. You may want to balance your work life with your exercise time and your play time. Balance is important to you and your children. You may feel your children should have both male and female teachers in school. You may even feel that there should be both male and female representatives in the U.S. Congress or your local State House. You may feel that your church should have both female and male preachers, and not just men preaching to a majority congregation of women. Why is this? It may be because you feel it is healthier, in some way, to have the input of both genders or the dual perspectives, or the yin and yang balance. To many of us, balance in our spiritual lives, and in our deities, are just as important—if not more so, because it is our spirituality that is the framework of how we live for our quality of life. So, in essence *"As Above, So Below."* This means that what balance we find in our material world we also need in meditation, magick and connecting to Spirit. The Yin and Yang aspect of the Universe is the representation for ultimate balance in all things. It is the symbol of extremes and opposites coming together and forming the base of all there is.

The Goddess

 When I was a little girl, I used to have dreams of a land where people venerated, *SHE*. She was adored and worshiped by Priestesses an d Priests. Her image was all over the land with statues and other engraved images.

Perhaps that was why I had no desire for church, because the *Goddess*, that I had always known, was not there. My search for the Goddess started early but it was not unique because seeking Her is innate to many. Goddess worship has always existed. It has merely been suppressed for well over 2000 or more years. The celebrated so-called *"Venus"* Paleolithic statuettes were found all over the world, and known to be representations of the Goddess, and some are estimated to be as old as 35,000 years (Liew, 2020).

A "Venus" Paleolithic Statuette Shown Above

The first written documented record of tributes to the divine Feminine was written by a Sumerian *High Priestess*, poet and princess named *Enheduanna*. She wrote in the ancient Sumerian language. Their early culture and writings were only rivaled by *Kemet/Egypt,* as an advanced civilization, in their time. Enheduanna, wrote about the goddess *Inanna,* and Her shining namesake star, to be *"the Queen of Heaven and Earth"* in the 23rd century BCE. The star of Inanna, in those days, was what we now know today to be the star of *Venus.*

The goddess Inanna was also referred to as the *Morning Star.* Inanna was a very popular *goddess of Love, Justice, Wisdom, War* and She was a symbol of *Sexual Prowess.* It is said that She would drag mortal military soldiers out of taverns to have sex with Her. Inanna was so popular that other cultures renamed Her and claimed Her as their own. Th e Akkadians called Her *Ishtar.* Th e Greeks called Her *Aphrodite* Th e Assyrians called Her *Astarte.* The Romans called Her *Venus.* Personally, when I go stargazing, I hail the planet Venus as Inanna, because I believe this planet deserves to be called by its eldest known hail.

An Image of the Goddess Ishtar-Inanna Above

There is a lot of lore about Inanna. The most famous story is about Inanna journeying into the underworld to rescue Her sister while having to shed articles of clothing the deeper She traveled. I love this story because there is real speculation that when Inanna journeyed into the underworld to rescue Her sister, She was really going within, to rescue *the Self,* and that

Her story was merely an example of what is called by Pagans, *shadow working,* which is based off of *Carl Jung's* theory of the unconscious-self. Shadow work is meditational introspective work that practices looking deep within oneself in order to create self-improvement, healing and change.

Goddess worship and study offers stories about goddesses like Inanna that are empowering because they give heroic stories of the divine Feminine. Goddess worship and study also brings balance especially in a world where the female aspect has very little mention or voice in history and religious text. Close your eyes and imagine a world where men were cut out of history books, and men were cut out of religious tales, and women led all or most spiritual events, devotions and rituals. Men were thought of as little more than an asterisk in society. Strange huh? Now open your eyes, flip the script, and look around. If you are a woman or girl, this is your experience.

As mentioned in module two, *Goddess Centered paganism* is the practice and or study of journeying into the realm of the *divine Feminine* and engaging in Her Mysteries, and it is studied by both women and men. It is about seeking the divine Feminine within and without. It is about men getting in touch with their other side. It is also about leveling the psychological and spiritual scale and allowing for the *Female* presence of divinity.

Goddess worship includes Universal *Dualism.* This means it allows for the female attributes to thrive as well as the male attributes. But it also allows the flowing of creativity, creation, inwardness or introspective, motherly love, healing, pliability, Priestess magick, nurturing, artistry, liberty, nuance, spiritual womb energy, protection, and it allows the freedom to be unstructured. She is also a protective mother and a defensive warrior. These are the attributes of the Yin. Below are offered a few names of goddesses that are mentioned to be popular with African American Pagans. The names are listed by cultural origin. I will not give detail about them because they are all easy to explore online or in metaphysical books. One good book to begin studies for the African divine feminine is a book called, _Orishas, Goddess, and Voodoo Queens: The Divine Feminine in the African Religious Traditions_ by _Lilith Dorsey_ (Dorsey, 2020). This book gives detail on some Orisha and Loa goddesses and much more. When seriously looking for patrons, it is important to look up the pantheon, the stories and lore behind each god one has an interest in, and their likes and dislikes. The starred ones are African or African-based.

SOME WORLD GODDESSES

American Indian: (_Multiple Nations_) Corn Maiden and Corn Mother

Asian: (_Buddhist and Hindu_) Kwan Yin and Tara

Celtic: Brigid and Morrigan

***Dahomean:** Mawu

Greek: Aphrodite, Athena, Demeter, Hecate (Hekate), Hestia and Persephone

Hindu: Lakshmi, Kali Ma, Parvati and Shakti (Primordial Creator Goddess)

***Kemetic/Egyptian:** Auset (Isis), Bastet (Bast), Hathor, Heqat (Heqet), Ma'at, Nuit and Sekhmet

Roman: Artemis, Diana, Venus and Vesta

Sumerian or Mesopotamian : Astarte, Inanna and Ishtar

***Voodoo:** Erzulie and Maman Brigitte

***Yoruba Orisha:** _Aja, Oshun (Osun), Olokun, Oya and Yemaya_

***Multiple Regions of Africa:** Mami Wati

THE POWER OF DIVINE FEMININE MYTHS

I know that for most people Ancestral deities are very important to learn about and for their personal veneration. A lifetime of not seeing oneself in a divinity is not nurturing for one's soul. Ancestral mythical stories are like that chicken soup we hear so much about. For me it was not seeing an African or a divine Feminine for inner self-image. I was first called by *Oya*, before I even knew who She was. Surprisingly to some, however, I was also called by 2 other goddesses who were not African, although one of them, *Hecate* (goddess of crossroads), is said to have originated in Kemet as *Heqet* (the goddess of midwives) and became Hecate in *Greek mythology*.

From these sacred experiences with the goddesses, I have learned that the Universe, in *Its* most ultimate and supreme wisdom may choose to assign the best patron to guide for the needed period of one's life. In such cases the genome of the devotee or the patron is irrelevant. This is the test in which proves one's depth into a spiritual practice. If one is truly in tune with the Universe, and allows oneself to flow with the Universal frequency, the Universe will shock and amaze with the wonders of unpredictability. Then diversity and synchronicity will happen. Such is the conundrum of a seeker of truth, and when one's expectations are different. This is not to say that seeking the Ancestral truth is not important. Indeed, it is for all the obvious reasons, and reasons that I previously discussed. But, know that often on the journey for truth, the Universe may give detours, and at a time when one least expects them. Sometimes the true Ancestral spirit guides, to assist a practitioner, may not be of an expected Ancestors. Why is that you may ask? It depends on one's spiritual ascension. Like Inanna, when we ascend or descend, we shed our psychological layers until we become pure spirit. At some point during our ascension, we realize what our Ancestors have already found out, and that is that all spirits are our Ancestors, and that we have all known each other at some period of time within the spiritual realm, no matter who or what we are. At one point at the beginning of my ascension (or higher vibration of knowledge) I was assigned the energy of the goddess Oya. Ancestor familiarity was important to me. But as I continued to ascend, my spirit became more open, so the Universe granted me some guides outside of my known Ancestry who would best help in my growth. While this may not jive with many who engage in strict ethnocentric practices, those who are more open for diversity may experience this regardless if they expect it or not. Thus is the challenge, or even the reward, for those who have a determination not to limit oneself within that which may be only at Earthly planes of illusions. To the Universe, spiritual energy is spiritual energy. Limiting oneself from all other possibilities means limiting oneself from the vastness of what the Universe has to offer.

More About the Triple Goddess

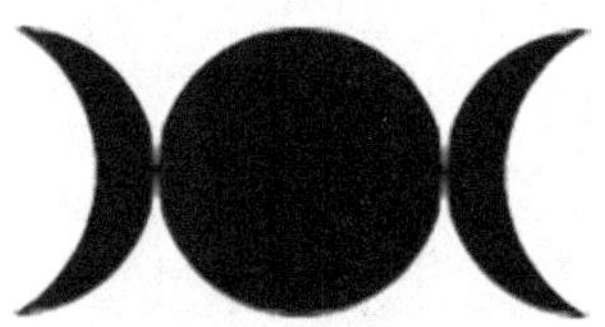 So, in a previous part of the study we discussed *The Triple Goddess* when applying to esbats, spells and rituals of the Moon. Now let's apply them to Goddess studies. As stated in a previous lesson, the triple goddess represents the Goddess' aspects of *Maiden, Mother and Crone.* Let's break down what that means. These three aspects are in no way the only aspects of the Goddess; however, they are the major framework to which all other aspects and attributes reside. Some call these the three phases of *the holy trinity.*

The Maiden aspect is the youngest of the *Trinity.* She is the *New Moon.* She represents newness, innocence, passion, a fresh start, naivety, virginity, trust, birth, positivity, rebirth, initiation, inspiration, truth and hope. She is the season of Spring, the return of its light and its green regrowth. She is the Phoenix rising from the ashes of the old, marking a renewed spirit. She is that which is pliable, intoxicating and witty. She is the smell of freshness after the rain and the smell of flowers in bloom. Her colors are pastels, like pink, green, baby blue and baby chick yellow. Notice that these are also the colors of Easter and the Pagan sabbat Ostara. These are Her favorite times of year. The oldest Maiden would be in Her mid- to late-twenties. Her symbols are the New and Waxing Moon. Goddesses like *Aja, Corn Maiden, Artemis, Oshun,* and *Persephone* are commonly considered goddesses with the Maiden aspect.

The Mother aspect is the second aspect. She is the Full Moon and She is considered the physical protector of the other two aspects. She is the *Warrior* aspect in many African Diasporic Traditions, African Traditional Religions, American Indian traditions and European Pagan traditions. She has gained strength. She is cunning. She has acquired vitality and survival instincts. She is a *Witch,* and She roams in and out of the *otherworlds and netherworlds.* She is the *Priestess* of Her tribe. She has a mate, and She is fertile and nurturing. She is ripe sweet fruit to the Maiden's bloom. She is the daylight, after the dawn. She is Gaia in the middle of Summer. She is strong, determined, and at the pinnacle of spirit. It is that spirit that gave birth to the Universe. Her colors are blood red, Earth green, soil brown, vibrant lavender and ocean blue.

The oldest Mother would be roughly in Her mid to late forties, though it could be a little bit later. Her aspects are represented in goddesses like *Auset, Aphrodite, Bast, Corn Mother, Freya, Inanna, Kwan Yin, Hera, Nuit, Morrigan and Yemaya.* Note that some of these archetypes of Mother spirit may also be found in the Maiden and the Crone too. For example, it is said that Hecate may be seen in all three aspects (Maiden, Mother and Crone.) Corn Mother is often thought of as Corn Maiden, and Oya, while often considered a Crone, can also be thought of in the Mother aspect. It depends on the perspective of the devotee.

The Crone represents the Dark and Waning Moons. She has always been my personal favorite of the trinity, and She is often misunderstood because She is the most mysterious. Yet Her mysteriousness and complexities are why I have always been drawn to Her. If the Mother aspect is the *Physical Protector* of the three, then, the Crone is most certainly the *Magickal Protector*, the *Cerebral Warrior* and the all-Adept *Sage*. She is the essence of time-tested experience, and it is Her experience that puts Her at the height of wisdom. She has existed in all three aspects of the trinity. Perhaps that is why She is sometimes depicted with three heads or with a three headed dog. Her favorite number is often three, or the triple three number of nine. She does indeed complete the symbol of the *Triquetra*

Triquetra Symbol Above

The Crone is the *Sorceress, Witch doctor, Shaman, Grandmother, Midwife* and the *Wise one*. She is the spirit that all other aspects seek for answers, guidance and comfort, although She often holds court in judgment and for discipline. The Crone is the magickal twilight and She is the guide of the *three-way crossroads*. She is the beginning of an end, and She sits at the portal to new beginnings. The Crone is in constant contact with the Ancestors, and it is Her spirit that guides us all through the veils into the spirit world. Elder High Priestesses embrace the aspect of the Crone because they seek to emulate Her knowledge and direction. Her colors are soil black, twilight gray, dark brown, third-eye purple, and midnight blue.

Her age is past that of the Mother's. Her favorite season is the harvest time and the dark side of the Wheel. Her favorite Pagan sabbat is Samhain. Some goddesses representing Her aspects are: *Oya, Kali Ma, Sekhmet, Hathor and Hecate.*

The God

"Know God" African Adinkra Symbol Shown

With all this talk about the Goddess, at long last, let's now start the discussion about the *Male aspect of the Universe. The Pagan Lord* is not at all like the *God of Abraham,* who most of us have been taught about. He is not a jealous God. He is not one to inflict vengeance. Diversity in all things, and beings, to him is balance and is as it is meant to be. It is not His judgment that women are subservient, and He doesn't dwell in Heaven awaiting the obedient or the non-obedient to arrive for judgment. Our Pagan Lord dwells within and without the Universe. Our Lord is the Universe, and He is in each and every one of us, just as the Goddess is in everyone.

The Pagan Lord has many aspects. He is popularly known as *The Green Man* of the *forest and The Horned God of the woods* protecting the green Earth, Gaia, and Her animals. He is also known as *The Hunter* because He is a skilled *Gamesman.* He is also a *Sportsman* with fair mindedness and consciousness. He is a Protector of all He surveys and a Noble Warrior when He is needed. The Pagan Lord prides Himself on being a *Magician* and *Sorcerer* and can *shapeshift* whenever necessary, and therefore is often a *Trickster.* He is also the *High Priest.* The Pagan God has many other attributes including *Lover, Father, Hermit, Hero,* and He is a *Wise King.*

The Pagan Lord is also known as the proverbial *Holly King* representing Autumn and Winter, and He is also known as the *Oak King* representing Spring and Summer. It is said that both kings do battle during the *Equinoxes*. At the beginning of the *Spring Equinox*, or *Ostara*, the Oak King has conquest, over the Holly King. He then reigns until the *Autumn Equinox* or what we discussed previously as *Mabon*. At the beginning of *the Autumn Equinox* the Holly King returns and has conquest over the Oak King. This lore of conquests represents the transitioning of powers between our Lord's aspects, which represents the light and darkness at the turning of the Wheel.

The aspects of the Pagan God are not judgmental because He believes that all living things have purpose, no matter what they are. He deems that what one doesn't learn in the present incarnation they will learn in any future reincarnation. He knows this because, in His Elder Sage form, He stands at the crossroads as a guide. As stated before, the Pagan Lord arrives as the Sun, only to later travel into the *Underworld on the dark part of the Wheel.* He is then reborn to the Goddess year after year, so He knows that the Universe is full of lessons, and that we each have an opportunity of learning those lessons over and over again. Other archetypes of the Pagan Lord are *Gatekeeper*, *Overseer* and *Loving Mate*. He is a Gatekeeper because He seeks to keep balance and order in all things. He is an Overseer to protect Earth's wildlife and the environment, and most of all Our Pagan Lord is also a Loving Mate to the *Queen of Heaven*.

Now, just as giving for the goddesses, let's give a few names of patron gods that are mentioned to be popular with African American Pagans. There are countless more, but this is just to get one started on research. Again, this study does not give detail about them, because they are all easy to research online or in books. The Yoruba Orisha are very popular. One good book to get started on for learning Yoruba gods, and goddesses is called, *The Way of the Orisha* written by *Philip John Neimark*. Below are some names that can be researched. The starred ones are of African origin.

SOME WORLD GODS

Buddhist: Buddha

Greek: Adonis, Apollo, Ares, Hades, Poseidon and Zeus

**Haitian Vodou -Loa:* Baron Samedi and Papa Legba

Hindu: Ganesh (Ganesha), Shiva/Siva and Vishnu

**Kemet/Egyptian:* Amon (Amen), Ausar (Osiris), Geb, Heru (Horus), Tehuti or Tehutay (Thoth), Set (Seth) and Ra

Norse/Heathen/Aesir: Freyr, Loki, Odin, Thor and Tyr

Roman: Bacchus, Jupiter, Lucifer, Mars, Mercury, Neptune and Saturn

**Yoruba Orishas:* Elegba (Eshu), Obatala, Oduduwa, Ogun, Olodumare, Oshosi and Shango

Below are Haitian Vodou sacred drawings called VeVe representing the symbols of the loa's spirit.

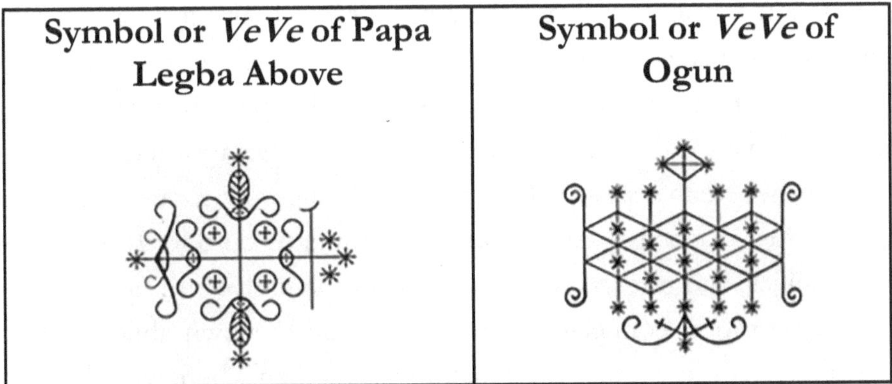

The Tools of Wicca

 My father used to say to us with old school *Ebonics*, "*If ya cut the munkey—ya act da fool!*" This was his way of warning us, when we were children, to behave and stop acting like fools before he had to hand down the corporal punishment. We always straightened up when he said that. That whipping used to hurt—*LoL!* I once heard a story that makes me wonder if that old saying really always rang true. I once heard a man telling a true story about a few scientists studying the behavior of monkeys and great apes. Apparently, one day, the scientists had a monkey in a room, and they decided to see if the monkey had the capability to use a tool. They took a banana and placed it up on a high shelf, and then they gave the monkey a stick to see if it would be able to use the stick to knock the banana off the shelf. What happened next was totally unexpected to them. The monkey used the stick to balance itself upon it. The monkey then reached up and grabbed the banana off the shelf. The scientists were expecting the monkey to teach them something about the world of apes, but in an unexpected twist the monkey taught them all a lesson about their own way of thinking. As human beings we tend to put emphasis on tools, be it cars, calculators, computers, cell phones or the latest television. We passively believe that we should let the tool do the work for us. We neglect to think that maybe we should put more emphasis on ourselves and our own abilities, and not so much on the tools themselves. In fact, I would say we are too disconnected from Nature and our own abilities. But I digress. Tools break, get lost or malfunction—then where would we be? Universal magick doesn't just consist of magickal tools. We as Magi imbue the tools with our own energy so that it flows with our will. The true Magi is not inertly on the end of a tool. Magickal use tools alone have no real power. If created and used correctly they can be conduits that will allow our energy to flow through them. We are what gives them their true

effectiveness. If my father were alive today, I guess I would have to ask him what he thought about acting like that smart monkey.

Wiccans use specific tools that other Witches may not necessarily use, and they use them in certain ways to manifest what they need. Wiccans use them in ritual, spells and ceremony. In case you are wondering, you don't have to spend a tremendous amount of money to purchase these tools. Tools for magickal uses are found cheaply at flea markets, yard sales, fairs, thrift stores, neighborhood Asian or West Indies stores and craft fairs. You can even find some great items in dollar type stores. The best tools are the ones you can make yourself, because you put your energy into them when you make them. Others can be found in Nature and when foraging. As you become more adept in your magickal practice your inner spirit will direct you to what you need for your workings. The following is a list of tools that are used by Wiccans and Witches.

The Ankh

The *ankh*, also known as the *"Key of Life,"* is one of the spiritual symbols most valued by many black Americans and many others of the esoteric spiritualists' cultures. The ankh is shaped like a closed *oval loop* sitting on a *cross bar*, and another bar or staff pointed downwards. This Kemetic symbol originated in Africa, and is said to be as old as 5000 years, or originating in 3000 BCE. Similarly, a symbol called *"the rod and ring"*, is found on the famous terracotta Sumerian plaque called *"Queen of the Night"*, showing the goddess *Lilith* (or some say *Inanna*) holding them. This plaque is said to be from 1750 BCE.

The ankh is a magickal icon, or instrument, which was used by the Kemetic (Egyptian) dynastic rulers and their Priests symbolizing both the human lifetime on Earth, and the eternal life afterwards. Many hieroglyphics and depictions were found of *Anubis, "god of the Underworld"*, placing the ankh against the lips of the dead as to invigorate them. Other depictions show other gods doing this too, such as *Ma'at, Ausar and Sekhmet*. This is the reason the ankh is called the *Key of Life* or the *Breath of Life*.

The ankh is also popular with the *Coptic* Christians and the *Golden Dawn*, and they both call it *Crux Ansata*, which in Latin, literally means, *cross with a handle,* or *handle-shaped cross*. The Coptic Christians continued their Egyptian heritage theme by using the ankh as a symbol of Jesus' promise of everlasting life. The Golden Dawn believes the ankh is the symbol of *the manifestation of the divine Life Force* and represents the *divine Union*. This is because of the way the ankh combines the *masculine* downward staff and *feminine* closed oval ring. To the Golden Dawn this is the key to where creation is manifested. In addition, this *key of life* is shaped like the symbol for the planet *Venus*, which is of great spiritual importance in their theology.

To many Witches/Wiccans the ankh is a very important magickal icon. They understand the ankh to be a symbol of immortality and eternal life. Because the shape of the ankh is reminiscent of a mirror, many believe it to be a key that reflects many universal worlds, time and space, and the realm of life and death. Because of this it is also considered a symbol of regeneration as well as the symbol of creation.

Witches utilize an ankh for many reasons. Some use the ankh as a symbol to ward, and some use it as a luck charm symbol. Because of its unique attributes it can be used both ways. Some use it as a wand in ritual or magickal practices to direct energies. Some use it as a scepter in magick and ritual to show mystical or priesthood authority. Some place it on their altar to make their altars more sacred or to bring more energy to their sacred space. Some wear the ankh as a pendant during rituals, for protection, or they just wear it in casual wear as a spiritual statement. Some draw the symbol as a part of their sigil work. Some even get tattoos of ankhs for added protections.

Athame

The athame is a dull (unsharpened) double-edged blade or knife used only for ceremonial purposes, and is used to direct power through it, much like a wand. This conduit projects the flow of energy in the direction of your choice by your will and command. Swords are sometimes substituted. An athame can be purchased in magickal brick and mortar stores or online. The Athame is the symbol of the God, and while many think of the athame as an element of air, when used as a wand its element is also fire.

Bell

The *bell* is the instrument of vibrations. Vibrations are very important for the Witch or Magi because the Universe runs on vibrations, speaks to us through vibrations, and spells are cast through vibrations. That is why *The Wiccan Rede* suggests that spells be written in rhyme. As explained previously, *The Wiccan Rede* is a combination of rhythmic axiom Wiccans refer to. The Rede will be displayed and discussed in another Lesson.

To continue, when a spell or incantation is written in rhyme it moves within the universal vibrations and the Universe is more receptive to it. That is because energy travels through vibrations. We could think of vibrational movement as highways with different speeds and frequencies. Because of their attractive sounds, bells are used during rituals to add positive vibrations but also to direct the energies that travel through the vibrations. For example, the bell can be used to signal the beginning and the end of a ritual or meditation, or the end of an affirmation or the end of a spell. It can also be used to *activate* the spell just after casting. It can also be used to ward off negative energies while casting a circle. Bells can be substituted for *gongs, chimes, Tibetan mini cymbals* or various *singing bowls*. For a more Afrocentric tool you may want to add a *GanKeKe bell* (cow type bell from Ghana), or substitute a bell for a dried *Axatse gourd rattle* instead. This ancestral instrument is also called an *African shaker*. You can also use an Egyptian *sistrum*. Some people use drums to add to the vibrational connection instead. The bell is a tool that is the symbol of the Goddess, and its element is air.

Boline

The *boline* is a knife or sharp, hand-blade tool that is used for the preparation of magickal workings. If the athame were a magickal flying horse, the boline would be the workhorse or mule bound by Earth and the physical world. The boline is used for everything from the cutting of herbs or cords, or used for the dressing of candles by marking symbols and objects into them. They can also be used for creating other tools like wands. This tool is not normally seen on an altar and is used for anything in preparation for magickal workings. It is often found in the Witch's magickal toolbox.

Broom/Besom

As stereotypical as it may sound the broom is a popular tool of Witches and Pagans. The *broom* or sometimes called *besom,* is an explicable symbol of sweeping away and cleansing, and it is one of the most beloved of all the tools. A decorative broom placed by, or over the door is deemed a protective medium. It wards off undesirable guests and negative energies. I once read many years ago that a Witch should purchase a new broom every Samhain for her *familiar spirit*. A broom is often considered to be a good resting place for friendly or helpful spirits. This explains the old adage of a Witch flying on their broom, as both fateful companion and as a mode of flying its Witch wherever they wished to go. I try to keep that tradition of buying brooms on Samhain, and I keep brooms sitting by my doors—some inside, and some outside. The besom is a symbol of the Goddess, and its element is earth.

African Americans have a spiritual history with the magickal broom too. In the days of American slavery, when slaveholders prevented bondspeople from being married legally, the slaves would turn to the spiritual laws, and they would jump over the broom into their own portal of matrimony, thus rejecting the slaveholders' statutes, and consequently embracing the Universal laws.

I facilitated my daughter's wedding years ago, but before doing so, my daughter and I decorated a cinnamon broom for her, and her husband, to jump over afterwards. In doing so she was following the footsteps of her African American Ancestors.

The Witch's besom is never really used for actual sweeping of physical material, but is used mostly to move or block undesirable energies away. It is normally moved above, but not touching the ground or floor, in a sweeping or counterclockwise movement or what Wiccans call *widdershins*. The opposite of widdershins is *deosil* or clockwise. Move the besom clockwise when gaining energy. Both words, widdershins and deosil, are of *Scottish Gaelic* language. Sweeping counterclockwise removes energies. Sweeping clockwise gains energies. As stated previously the broom can be used near doors and portals, to sweep away unwanted energies in areas to prepare for rituals, and to create a doorway on the outline of the ritual circle for the practitioner(s) to leave the circle when necessary. A smaller broom can be passed to different members within circles during ritual to indicate moments of authority, moments of speakership or as a medium used to cast with.

The broom is also a special symbol for the goddess *Oya* since She is the Yoruba *goddess of Storms and Winds*. Her symbol of a broom relates with Her charge of moving, changing, cleansing and sweeping away that which needs to be moved. In fact, Her name means *She Who Tore,* or *She Tore,* indicating a sweeping away.

Candle

If I were told that, as a Wiccan, I could only use one tool, I would have to choose the candle. Candles and fire, in my opinion, have to be the strongest of energies because of what fire elicits. We all use candles for magickal times.

We all use them as symbols for hope and peace. From our very first birthdays, and all birthdays thereafter, candles are lit on cakes and wishes are made without a thought that we were casting wishing spells. Many couples, all over the world, light candles together with hopes that the magick of the candlelight would initiate or ignite excitement between them. The very sight of a lit candle or a raging fire evokes passion, romance, hope, sensuality, prayer, and tenderness. These very same qualities can aid in the manifestation of one's needs and desires. So, when one thinks of it, this all makes sense, after all, fire was the first element. When the *Big Bang* ignited its first elements were that of heat, flames and molten fire. These were the elements that help to forge our known Universe today. Fire is where creation and energy all began.

A candle placed on the top left side of an altar is representative of the universal Goddess and a candle on the top right side is representative of the universal God. These place settings are distinguishably the signatures of Wicca. Designating space in the altar for feminine energy and masculine energy gives recognition to the *Law of Polarity* (Duality) and *the Law of Gender*. Between the two Genders is where it is believed that creation and manifestation is holy and fully possible.

Lit candles in the middle of the altar can be used for burning petitions and are often signals for initiating rituals or spells. Examples of candle colors for the Goddess candles are silver and white, which represent Moon energy. The colors of the God candles are yellow, orange and gold, which represent the Sun and the light. Depending on the ritual, a red candle may be used as a Goddess candle to represent the power of the Mother's Full Moon energy, and the nurturing strength of the Mother-Goddess. A green candle during the Summer can be representative of the *Green Man* which is an aspect of the Pagan Lord. Candles are also laid in the middle of the altar for the purpose of magickal workings. The color of the candle is contingent upon the purpose and or intentions of the ritual or spell. Later in the study, we will discuss colors and how they may be used for magickal workings. Candles are the elements of fire.

Cauldron

This next tool is as stereotypical for Witches as the broom. We all have the vision of Witches hovering about a bubbling black pot and spewing magickal incantations. I also have a vivid memory of myself as a young child playing outside around a huge black pot during my rural vacations with my family in North Carolina. This pot was the biggest *cauldron* I have ever seen to this day, and it was used by my

Ancestors to wash clothes outside by boiling them under an open fi re. The old folks called it *a wash pot.* But, when I think about it now, it was a huge black cast iron cauldron, and it was a remnant of the times before the washing machine. My mother and aunts would tell us about the times when their grandmother and elders made soap out of lye in the pot. They would ponder in sentimental voices about how nothing would clean clothes brighter than a hot, boiling wash pot, and good strong lye, back in the old days. They told tales of how the elders would stir the clothes and homemade lye with a huge stick or paddle. I still think about that pot and the good feelings I had as we played around it. Even then the old ways have always given me comforting and wholesome feelings.

There are some things that take on the energies surrounding it. They absorb the good times and echo those energies to people of whom are in their presence. Cast iron cauldrons are just those types of sponges. They give off the same feelings you would have when looking at a vintage pot that you know your grandmother had for many years, and your memories of all those good meals she cooked in it leaving delightful wholesome thoughts. They relay the sentiment that something good is or is about to brew. Cauldrons are symbols of the Goddess. They are the representations of a matrix or vessel. The vessel is the representation of the primordial ocean, and the ocean is perceived to be the *Mother of Life*— Her womb. In short, it represents the vessel for all of creation.

Cauldrons are used to burn ceremonial herbs, to cook magickal brews, to burn petitions in or to cast a bounty of spells. I have a large cast iron cauldron that I use to cook some recipes that I call my "Witch's pot". I have a larger one that I sit by my back door to bless the home, and to do special potent spells within. I have a tiny cauldron to use to burn herbs and incense on my altar. Cauldrons can be found online, in flea markets, yard sales and thrift stores. The element of cauldrons is water.

Censer and Incense

 *Censers* are containers or vessels made for burning or to hold smoldering incense to cleanse areas of negative energies and to bring pleasant smells to ritual. They are usually insulated containers that can hold self-igniting charcoal. Special charcoal for the censer can be purchased at any botanica or metaphysical store. Incenses can come in resin, stick, cone or powdered form for burning. Once the charcoal is ignited, powdered incense, dried herbs or resin incense can be placed on the charcoal to burn in a censer or small cauldron. In stick form incenses go into a type of incense holder. Some of the types of resins that can be used in censers are copal, frankincense, dragon's blood, myrrh etc.

Sage is a dried herb that can come in loose form or in what is shaped into a *sage stick or sage wand*. Sage is often used to eliminate negative energies or spirits and is used to cleanse and blessed the home. Sage is also used in magickal circles or rituals to cleanse areas for magick and members of circles. Spiritual cleansing with sage and other incense is called *smudging*. Smudging can also be used to purify tools. Others used to smudge include palo santo, lavender, flowers like roses and chrysanthemums, and herbs like rosemary and mints. These plants can be tied, dried and used loose as incense or as smudge wands. These wands are often incorporated with various flowers and herbs. The pleasant smell of smoldering incense places one's mind into a favorable state that is conducive for magickal workings and meditation. Incense represents the element of air and is usually placed on the side of the altar representing masculine energies. However, if incense is placed in a censer or cauldron, it is normally placed on the divine Feminine side of the altar.

Cup

The *cup* or *chalice* is similar to the cauldron for the reason that they are symbols of the Goddess and represents Her vessel. The cup is usually filled with liquid like milk, water, brew or wine and placed on the altar for ritual offering. In some rituals, the Moon is reflected into the wine or water to be fortified with its power for drinking. The most practiced ceremony is the act of gently placing the athame into the cup or cauldron, at the near end of a ritual or ceremony, representing the joining of the God and Goddess in *divine Union*. In many cases a male member inserts the athame while a female member holds the cup. This creates a gateway or conduit for manifestation. To give one's altar a more Afrocentric flare, find a wooden or African cup or a dried gourd that has been cut in half and use it for an altar cup. The element for the cup is water.

Pentacle

Of all the tools mentioned, this one may be the most maligned by people opposed to Pagan practices. In popular culture, and in the movie industry, this spiritual charm has been morphed into a symbol of evil, yet many people are unaware of the origins of this icon.

The *pentacle* is a 5-pointed star depicting points of equal lengths. The points of the pentacle's star are encased or set within a circle. It is said that the pentacle was first designed by a group of people, said to have originated from Italy or Greece and moved to Egypt sometime during the 6th century BCE. They were called *Pythagoreans* and led by their teacher, Pythagoras, an ancient Ionian Greek philosopher. Pythagoreans were philosophers and mathematicians who designed images in the category of what is now referred to as *sacred geometry,* and one image they were given credit for was called a *pentad.* Th e pentad is a 5-pointed star and often encased by a pentagon. Th e Pythagoreans believed that each point of the pentad represented an element: *water, earth, air, fire and idea (spirit)* (Hobgood, n.d.). Later, Christians adapted the emblem to symbolize the wounds of Christ before taking the cross as their official symbol. Pagans continue to use the 5-pointed star for its original meaning.

Decorative renderings of the pentacle or *barnstars,* can be seen on barns as one travels through the countryside, or American Dutch farmlands. To these farmers the symbol has the power to ward off evil.

Eastern Star members use the inverted pentacle as their official sign or logo. Many churches display the pentacle in their architectures like the *Parish church of St. Barnabus* in *Bethnal Green, London, the Mormon Temple Nauvoo* and *Marktkirche,* and the *Lutheran church* in *Hannover Germany* just to name a small few.

For Wiccans the pentacle is a symbol of the Goddess or the Lord and Lady and or the Earth. It is used as a symbol of protection and is said to keep away negativity of all forms. It can be made from wood, copper, brass, silver or any type of metal. It can be drawn or carved into items like candles, stones and crystals. It can also be worn as a pendant or embroidered into garbs to be worn for rituals and magickal workings. Many Pagans place the pentacle on their altars, hang it on the walls or carry it with them. Pentacle tattoos are very popular now as both decorative and spiritual symbols of power and protection. The element for the pentacle is both earth and spirit.

Petitions

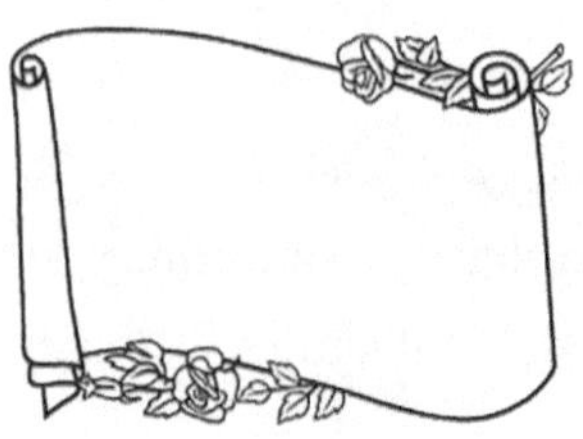

Have you ever written a note to someone or even God, and after you have finished you either burned it by fire, or thrown it to the wind, or floated it in a body of water hoping that divine intervention will hear your prayers? In magick this is what is called a *Witch's petition*. A petition is a written declaration, request or statement of intent. It is then used in a spell or ritual by activating it in some way. Usually, it is activated by the elements of air, water, fire or earth. Different traditions and practices perform the petition spell in different ways. A petition can be its own spell, or it can be used in conjunction with a larger ritual. A petition may be addressed to an individual spirit, Ancestor, patron god or the Universe in general.

Petitions are usually written on any paper, but the most preferred type of paper, in an African Traditional Diasporic Religion, and some other Pagan traditions, is parchment, craft paper, brown bag or butcher paper. For most Wiccans petitions sent through the wind or on water are usually written on natural material like basic leaves, bay leaves, bark or other biodegradables. Petitions are usually activated by burning it during a spell being cast.

Sigils

The word *sigil* is a Latin term which refers to an inscribed or painted symbol created for the purpose of magickal workings. Sigils are pictorial and often hieroglyphical type signatures considered to have magical powers. Sigils are among the most common kinds of magick in which we all have seen, at one time or another, in the modern world and ancient caves, tombs, and pyramids, as well as, walls and buildings along the city streets. These markings and tags are often sigils which go unnoticed. Sigil magick is the artful use of symbols, shapes and imagery to manifest a specific outcome or intent. A sigil is often a meaningless drawn symbol that is given meaning to by the practitioner when casting spells.

More often than not, a sigil is meant to have a meaning only to its creator, so as to cloak the meaning of the conjure to others who happen upon the written spell. Sigils are often used as tattoos, temporarily drawn on hands, arms, feet or clothing, like inside one's shoes. They can be carved into candles, drawn on petitions, and recorded into a *book of shadows*. A sigil can be created by the magician themselves, discovered online or given to by another practitioner.

Some symbols can be used as sigils, while not truly considered sigils, such as the African *adinkra* symbols, or alchemy symbols for air, water, fire, earth and spirit. Heart shapes are used for spells of love, as well as for works with goddesses. There are examples of sigils below. The first is a common type design for conjuring or calling to spirit for manifesting intent—showing arms and legs spread to the heavens. The second is a basic heart shaped sigil for matters of the heart. The third is a *West African Adinkra* called "the leg of a hen", referring to chicks being under the mother. The fourth is also an Adinkra called "seed of the wawa tree", showing the hard shell of the seed which is known for its impenetrable protective qualities. The fourth sigil looks more like a turtle to me, so I think of it as the hard shell of a turtle. You can find more than 60 adinkra online. These sigils can be used alone or with other markings to personalize one's magick.

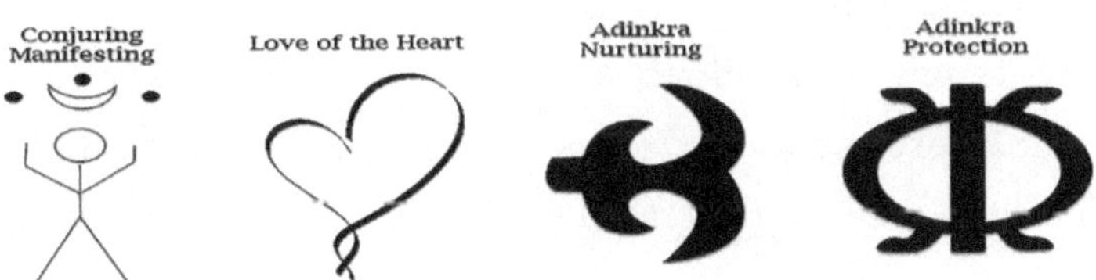

Wand

Wands, as seen on <u>*Harry Potter,*</u> are primary tools that can be used by practicing Wiccans. I am sure that as children we have all made our own share of imaginary magickal wands, hoping to make our irksome little sisters and brothers disappear. I know I have. Just as in the other tools, it should be remembered that the power is not with the tool but within the person commanding the flow of energy through the tool. The wand is a conduit to direct the power generated from the hand of the user. Wands are more often made from any type of wood, but some people are now also using wands made of crystals or mostly crystals. Copper is also a very popular medium for creating wands. Wood wands are carved and/or painted with any design, and crystal gems are often added to the tip of the wood for balance, focus quality and to make it more conductive of magick. Wands are mainly purchased, but they are usually a little pricey. You will find that the tool you make yourself is more effective than one you purchase in any store or online because of the energy you place into the tool as you are creating it. It does not have to be fancy. It just has to be a stick that resonates with you. A branch that you find in the backyard or in the woods can work just as well. Some woods that are said to be the best for creating wands are *Elder, Black Walnut, Apple and Holly.* But in truth, the best wood is any one which speaks to the individual. Wands carry the element of fire, and are considered a tool of the *divine Masculine* energy.

The Altar

Since we have discussed some of the most important tools used for magickal workings, it would be appropriate to next discuss the place where one may use the tools. It was once suggested to me that the entire world is a sacred *altar* to present to the Divine, and that everything we do should be in reverence to that sacred altar. This means that the way we live our lives, the way we treat and respect others and the way we engage at living our best lives, for our highest good, is an offering we place on the *virtual universal altar*. There are times, however, when we may want to privately reflect, pay homage to a season or an Ancestor, worship, and or perform a ritual. A private altar is often used as the focal point for those times of magickal workings and meditations. We can also use them for communing with our *higher self* or *one's divine Spirit.*

An altar is normally placed anywhere that is convenient and accessible, and it can be made from pretty much anything. Altars can be made from desktops, crates, folding tables, elaborate furniture, or wooden planks. I have even seen people use bookshelves or the floor of their back porch. You can even find custom-made altars by specialty makers. My first altar was my old college trunk, but I have since upgraded to an older, oblong living-room table. Although it is more highly desirable to have altars made of all-natural materials like stone and wood, an altar can be made of almost any material or table one has available. I keep my altar in my bedroom for privacy, but many people place altars throughout their homes and may even keep a small one in their kitchens. Altars can be placed in closets, living rooms, spare rooms and halls. Some practitioners even have altars in their backyards. Some people like the convenience of having a portable altar, meaning that they keep it in a box or container and pull it out when they need it. This is helpful for someone who lives with others, and for whatever reason doesn't feel comfortable keeping one in the open. A portable altar can be carried when traveling and packed up when not in use. Portable altars can be assembled by the practitioner or it can be purchased ready to use from metaphysical merchants online or at metaphysical or botanical stores.

Altars are often designated for all different purposes. One may be used for general workings, prosperity, self-improvement, and one may be used as a love altar. I have even visited a Witch who had a love altar in her bedroom in order to keep the relationship between her husband and herself fresh and loving. One quick note for Wiccans who are vigilant in light working. For Wiccans, love altars are used to ask the Universe to bring love or relationships into one's life. It may even be a self-love altar. For most Wiccans there is a common belief that if two people were meant to be then the Universe will most certainly make it happen without the need to direct energy towards a specific person. Wiccan love spells have no direct target, because it is considered baneful magick to direct a love spell towards anyone against their will. Spells that have no direct target leaves that discretion to the Universe.

In this way it is assured that the results will be for the highest good of the practitioner. I call this ethical practice a type of *broadcasting* spell. A broadcasting spell is a spell sent without a target, but is answered by the one who is meant to hear it.

In my personal opinion, broadcasting spells are more ideal, especially in a love spell, no matter what tradition is used. For example, say that someone wants their baby daddy, or baby mama, to come back to them. They place a love spell on them to do this, and it works. They are then, most likely, in possession of a miserable love zombie, especially if they didn't want to be there before the spell was cast. This means that they are only there because of the spell. They are spiritually tied to the Witch, but there is no true heart in the relationship. Eventually the Witch comes to know this, and begins to feel the emptiness. If a broadcast spell goes out, then the Universe sends the person the Witch was meant to have, and who truly loves them, even if it is the baby daddy or mama coming back. The reason for this is because they are there because they want to be there and are meant to be, and not there because they were forced to by a spell.

Creating the Altar

Before erecting an altar, you might want to ask yourself a few questions. The first question is will you allow everyone to know that you are Wiccan or Pagan? The reason for this question is because if people you are living with don't know that you are Pagan, then an altar will definitely give them clues. If you don't want anyone to know, then you may want to place your new altar in a private place, or you may want to create a portable altar that you can use in private times and private places. You can then place it away when you are done. If you have *come out of the broom closet* (or have told your family or roommates that you are Pagan) you may still want to let them know about your altar. If they happen to stumble upon your altar (and they in all probability will) it could be a culture shock to non-Pagans, to say the least, and to others who are uninformed, it may be downright scary for them. It is always best to have a frank discussion with roommates and family and explain why an altar is right for you. Unfortunately, family members may never accept a Pagan altar in their home, and that is okay. If you are living in their home, or just sharing a home, it is always best to consider their feelings and concerns. One can never be at peace with one's practice if there are hard feelings from others about your altar in the home. Having peace of mind is very important when engaging in mystical practices. There are other options like making use of a portable altar to use outside in Nature or to use it somewhere you can do your own private workings. You may want to create a magickal circle or shrine with other Pagans or Witches and share an altar outside of your home. Know that *"where there is a Witch there is a way"*.

Once you have erected your altar you may want to decide if it would be a *general-purpose* altar or *specific-purpose* altar. A general-purpose altar is used for all intentions, including meditations, magickal workings, *spiritual devotion* or just seasonal offerings. *Seasonal altars* are altars made to pay homage to the seasons, esbats and or the sabbats by giving offerings for the seasons and or displaying such as flowers, fruit and seasonal decorations. A *specific-purpose altar* is created for a particular intent and is displayed for an extended period of time, like for example a healing altar for someone who is sick. A practitioner would go to this altar for the purpose of meditation and magickal workings towards healing.

Another type of specific purpose altar is a *dedication altar,* which is specifically dedicated to a particular patron deity. This deity may be a beloved patron in which an altar would be dedicated indefinitely for their veneration. Some practitioners call these altars *shrines.* In some ATRs, some dedicated altars are called *thrones.* Another dedicated altar may be a *combination altar* for both veneration and love. One Pagan once mentioned to me, many years ago, that she had dedicated her *love altar* to the goddess *Aphrodite.* In that same vein one may wish to dedicate a *healing altar* to the goddess *Kwan Yin,* or whatever patron one may feel is appropriate. Whatever you may decide, indeed know that altars are very creative vehicles. Creating your own altar, in your own space, for your own desire and in your own design can be an amazing experience, be it a temporary altar, or one that is dedicated for your own whims and or spiritual needs.

Once you decide where you want your altar, how you want your altar to be made, and what type of altar you want, you may then decide what direction you would like your altar to be in. As in my case, often providence decides what direction the altar faces. If you have limited space, like me, you may have no choice but to place it facing in the only direction available to you. However, if you are fortunate enough to have a choice, perhaps you may want to consider placing your altar in the direction that is more favorable to you and your own elemental *Feng Shui.* To Pagans each direction, *North, South, East,* and *West,* has its own characteristics, which also happens to correspond to the four elements. So, if you know what type of workings you will be doing at your altar then, if at all possible, you can choose a direction that is right for you. The following may help guide you in what direction is best for your altar.

Altar Directional Correspondence

- *East* corresponds with the element of air. *Air* is the symbol representing dawn, intellect, newness, divinity, Spring, and the Maiden aspect. This energy is good for starting new beginnings, new ventures, truth seeking, learning new ideas and practices, clarity, transparency, clairvoyance and communications.

- *South* corresponds with *fire*, and it represents manifestation, action, love, kundalini energy, creativity, Summer energy and the fire of the masculine energy. Since South is fire energy it also represents the Sun, the Warrior aspect, removing blockages, charging to a cause and defeating that which is holding one back.

- *West* corresponds with *water*, and water is associated with flowing emotion, purification, cleansing, Moon magick, tidal energy, romance magick, adventure, flexibility, sunset, Autumn, endings, and maturity. Since it is water, it relates to the Mother aspect of nurturing, childbirth and healing.

- *North*, the last direction of course, represents *Earth* and the wisdom that is associated with its grounding. It also represents fertility, knowledge, prosperity, balance, Winter and the Crone. This altar direction is good for planting and sowing one's future, growth, seeking knowledge and learning, justice, meditation, finding equilibrium, mediation in decision making, and is also conducive for healing and good health.

If there is a particular goal you wish to achieve for yourself, you may want to carefully choose the right direction and point your altar in that direction. This would aid in achieving coming goals or aspirations.

When you choose the type of altar and the direction, perhaps then you will be ready to decide what you wish on your altar. While Wiccans use special tools for their altars you can still have an altar representing your style and your flare. After all, the more pleasing your altar is to you the more likely your altar will successfully work for you. Magick works on the frame of mind, and a gratifying altar sets the mind on to spiritual success.

Claiming Your Cultural Altar

Much of the African American mystical culture incorporates ethnocentric altar settings for one's spiritual roots, ancestral grounding, and spiritual identity. While Wicca brings to mind European customs and conventions, because its concept of witchcraft started with European ideas, pantheons, Ancestral worship, ethnocentric garb etc., there is a Wiccan cultural movement that is evolving, and allowing for other cultural designs and needs. Included is the movement of *Afrocentricity* and other *cultural diversities. It* also allows for *eclectic* ideas. For example, on my altar I may have a statue of Oya or Baste or *Aku-Aba,* depending on my spiritual intent or purpose. I also keep ankhs and cowry shells on my altar. I sometimes have seashells for Yemaya. I also have an African drum and African shaker near the altar. These things connect me to my Ancestors, DNA and my spiritual identity. Regardless of one's culture, adding a piece, or perhaps better to say *"a peace",* of oneself to one's altar, makes all the difference, and makes the altar feel even closer to home.

As an example of eclectic practices, there were times when I wanted *Buddha* for meditation or a statue of *Ganesh,* who is the *Hindu god of Luck* and *Wisdom*. I have laid acorns and pinecones on my altar for the season. I have also laid leaves and stones on my altar that my grandchildren gave me when they visited. Gifts like those are the most spiritual and nothing is more enchanting than to see children placing flowers and items that they found in a field on an altar. This is why many Pagan parents create altars for their children. It also keeps them from playing on your sacred altar if they have one of their own.

A Wiccan altar is basically a small symbolic interpretation of one's world and one's environment. You may want to place representations of each element on your altar. This is a wonderful way for grounding. This is your time to be creative with your link to the Universe. Do this the way your lifestyle, and your wallet tells you to. Do not feel discouraged if your first altar is not everything you want. In time, you can add to it or build it just as you like. There is no need to run out and buy everything you see to place on it at first. Many things you can get inexpensively at a dollar priced store. Why not allow the Universe to give them to you? Natural touches that you find while hiking, taking trips, or by the side of a road are perfectly wonderful. An altar, that is not use for Wiccan rites and magick, can be as basic as a couple of candles and some flowers on a table, or it can be the greatest work of art. Keep in mind that you can choose, and never allow anyone tell you that your altar is incorrect. While anyone can make suggestions, it is only you to whom the Universe connects through it.

An altar is a place where you can reflect on your magickal practices, so take the time to consider the wonders and the possibilities that are all yet to come. Make it yours and make it right for you.

General Outline of a Wiccan Altar

A general-purpose altar fully adorned with items and offerings is charming, however, in Wicca there is a basic template or outline on where items and tools are placed in relationship to the Goddess and God or the feminine and masculine energies. Different books may vary with suggestions on a tool placement here or there, but basically, they follow similar formats. Previously we discussed the tools of Wicca and their relationship to the Goddess and God. **Exhibit 3.2** is a suggestive outline that explains how the tools can be placed on the altar for ceremony or magickal workings. This diagram is not written in stone, but it can give ideas on how to create a working Wiccan altar.

So, sistars and brothas, here are the nuts and berries so to speak. It distinguishes what a basic Pagan altar is, and what a true Wiccan altar is. As stated previously, a Wiccan altar works on at least two *Kemetic* or more often called *Hermetic* spiritual principles. These are called, *"The Law of Gender"* and *"The Law of Polarity" (Duality)*. There are other principles you can research, but for now these are the ones that are most important to know for creating your altar. With these laws it is understood that all things, in the known Universe have a feminine aspect and a masculine aspect—a Yin and a Yang. These are the elemental basics for all creation. In order to manifest anything, we need to balance these energies within ourselves, and without, in order to create and manifest. So, in Wicca, in order to connect these energies, we arrange our altar to achieve desired change and manifest our intentions. We set our altars to the pulse for both *active engagement* and *manifesting*. We do this by dividing our altars into duo sides. The left side of the altar is dedicated to the Goddess, and the right side of the altar is for the God. Recently though, I have read where others use a reverse format, whereas the Goddess and Her symbols are placed on the right and the God and His symbols are placed on the left. While this is different from what I have been taught by the old Witches back in the day, either way is perfectly fine, and one can choose the placement that feels right for them. However, for the purpose of this study, this book will demonstrate with the Goddess—left format, and the God— right format.

Again, all tools related to the feminine are placed to the left with the Goddess. All tools designated for the God are placed on the right. The center of the altar is offered as neutral space allotted for magickal workings and sowing the seeds. As you can see in the sky view of an altar in **Exhibit 3.2**, the Goddess' tools, such as the bell, cauldron, cup or chalice are placed below the Goddess' candle. The incense, sage, athame and wand are placed below the God's candle. All spaces in between the two candles are working spaces. Directly between the two candles allows for the depictions of deity, Nature or the season. For example, if male energy is needed perhaps a likeness of *Ogun, Shango, Baron Samedi, Ausar* or other. If one wishes feminine energy, for example, an image of *Oshun, Bast or Auset* would adorn there nicely. An optional image of yoni or phallus items could also be substituted depending on the desire or the intent of the altar. Below these images here one may add a pentagram, pentacle, offering or ankh. As with all items on the altar they are totally optional. What is only important is the arrangement of the items. While an athame is an important item to Wiccans a wand will do just as well as a substitute. While a bell or a gong is great, a shaker can do the trick also. Again, what is important is the way the items are assigned in recognizing the polarity (duality) of energies, or the principles of gender. This is the way of a Wiccan altar.

When you are not working with your tools or your altar you can carefully store your working tools away until you are ready to use them again. Storing tools away is a good idea especially if you have children around and you don't want them to play with the sharp items like an athame or a boline. Putting them away also keeps the tools from picking up adverse energies from other people in the home.

Think of the next diagram, **Exhibit 3.2**, as your altar table. The altar table is divided into sections. A Wiccan can place their tools to their corresponding suggested section. Working candles, petitions or spell items can be placed in the "working space" or "neutral" area.

Before assembling your tools and altar you may want to cleanse and consecrate your tools for use. This is an important step when creating your altar for a couple of reasons. Tools bought from stores may have passed through many hands and may have picked up energies that are not conducive to your needs. Cleansing the items eliminates those energies. Consecrating one's item tells the tool what is expected of it. It also informs the Universe that the tool itself is sacred and is meant for sacred use. Oftentimes we are in a rush to use our tools for certain missions and may not have time to do a full cleanse and consecration. I know, I have been there. The need for a quick spell has happened to me a lot. I do wish to emphasize that even when one is in a rush a quick one-minute cleansing to remove any negative energies is very important. Some people believe that the consecration aspect can be done while doing the spell because the energy used to cast the spell and the energy that flows through the spellcaster into the tool is informative enough to the tool. Instructions for cleansing and consecrating tools will be discussed in Lesson 6 of this study.

Wiccan Altar Exhibit 3.2		
Goddess Candle	Goddess or God Patron Icon Or Yoni or Phallus Symbols	God Candle
Censer Cup or Chalice	<u>Neutral Space</u> Pentacle or Ankh or Offerings	Sage Stick Incense
Cauldron Bell	<u>Neutral Space</u> *(Example tools):* Working Candles, Petitions, Spells or Affirmations	Wand Athame

LESSON FOUR

Journeying into Magick

So previously we discussed witchcraft and we briefly touched on the word *magick* here and there. In this section let's discuss the nuts and bolts of basic magick that is performed by Witches and Wiccans and other Pagans. Let's first start with what magick really is. It would be an easy wager to state that, after you read this study, any magick that is performed by you afterwards would not be your first spell. Do you disagree? Well, let us challenge that shall we? If you ever wished upon a star, blew out candles on a birthday cake, crossed your fingers, threw salt over your shoulders after spilling it, carried your bride over the threshold, or did the infamous knock-on wood, then you performed a magickal act or spell. Each of these acts are either to gain fortune or to prevent misfortune. Chances are they may have worked for you without you having a second thought about it. This Lesson will discuss magick, what magick is and why it works. This study will also briefly touch on just a few basic magickal mediums, used by Witches, to assist the practitioner in magickal workings. These mediums are: *Meditation, Dreams, Divinations, Herbs, Crystals, Numerology, Astrology and Colors* Magick is more than wiggling one's nose or waving a wand. While there are some practitioners who have that fine-tuned adept connection to the Universe to do that, either by birth or by incessant practice, most practitioners must grasp the actual act of the *"conjure"*. I am sure you have heard some people call themselves conjurers, and I described what a conjurer was previously. The name conjurer comes from the word conjure which means the act of calling forth using one's power or energy *from within,* or evoking in order to manifest. This is an interesting dichotomy. Many people associate conjuring as calling forth externally to manifest. The dichotomy is that in order to call forth externally to manifest, one has to conjure within and conceptualize before manifesting. That is to feel one's natural internal vibrations, draw the energy from the deepest resources and recesses within, and use that energy to send the message so it can be heard and to resonate into the beyond. This is not always an easy task, but if it were easy anyone could do it. Magick takes practice. But, as *Paulo Coelho* stated in his book, <u>*The Alchemist,*</u> "…when you want something, all the universe conspires in helping you to achieve it" (Coelho, 2014). So, when you get right down to it, the Universe listens. It is just a matter of getting our message across in order to make the changes we want in our lives.

Magick is the act of engagement with symbolisms, actions, INTENTION, and the demonstration of WILL. When this is done the practitioner can manifest their desires. So magick is not prayers or pleading to a god or spirit. That is a different practice. In magick the practitioner assumes the role of their own divinity and declares that their intention is done or that their desires will be done. Even when working with a patron deity the practitioner works in partnership or collaboration with deity to manifest.

Magick works through *Universal Laws*. Previously I discussed the *Law of Gender* with regard to the arrangements of the Wiccan altar. However, for the purpose of creating magick, we will discuss the *Universal Law of Vibration, the Law of Correspondence* and the *Law of Cause and Effect*. There are approximately seven laws but, for the purpose of this area of study we will just concentrate on the 3 Laws last mentioned. Apply these 3 laws for a successful witchcraft practice, because these laws will make the *Law of Attraction* happen for you. If you have heard of the Law of Attraction, it is because it is commonly discussed in popular and New Age culture. While the Law of Attraction is not part of the ancient Hermetic mystical laws, it is what happens when other Universal Laws are applied and performed through spell work. These laws will be discussed further in this section.

Cone of Power

The *cone of power* is the psychic energy that most adept Witches raise within themselves for the purpose of conjuring, directing and casting energy. This creating and directing of energy brings about the best results for intentions and or spells. For creating a cone of power some Witches use the mediums of music, singing, dancing, drumming and or meditation to raise this energy. It is a way of placing oneself into an altered state. These techniques are particularly popular with group rituals. Spiral dancing for example, is a good way for groups to raise energy. But the cone of power is also used by the solitary practitioner in spell castings and workings.

Temperament Magick

There are 3 categories of what I call *Temperament Magick*. These categories are *Light Magick, Grey Magick* and *Dark Magick*. I call these categories Temperament Magick, because the type or shade of magick that is cast is based on the desires, the nature, choices, and the overall outlook of the Witch. Some Witches may use all the temperaments. Some may only use Light Magick, but will use Grey or Dark Magick when pressed to. Other Witches would only use one no matter what. Wiccans tend to stay within the temperament of the light since they are mostly Lightworkers, but to reiterate, it really depends on the Witch and their practice. Know that this part of the study is in no way in judgment of a particular temperament. It is only for the explanation of the types of magick there are.

Light Magick

Commonly, *light magick* was formally referred to as *white magick*, and *dark magick* was formally referred to as *black magick*. While some Witches still use the former terms most African Americans Spiritualists tend to use the words light and dark, so as not to conflate the words with racial or ethnical magickal identity, and *white being good and black being bad. Light magick* refers to the magick that is suitably done in the daylight (the light of day), and magick that is agreeable with the majority of people. This type of magick is allied with healing *Sun* energy, and or magick that is antithetical to *hexings, crossings, or curses.* Light magick works for common welfare such as for therapy, wellness, self-help, self-development, blessings, dedications and celebrations. Light magick works in the realm of *doing no harm* to others

Grey Magick

Grey magick is considered to be neutral, impartial, or a magick that seeks protection without causing harm or total harm. It is more than often the *magick of defense*, but with the purpose of *harm reduction.* Grey magick teeters between the line of light and dark magick, because it is usually magick directed towards a person to go against their *will,* however it is performed specifically for beneficial reasons or reasons of protection. It is not necessarily focused with vengefulness, hostility or harmful practices. On the contrary its purpose is usually to prevent harm in the least noxious way. The most common example of a grey magick is a *binding spell* to halt a stalker in order to prevent them from doing harm to a person that they are pursuing. While the stalker may have been prevented from acting on their desires to do harm, the act of keeping the stalker away from their intended victim is not with the intentions of harming the stalker physically or theoretically.

Dark Magick

Dark magick refers to magick that is commonly done away from the light. It is that which is often hidden, not done in plain sight, or not done with the favor of most people. It is conjured in what most people may consider the *darker recesses of one's being.* This magick is forged within *the darker energies of the spirit.* Some Witches may not agree with me on this, but when discussing hexing and cursing with other Witches, their desire to cast dark magick appears to stem from times of fear, revenge, desperation, anger and jealousy. They speak of hexing people, for example, when their mates are cheating on them, or when they are tired of their bosses or co-workers, or when they are angry with someone, or when they are in the middle of a court case. This type of magick is powerful, because the intensity of their animus conjures strong vibrational energy that brews long before the Witch can cast their spell. This magick is often more potent than light magick, or even grey magick, because of the ease most of us have to summon this type of energy. It has its own cone of power. In contrast, and depending on the energy of the Witch, light magick tends to take longer to conjure and does not have that feverous cone of power or energy that comes to us easily with feverish emotions. Dark magick crosses the line of grey magick and delves into the world of what is called *baneful magick.*

How Does Magick Work?

*To me, the Universe is simply a great machine which never came into being and never will end. ~ **Nikola Tesla***

Magick has been around since time. The very existence of the Universe itself is beyond the magickal and the mystical. Even as scientists informs us of much of which we know, they themselves are marveled at the interworking of the *"Here"* and the *"All"*. Whereas, while science can explain the basic framework of how one part hydrogen and two parts oxygen make water, they are hard pressed to explain when, why and how these elements first came into existence, in the Universe. To quote one of my favorites, Albert Einstein, who said, *"To know what is impenetrable to us really exists, manifesting itself as the highest wisdom and the most radiant beauty, which our dull faculties can comprehend only in their most primitive forms…."*

Basically, Einstein was saying, we know the basics and the beauty of the Universe, but there are some things that we cannot begin to fathom, and are far beyond our grasp. We as human beings know that the Universe works, but regardless if it is the physical or the metaphysical, we don't know the details as to the why, and may never really know fully. This is fine. As long as it works. Let's say you go out of your home to your mailbox and find a check written to you for one million dollars. The check is certified and the letter that came with it is stating, *"Hello, I am a billionaire and I wanted you to have this check because I just wanted to give it to you. Enjoy your life!"*

There is no name on the check or the letter that came with it. Sure, you would question who gave you the check, but in the final outcome it still cashes. This is what magick is all about. You perform the magick and the Universe anonymously grants you your desire. You may know the how (you cast a spell) but you don't know why it works or who actually cut you the check.

There are some aspects of performing magick that we do understand, and the mechanics of what is functioning. We know these aspects because there were *Sage Mages* and *Vedics* who have come before us, and spent lifetimes mastering the ancient arts of magick. For example, in ancient times there were magickal teachings taught by a particular spiritual teacher who was called *Trismegistus* or *"Three Times Great."* The Greeks referred to him as *Hermes,* in Grecian Egypt He was called *Thoth,* but his name was *Tehuti* (Tay-he-tee) in the ancient land of Kemet. Tehuti spent his lifetime learning and teaching magickal universal mysteries, and He had countless students who dedicated their lives to the mastery of the Mystery School. His students vowed silence about the mysteries they learnt.

From this remarkable school came the *Seven Universal Laws.* For the purpose of this lesson and the understanding of basic magick this study will briefly touch on the *Universal Law of Vibration, the Universal Law of Correspondence* and the *Universal Law of Cause and Effect.* These laws can also be referred to as "Principles," Some call them the *Hermetic Principles.* These principles were published in the book called <u>*The Kybalion*</u> (Initiates, 2018).

These principles assume that the Universe itself is alive, and that the Universe is both a receiver and transmitter, the way space receives and transmits radio waves. It receives information from us, not just from magickal spells and meditation, but from our everyday lives. It is believed that the Universe picks up the vibrations and frequencies of our existence and sets the current of those vibrations and frequencies to automatic. In other words, it sets its transmission to one based on what one transmits to it. To Witches, this is a part of what is called *The Law of Returns.* I know. I am throwing a whole lot of laws at you. Just know that the *Law of Attraction* and the *Law of Returns* are not a part of *The 7 Universal Laws.* For now, just think of *"The Law of Returns"* as that old school law your grandparents preached to you about - *"…what goes around comes around!"* To Wiccans it is called, *"the threefold law"*.

Universal Law of Vibration

The Universal Law of Vibration states, *"Nothing rests; everything moves; everything vibrates."* This principle means that "everything is in motion" and that "everything vibrates"; "nothing is at rest". Thousands of years later, contemporary day science has proven this to be true. Everything is a vibration of atoms and molecules moving and never resting. They vibrate and calibrate to a certain frequency in order to manifest into a tree, an animal, an object or into human form. Know that everyone is made up of vibrations which are calibrated into a certain frequency, as well as everything that makes up the Universe. Vibration and frequency are the languages of the Universe. When the Universe hears a practitioner's thoughts, spells, intentions, and/or desires it hears by the practitioner's vibrations and frequencies. The higher the frequency the more likely it is that one's intentions will manifest. So, in essence, it is advantageous for the practitioner to repeat their incantations over and over during a ritual or spell in order to be certain that the frequency is sufficient enough for reception and manifestation.

Universal Law of Correspondence

The Universal *Law of Correspondence* in essence means: *"As above, so below; as below so above; as within so without; as without so within."* This principle means that there will always be a universal connection between various planes of existence, spiritual realms, things, beings and/or life. To reiterate from a previous part of this study, the Native American philosophy, *"We are all related"* in the circle of life. This means we are all similar and connected in some way. So, in relating this with magickal spells or intentions, the preparation of the psyche is important for this principle. Let's further dissect this principle. Let's say that I had a bad month, so I wanted to take a vacation to ease my mind. Perhaps I would like to go to the mountains so I could see the trees and the peaks. Perhaps I want to go swimming in the lake or take a drive through hills. These events on my trip are therapeutic for me because I deemed them to be. If I had a phobia about the mountains, then the trip would have an adverse effect on me. But I chose to go somewhere that I enjoyed. At the end of my trip I was ready to go home and back to work, and my positive vibrations informed the Universe that I was at greater peace. But what gave me peace? It was the trip of my choice. It was the swim in the lake and the drive through the hillsides. I chose this trip because I related it to relaxation and peacefulness. In the *Law of Correspondence,* I associate relaxation with a mountain trip. I believed the two to correspond. In practical magick this is also called *Sympathetic Magick.*

Sympathetic Magick is performed with items that bring to mind the practitioner's desired outcomes. Tools often used for this are colors, images, the Moon, poppets, sigils etc. For example, suppose the practitioner wishes to receive money. The practitioner may want to light a green candle since the color green represents fertility, prosperity or luck or money. As another example let's suppose the practitioner wants their true love to come into their lives. The practitioner may want to, for example, cut out a cardboard red heart and use it as a part of the spell. The heart represents feelings of the heart and red represents passion and love. Sympathetic magick is the art of using certain symbolically related items that leads one's psyche into a certain vibration and corresponding frequency for the best magickal outcomes. And it works through the *Law of Correspondence.* More will be discussed about Sympathetic magick later in this study.

Universal Law of Cause and Effect

The Universal *Law of Cause and Effect* means: "Every cause has its effect; every effect has its cause." In other words, it emphasizes the basic law of "causation". Everything happens for a reason. For magickal spells the best way to look at this is, "for every action there is a reaction". This principle informs the practitioner that one can master their own destiny if they take control. For most spells there is a reaction depending on their execution. Well-prepared spells, rituals and intentions have influence over a practitioner's outcomes. The Universe is a part of the *All,* and it works for us as an exquisite apparatus or a magnificent engine. It passes no judgment. It has no opinion. The Universe seeks no vengeance. It is not Santa Claus checking in to see if we are bad or good. The Universe is more like a karmic echo or a reflection of our eternal existences. It works in a cyclical process like the breathing of the tide. It works in divine order with the multiverse we call the *All.*

Mediums of Witchcraft

Meditation, Dreams, Divinations, Herbs, Crystals, Numerology, Astrology and Colors.

Every established practicing Witch or Wiccan has what I call a basic *working framework.* One Witch may be a Wiccan who works with tarot, casts spells with crystals and feels a close relationship with numbers. Another Hedge Witch may not follow the Wiccan Rede much but does light work, brews and potions and does meditation to facilitate his walking between the worlds. Another may be a Conjurer who is a devotee to the Orisha, prides herself as a healer, refers to herself as a *Bruja* and throws bones for divination. This Witch may also participate in *Powwows* with Native Americans on the weekends and work with the Medicine Wheel for clients. Each of these 3 Witches mentioned, works with a Witch's framework. The framework is a combination of mediums they use for their spiritual workings. This section will briefly discuss a few mediums that a Witch may use. There are some Witches who use all of these and more. The framework can be as big or as small as the Witch desires their framework to be. Take a minute and think about what you would like to encompass into your Witch's framework, or what you practice presently. What are all of the mediums you would like to add to your craft?

Meditations and Visualizations

One of the most important practices of witchcraft is *Meditation* and *Visualization*. It is so important that I will go out on a limb and say that if a Witch has no other *medium technique* in their framework, this would be all that they would need to become an adept Witch and Conjurer. I would also go out on a limb and say that I believe every Witch should learn this before they buy any tool, use any other medium, cast any spell or have any other framework. The reason for this is very simple. Witchcraft is primal and vibrational. It is the act of getting in touch with one's inner self, psychological self, *shadow self* (the self that one doesn't know or understand). It also helps to develop the *clair-senses.* The clair-senses are those psychic sensitivities corresponding to seeing, hearing, feeling, smelling, tasting and touching. One example of a clair-sense is *clairvoyance,* or *second sight.* But, most importantly, meditation can help guide one to *higher self* or one's *goddess* or *god self.* It also helps with finding one's *spirit guide* or one's patron deity.

Meditation can be a psychic cleanser; a power enhancer, it could lead to *spiritual awakening*s, or awaken what the Yoruba spirituality calls our *Ori.* The Ori is the West African metaphysical concept referring to one's spiritual intuition, personality and destiny. Ori literally means *"the head"* and is the reflective spark of human consciousness. It is one's inner divinity. Once a person is in touch with their inner divinity or higher self, and uses meditation to cleanse the spirit and soul, magick will become more innate and intuitive because they have awakened that which has been lying dormant.

Visualization, during meditation and magick, teaches one to focus energy through the imagery of the imagination. Visualization during meditation can take a Witch between the worlds. Visualization in spell casting aids a Conjurer to cast spells with nothing more than inner energy and external visual powers. The practice of visualization can be fine-tuned with regular meditational practices.

Different Meditation Techniques

There are 3 different meditation techniques that we will touch on in this part of the study that I feel are important for practice. There is *Mindfulness, Spirit and Visualization.* My students sometimes ask me what is the best way to position oneself while in meditation. I always tell them to sit if they are comfortable or lie down if they are comfortable. It is not necessary to sit up in a lotus position to communicate with Spirit, as long as your posture is comfortable and not injurious to your neck and back. I personally do my best meditation lying down.

In **Mindfulness meditation**, one pays attention to their thoughts as they reflect through the peacefulness of their mind. This is not a time for judging your thoughts or engaging with them. You play the role of an observer and take note of the thoughts and patterns that randomly appear in the consciousness. This is a time to be a student of oneself and one's mind. It is a time to use stillness as well as awareness while regulating the breathing. This can be a scary endeavor since most of us tune ourselves out to what we don't want to think about. Instead, you play the part of an eavesdropper, listening into that which is normally forbidden by the subconscious self. When participating in this exercise, we allow those same thoughts to flow freely. This can be a very healing experience, but at the same time it can be very triggering to some. So, if necessary, have someone handy you can call to discuss your findings and feelings about the experience. The purpose of mindfulness exercise is for reconciling who we are, by later processing our thoughts and healing what needs to be healed. It seeks the truth, and allows it to flow. This is a good technique for *shadow work* (finding the shadow self), and it helps one to understand their authentic self.

In **Spirit meditation** (many call it *Spiritual* meditation) one reflects on the quiet and the silence around them to seek a deeper connection with something that is greater and deeper than the individual self. This meditation can connect one to *Divine Being* or *Source* or the Universe by allowing divinity the opportunity to connect with them. It is mostly in the state of silence in which divinity connects. It is best to start with a series of Mindfulness meditations first, for psychological enlightenment, and better knowledge of the self, before engaging in Spirit meditation. The reason for this is when one comes to *Spirit* one wants to come correct, with clarity and less psychic baggage.

Visualization meditation is the practice of drawing from the inner sight senses to become more adept in visualization. This exercises the brain and sharpens imaginative focus, thus giving clearer visualization for magickal workings. Visual meditation is used to harness and enhance energy. These abilities strengthen the concentration needed to cast spells and manifest one's desires. For example, one visualization session may be the action of sending flowing light through one's fingertips, and having the light surround an object on a table or floor. Another may be a meditation of finding a pool of pure energy and stepping inside that pool to have a healing experience.

Within all types of meditation, it is important to have regulated breathing, to sit or lie comfortably and to wear comfortable clothing, if any clothing at all. *Sky-clad* or naked is optional. The practitioner needs a quiet place with uninterrupted allotted time. Incenses and or essential oils can be used to aid in placing the practitioner in a meditative mood or tranquil state. It is important that the incense is not overpowering and allows for proper breathing.

Dreams

Dreams are the magickal portals glimpsing into the secret corridors of our own minds. They allow us to sort out the events that we have in our awakened hours. They relieve stress by taking us away to extraordinary places, and they assist us in knowing our inner thoughts even when we are uncertain of them ourselves. After the father of a person I knew died, some years ago, he began to take on some responsibility of helping his mother. One day he had a dream that he tried on his father's shoes and no matter how hard he tried they just didn't fit him. They were too big. Well, I suppose it doesn't take a rocket scientist or PhD level psychologist to figure out that he was concerned that he could not take care of his mother the way his father did when his father was alive.

Dreams often send us messages like that. Sometimes they are not presented with the clarity of the shoe story. Most messages are in code and it is up to the individual to break that code. A dream with lots of snow, for example, may mean fun and wholesomeness to one person but it may mean danger and harshness to another.

There are several types of dreams. For the sake of magickal references this section will review the dreams of *Out of Body Experience (OBE)*, *Healing Dreams with Subconscious Dreaming*, *Prophetic Dreams and Visitation Dreams.*

The Out of Body Experience Dreams or OBE (Involuntary)

An *Out of Body Dream* or *OBE* for short, is a dream that connects one into the astral plane. It appears very real and one may feel oneself in a levitation state or flying in the dream or may even find oneself in familiar or unfamiliar territory. An OBE can be *willful*, meaning that the practitioner performed actions to create an out of body experience, or it can be *involuntary*, meaning that having an out of body experience was totally unintentional. Personally, though, I sometimes know when I have been on an astral plane, because I would remember going downstairs or descending down a chimney or taking an elevator down just before waking up. Often though, one may just wake up after experiencing the levitation. Some people believe that the falling and jerking sensation one sometimes feels, just before waking up, is the end of an astral travel event, and the spirit merges with the body abruptly. This is the consciousness or spirit going back into the physical body.

Another indication for me is waking up and not feeling my legs for a few minutes. This indicates to me that my spirit had not totally and fully integrated back into my body, and I would then lie there and wait for my body and spirit to realign. This is because it is said that the head is integrated first and the legs and feet are last. I have even, at times, felt a spiritual hand tugging on my legs or waist, trying to keep me from integrating back. Perhaps it was someone I had befriended on a plane and we had a mystical adventure together, but sadly I never remember it. I can tell you that *pending integration* is the best feeling. There are tingles throughout my body, and it is a lovely euphoric experience. It brings to mind the feeling of afterglow.

Healing Dreams

Healing Dreams are the dreams that aid us through the rough times. They give us what we need when we are deprived of things such as food, water and sex—which can include wet and erotic dreams. These dreams also include psychological healing during times of anxiety and stress. They take us away on mini vacations and planes of relaxation. Because of this, healing dreams will often give people good ideas for relaxing and meditative practices. If your dream feels good, then remember that your mind knows what is healing to you. Use it in the material world.

There are some healing dreams that are not so pleasant, but they are still healing, nonetheless. These are called *subconscious dreams*. These are the dreams that alert us to our inner thoughts like not being able to fill our father's shoes. They bring out irrational fears or thoughts we try to bury deep inside our minds. These dreams are informative because many times they give us the hidden answers that we seek within ourselves. They treat us with *exposure therapy*, forcing us to face our phobias, dreads and fears in order to normalize them in our minds, and to move us to analyze them and perhaps even reframe them to a balanced level. In other words, they expose what is trapped deep inside the hidden recesses of the inner thought. Let them be your guide to what you can do for self-development and self-healing.

Healing dreams can sometime have *deep subconscious* elements to them, showing symbolic meaning to the dreamer. Because of this these types of dreams are sometimes the hardest codes to crack. However, if your dreams are showing you aspects about yourself, it may be because it is in a self-healing mode exposing you to what needs to be dealt with. Healing dreams can also help a practitioner with any shadow work that needs to be done.

Prophetic Dreams

Prophetic dreams are the dreams that connect us to our *third eye* or *pineal gland.* They are messages that the Universe wants us to know. They are usually very different from any other dreams, because they are more lucid, and clearer and much more real. They are dreams that give information and warnings about the future and the present. To give you an example, one day I was in the midst of waking up, but just before I did, I felt a burning sensation in the middle of my forehead. It felt like a tiny bit of hot oil that had splashed while cooking. I had accidents with drops of cooking oil before. They hurt, but never before on my forehead. I thought it was strange but didn't think much of it, and I had actually forgotten about it as I went about my day. I later decided to fry something. I don't recall what it was, and it could have been potatoes or eggs. In the middle of frying, drops of oil splashed out of the frying pan and splattered me in the middle of my forehead. It wasn't serious, just a few burning drops, but I immediately remembered the dream because the drops felt just like the sting before I woke up that morning. The dream warned me about the splash that was coming.

Prophetic dreams also come to us in codes and not as clear as splattered cooking oil. This is because the Universe often transmits information symbolically to our right brain, and it gives us imagery that it believes we can interpret. I often think that the Universe gives us too much credit for interpretation of dreams. Some coded dreams are harder to crack. But with determination symbols can be interpreted and prophetic dreams can be, for a Witch, another way of divination.

Visitation Dreams

Visitation dreams are dreams with etheric visitors such as Ancestors, spirit guides, recently departed family members or celestial messengers. Frequently the reason for the visitation is to give messages or to take care of unfinished business. Transitioned family members may just want to give loving partings before crossing over into the light plane. Half the time for me the visitor's face is distorted and some of their words are muffled. I find it interesting that the Universe will block what it really doesn't want us to know. These dreams can be endearing and heart wrenching at the same time and the feeling of these dreams are very distinctive. It is usually a dream of clarity and the dreamer finds themselves within a whole different spiritual dimension. It is usually set in a place that is familiar to both the dreamer and the transitioned person. It is always important to hear what the visitor is saying if it is at all possible. The messages are often very important.

Nightmares

Finally, let us discuss *nightmares*. Nightmares are also subconscious dreams. They are the shadows of the things we profoundly fear and the things we store away in the dark corners of our minds, like the proverbial monsters we keep in closets. Sometimes these monsters tend to come out in our dreams, forcing us to confront them. Understanding and confronting these anxieties can be the first step to healing. As a mental health worker, I know that one of the best treatments for fear is exposure therapy (exposing the person to their fears and normalizing them.) Use this monster in your dreams and look at it as your ally for self-knowledge. Unmask it and interpret its meaning, then reframe the narrative in a positive light. Once you understand the irrational fear, know that it cannot hurt you. And only then can one be released from its restraining shackles.

The Boy and the Monster Dragon

 This brings to mind a story concerning a little boy who constantly cried because he had the misfortune to dream about a fi re-breathing dragon chasing him every night. This was not only a concern to the boy but also to his family. The boy was so distraught he didn't want to go to bed at bedtime or go to sleep. One morning, at the breakfast table, the boy's father made a suggestion to his son. His father told him that maybe the only reason the dragon appeared so much was because the dragon wanted the boy to ride him. The father suggested to his son that the next time he should try facing, and then mounting the dragon. The boy was completely rattled by his father's suggestion. Facing such a monster would surely be too much for him to even contemplate doing. But eventually the boy relented to his father and promised him that he would give it a try.

That night the little boy went to sleep and dreamt about the dragon chasing him again, but this time the dream was extremely lucid, and the boy remembered his promise to his father and turned to face the dragon in a staring contest. This made the dragon become so mesmerized that he stopped chasing the boy and stood totally still. The boy then mounted the dragon. The dragon succinctly spread his wide and scaly wings and took the brave little hero on a magickal sky-ride all through the night.

One morning, about a week later, the father woke up to the screams and cries of his son again. *"What's da matter? What's up?"* asked the father, alarmed at the sight of his distressed son. *"Did you dream about the dragon again?"* *"No!"* cried the boy. *"And that's why I am sooo… upset!"*

Interpreting Dreams

It is important for us to interpret our dreams. It keeps us Witches healthy mentally when we understand them, because understanding one's dreams is a step to understanding oneself in a present-day snapshot. The first leap to understanding dreams is remembering them. It is very easy to wake up and not know what we were dreaming in the next few minutes or even seconds. One way to counter this is to make a determination to remember them. One technique is to place a pad and pencil beside the bed, so that upon awakening one can immediately grab them and write the dreams down exactly as they remember them. We can write down details like who was in the dream, if we recognized them, what they were wearing, how we felt, the colors we saw and so on. We may even want to write down what type of the four dreams we believed them to be—*Out of Body Experience, Healing Dream, Prophetic Dream, Visitation Dream* or if none of these types at all. An easier way may be to place a recorder by the side of the bed so to dictate and record what was dreamt about, and one's feelings about it.

Here is another trick that often works well for remembering dreams. Before you go to sleep, say to yourself over and over *"I will remember my dreams"*. Also, placing a sprig of fresh lavender or rosemary or a few drops of sandalwood oil on a pillowcase may assist in recalling dreams and helps to put one in a *lucid* dream state. Lucid dreaming is the art of one being cognizant that one is dreaming and knowingly engaging in the dream. In other words, lucid dreaming allows one to be actively conscious in the moments of the dream.

Understanding Symbolism in Dreams

Some of the symbolisms can be indeed challenging. For example, a dove in a person's hand, in a dream, may mean love to some people, or peace to others. It is up to the individual to determine the meaning of their own symbolic dream. To give a personal example, I love snakes and I believe them to be my spirit animal, so the sight of a snake in my dream may mean a message from spirit guide or a symbol of luck, sensuality or prosperity. It would all depend on the context of the dream. Another person on the other hand may fear snakes so the symbol in their dreams may represent a whole different message.

The practice of dream interpretation expands the skills and the intellect of a Witch, but only if we engage in the challenges. Like anything else it takes practice. Remember to determine the reasons for the colors and how the colors made you feel. Try to figure out why there was a rabbit riding a donkey in your dreams. What is your dream trying to tell you? Have you been around these animals lately and why? What do they remind you of? Who do they remind you of? What is the first thing that comes to mind when you think of them? Utilize what you know.

They say that confessions of the soul are half the battle. Often, I find it very hard to admit what my dreams are trying to tell me. My first instinct is to deny everything. Utilizing one's dreams can show us feelings that we never knew we had. They show us our good sides, but they also show us our unattractive sides too like envy, bias, apprehension, prejudice, jealousy, fear, trepidation, low self-esteem, hatred, resentment, desire, targeted lust, selfishness, and frustration. We know these things because of the emotions we feel when we are dreaming and how we feel after the dream is over. Dreams can be a how-to guide for change, or at least give us a better understanding of who we are and what we are dealing with. One can attempt to master these feelings by dealing with the pain of them on a positive level. This can make all the difference in the world.

In Conclusion of Dreams

As practicing Witches, our practices will take us on small or large adventures. Many of them will be in, or connected to, our dreams. The reason for this is because of our genuine act of magickal discovery and active practices which opens up a signal to the Universe that we are ready to know. The Universe will respond to that signal in ways you won't begin to imagine. You will speak with spirit guides or be given clues to new spells. I was even given a stock tip by an Ancestor in a dream that turned out to be a wonderful tip. This is the way the Universe encourages us to continue our practices. You will most likely never get rich, but just the act of receiving messages, confirmations, affirmations, discoveries, and to receive the *knowing,* is so very fulfilling, it is enough for me.

Remember to interpret dreams. Remember that dreams are often the subconscious symbols of our thoughts. Remember that recalling our dreams can be therapeutic, informative and enlightening. Remember to keep a pad, pencil or recorder near your bed for better recall of dreams And finally, remember that our dreams are tools bestowed to us by the Universe to help us process our human lives and journeys.

DIVINATION

*~ Your vision will become clear only when you can look into your own heart. Who looks outside, dreams, who looks inside, awakes. ~ **Carl Jung***

What is Divination?

So, when you hear the word *divination* what do you think of? Do you think of fortune telling, omens, predictions of the future, or mediums? Yeah, well you would be correct. To quite a great extent divination has been associated with these practices. But this is not the entire story. While divination has been associated with mundane *predictions* or current events, for the serious spiritual practitioners of the craft, divination is so much more than checking in to see if Boo cheated last night. For those of us who seriously delve in the spirituality of magick, divination gives us a tool for the *true knowing*, a way to being linked and being aware. It is our way of having a finger on the Universe's pulse. It is our way of connecting to the divine energies. To many practitioners it is one way to tap into *Source* and to strengthen magickal power. And, for the most serious Sorcerers and Priest/esses, it is a way of having a direct relationship with *Source*.

The word divination comes from the Latin word *divinare* meaning "the Divine" or Goddess or God or "belonging to a god" or "from god" (Encyclopedia.com, 2019). The word 'oracle', which refers to the person who does the divination, comes from the Latin word *oraculum* which means "to speak." So together it means, *"to speak that which is of The Divine"*, or *"to be inspired by the word of The Divine"* (Melyn, 2014). So, for Witches, divination is more than just looking for predictions or working for a *quadrant* (one who ask a question to the oracle) and *throwing* tarot cards. Divination is a way to keep plugged into the Universe, or to *stay woke*, or to have a conversation with the Divine, or to seek spiritual guidance, or to look for the best way to cast a spell or doing a ritual, or to gain spiritual energy through connection, or receiving affirmation about one's spiritual journey, and or to stay in tune, in harmony and in rhythm overall.

Divination also works through the *Law of Correspondence*. If you recall from a previous section this principle means that everything is connected to everything else, *"as above so below - as within so without"*. As it relates to oracle work, divination is a way of connecting to our universal web that is connected to the *All*. Divination connects to this universal knowledge grid that responds to query. No one knows exactly why divination works, but some people believe that the Universe works through our *primal unconscious,* which is where the famous metaphysical psychologist *Carl Jung* believed creative and mystical knowledge of self, resides.

The history of divination reaches deep beyond the annals of hue-man history. So, this means no one knows its complete history. We do know that divination is innate and has been utilized all over the world, in all cultures, all races and throughout all civilization for a very long time. There are as many ways to perform divination as there are people. To give just one example, in Cameroon in West Africa, the Mambila people have a practice called *Nggam,* where the diviners watch the actions of spider crabs to interpret various readings. In other African Traditional Religions *cowry shells* are thrown (usually by a Priestess or Priest) on a table, a floor or a mat, and the answers of the inquiry is based on the way the shells fall. In traditional witchcraft, the African American community also does divination by using cowry shells for readings. I have thrown a few cowry shells myself here and there, but to only get a yes or no answer. True cowry readers, trained in the practice, do more extensive reading with this art. Other divination tools of my choice are the tarot, pendulum, scrying and dice. In this section we will quickly mention some basic popular tools of divination today. The divination tools to be briefly mentioned are *the Tarot, Dowsing (Rod, Pendulum, Ouija board), Throwing Mediums (dice, cowry and bones), Scrying, Tea Leaves, Palm Reading and Runes.*

The Tarot

The origin of the *tarot* is about as mysterious as the cards themselves. The tarot cards are said to have developed and come to popularity sometime between the late 1300s to the mid-1400s in France. There is an oldest surviving, and most complete, set of cards known as the *ViscontiSforza* deck, which was created for an aristocratic family around the year 1440. The cards were used to play a game called *trump,* and later spread to Italy during the fifteen century and was used to play a game known as *tarocchi.* This game was all the rage among aristocrats during their leisure periods.

As time went on, the cards began to be used for divination. According to *Joan Bunning* in her book, <u>*Learning the Tarot,*</u> between the eighteenth to nineteenth centuries the cards were discovered by occult scholars who reviewed the details of the cards. Their study revealed to them the "history of the tarot by connecting the cards to *Egyptian mysteries, Hermetic philosophy,* the *Kabbalah, alchemy,* and other mystical systems." Bunning went on to state that the cards were subsequently used by secret societies such as the *Order of the Golden Dawn.* (Bunning, 1998, pp. 3). It has been argued that the tarot actually originated or was connected to the ancient Egyptian/Kemetic magickal practices and connected to the secret wisdom and teachings of *Tehuti* (Trismegistus).

Here in the United States, the *tarot* is one of the most commonly-used divination tools. The tarot consists of 78 cards. The deck is partitioned into two sections. These sections are called the *major arcana* and the *minor arcana.* Arcana comes from the Latin word *arcanum* meaning *secrets* or *mysteries.*

The major arcana is made up of 22 cards and works closer to the universal energies, which means it works through the unconscious or that which is hidden and waiting to be revealed by one's own mystical spirit. The minor arcana is made up of 56 cards and is made up of *Cups, Pentacles, Swords and Wands.* These suits may vary based on the type of deck. For example, some decks may have *Hearts* as opposed to *Cups,* or have *Staffs* instead of *Wands.* It all depends on the theme of the deck, but the meanings and the energies are similar.

The minor arcana relates to the mundane and the events of our everyday lives. This means for example; the minor cards may concentrate on what work one does at their job or what is going on in basic family life. The major arcana may describe what the ether has in store for one in their career, or if there are other choices that can be made in regards to a career path, marriage or higher education.

Today there are many different types of decks to choose from as opposed to when I first started reading around twenty-some years ago. Most all decks in those days were the _Rider-Waite-Smith_, which depicted archetypes set in the Middle Ages of Europe. Even if there were a few other different decks, they mostly followed the same type of Middle Age theme, because this was what everyone was used to. Today's tarot decks are plentiful, and they can be specialized with the interest of the user. There are designs of _African decks, various ancient European decks, Latinx decks, Egyptian/Kemetic decks, Urban-centered decks, various cultural decks, LGBTQ decks, Goddess-centered/divine Feminine decks, Wiccan decks, witchcraft decks, Oracle decks_ (decks that are not tarot but give rules based on its creator), and all other themes in between. There are decks with the most beautiful craftsmanship and artwork, and some of them are truly breathtaking to see.

I have often been asked by new readers what deck they should get to start off with. One popular belief out there is, _"the best deck is the one someone else gives you."_ I am not quite certain about that one. What I tell people is what I have learned, and what some others have told me as tarot readers, and that is _to never pick a deck, but allow the deck to pick you._ What I mean by this is when you are sure you wish to be a reader, then do a serious search for a deck. Go online or to botanical/metaphysical stores. I do recommend that you take trips to brick-and-mortar stores, because in some cases you are able to limitedly look through the cards before purchasing them. There are many people demonstrating cards, and giving reviews of decks on *YouTube*. This is the best way to look over some without purchasing them.

I would recommend looking through at least 30 to 35 decks. Look for your deck as though you are looking for a lover to marry or a soul mate. If you search with this intention, one day you will find a deck that you will not be able to live without. Since the Universe communicates through the heart with the cards, and any other divination tool, the tool should be absolutely connected to the heart. This is what I meant when I said allow the deck to choose you.

This reminds me of my own story, except my story was both literal and figurative related to saying let the cards choose you, and the common belief to let someone give you the cards. Approximately twenty-six years ago when I was a novice in the craft, I decided that I wanted to begin reading the tarot. I went to a black-owned metaphysical store to purchase the cards, and even though it was a black-owned cultural store, the only deck the merchant had was the Rider-Waite-Smith deck (which was pretty much all anyone had at that time.) I purchased the deck and looked through it. It was the same deck that I had seen in books, but every time I picked it up to learn to read, I would quickly lose interest. After several attempts I placed them on a shelf, and there they collected dust for the next 3 years. I had pretty much resigned myself to the fact that reading the tarot was just not my thing.

One day I made the misstep of joining a book club without reading the fine print that I was to buy a book once a month. The book club would send me books and I would send them back, and this went on for approximately 4 months or more. One day the book club sent me something that I couldn't bring myself to return. Although it was not a metaphysical book club, something moved them to send me something—

why I could not explain. Most of the time I would send the books back and not even open the box, but this time Spirit moved me to open it. There in the box were the most gorgeous tarot cards I had ever seen. They were by far more picturesque, graphic and eye-catching than the Rider-Waite. I fell in love with these cards and found myself paying the book club for them. The cards also included a DVD explaining each card and a guidebook. From that moment on I was a reader. Because I felt the cards spoke to me, I fell in love at first sight. I immediately knew that the cards were sent to me by the Universe. In sending me those cards Spirit was saying to me, *"You have made a pact with me to walk your journey and you have been slacking with your practice of divination. I will aid you and send you your cards through this channel. It is up to you now to continue your path and communicate with me through this medium."*

With the tarot, remember to take your time to pick your cards, or for that matter any other form of divination of your choosing. There is no rush. Pick the cards as you would pick a lover. Choose the one that speaks to your heart, and one that you couldn't live without. Also try to find a tarot deck that comes with a study guide or video or both. This will ensure that you will not be as lax in your practice as I was. Believe me though. Spirit will show you when you stray from the path. Believe me. I know.

Pamela Colman Smith (Pixie)

The illustrator of the *Rider-Waite* tarot deck, now recognized as the **Rider-Waite-Smith** deck, was Pamela Colman Smith (nicknamed Pixie). *Pamela C. Smith* is said to have been the biracial child of wealthy American parents with an Afro-Jamaican genetic line, born in the 1800s.

Pamela Colman Smith was an artist, musician and storyteller. Pamela had interest in Jamaican storytelling and was a spiritualist with an interest in

Obeah (Jamaican Spiritualism), but she later converted to Catholicism. Smith was commissioned to create illustrations for the famous tarot cards by *Arthur Edward Waite,* which was published in 1909 by the publisher, *Rider.* With this little-known fact, it is interesting to know that the tarot deck, that we have all become acquainted with, was illustrated by a woman of color.

Pamela Colman Smith also wrote and illustrated two books about *Jamaican folklore* including: <u>*Annancy Stories*</u>, an expanded collection of West Indian folktales published by *Pamela Colman Smith* in 1899 (Smith, 2006).

Dowsing

While searching for a thorough definition of dowsing, I found that most definitions in the online dictionaries were incomplete. The best definition I could find was one in the *Oxford Dictionary* online, and it stated, *"A technique for searching for underground water, minerals, or anything invisible, by observing the motion of a pointer (traditionally a forked stick, now often paired bent wires) or the changes in direction of a pendulum, supposedly in response to unseen influences"* (Dowsing, 2020).

This was pretty close. So, dowsing or what is also called *rabdomancy,* is the art of using metal rods, copper, wire, any type of wood branches, sticks or twigs to divine for searching. However, this category also includes *pendulums* and *Ouija Boards* which are also considered dowsing instruments. Dowsing comes from the Dutch or German word *douse* which means to submerge or to plunge. According to Occult-World.com: *"Rabdomancy - The other word for dowsing, is derived from the Greek rhabdos (rod) and manteia (prophecy), and is a form of divination by means of a rod, wand, staff, stick or arrow"* (Rhabdomancy, 2020). It is not clear to me if this definition refers to the act of *plunging* or *submerging* into the cache of water, oil or precious minerals that divining often looks for, or if it is referring to the submerging of energy that the oracle taps into in order to bring them to what they are seeking.

Just a few years ago, one clear, beautiful day, I was writing at my desk on my computer, in my home office. I happened to stop and peep out my window. There outside my window was a gentleman with a metal divining rod walking around in my front yard and following the bend of the rod. What made me want to wipe my eyes to make sure I wasn't dreaming was the fact that he was wearing our town's official utility worker's uniform. My window was already open to the screen, so if anyone thinks this sistar Witch wasn't gonna shout out the window and ask what the heck was going on, guess what, they have another think coming! I bid the guy good day and asked him what he was looking for. He calmly told me he was looking for any underground cable, almost in the tone of—*isn't it obvious?* It was then I remembered that AT&T was going to dig the area and put their fiber down. The town's worker was checking for electrical cable in order to mark it, so that AT&T would not interfere with it. I asked him if he was using that divining rod to find the cable. The worker said yes. And he said, *"and it always works pretty good too."* I asked him if I could take a picture of him with the rod and he allowed me to do so. I lost that picture of him smiling and holding that metal fork rod when I broke my phone. I never saw him again, but I often think of him and wish that I had asked him to give me lessons on that art.

What this experience with the worker in my yard told me was that the arts of what is called the "occult" is spilling over into societal circles. Divination has been proven to work so well that even municipal towns and counties are utilizing their effectiveness. I am confident that this has been going on for hundreds if not thousands of years. We have all heard about how dowsers and psychics have been used by police on missing persons and manhunts for many years. Dowsers have been paid to find water and oil throughout history.

One of the clients I used to do tarot readings for, every week for years, announced to me that she was taking classes to learn dowsing. I asked her what she would be looking for. She said just to be her own oracle. She stated that she would have the metal rod, but the rod would give her yes or no answers to her queries, just as a pendulum would. I took this to mean that dowsing now extends to basic oracle work. Or can it mean that it has always been used that way but we in pop culture just limited the tool to minerals? What would be your guess?

Apparently, the African Ancestors may have a long history in dowsing. According to the *American Society of Dowsers* (ASD), dowsing has been practiced for thousands of years in many cultures and throughout the world. Also, according to ASD, in 1949, a group of French explorers, while doing a search for ancient civilizations in the Atlas Mountains of North Africa, found a massive cavern called Tassili Caves. In the caves they found walls that were covered with prehistoric paintings. The ASD website stated, *"Among the many fascinating wall murals…they also found a remarkable huge wall painting of a dowser, holding a forked branch in his hand searching for water, surrounded by a group of admiring tribesmen."* According to the ASD, the wall murals were carbon dated to be at least 8000 years old (The American Society of Dowsers, 2020).

While I can't prove how factual their interpretation of the murals was, I do agree that it is most logical to assume that dowsing has been with us for at least several thousands of years.

Other Tools of Dowsing

What many people don't know is that both the *pendulum* and the *Ouija board* are also dowsing instruments because they also point to the answers one seeks through energy.

The *pendulum* is a weight on a string or small chain. Oftentimes, for Witches, the weight is a small crystal or goddess symbol, but it could be a rock or a pendant from a necklace, or it could be absolutely anything. I've even heard one woman online say that one day "in a pinch" she made a "ghetto pendulum" with a toilet paper roll on a string. The weight of the pendulum usually has a point on it, but it doesn't have to. The pendulum is usually placed over a type of spirit or pendulum board but not always. In a case of the board the pendulum rocks to the direction of words or letters or numbers on the board.

For most people the pendulum is just straight-up, meaning it gives them the yes or no answer that they need without any board. For a pendulum to work, the oracle usually starts a relationship with it. Some people sleep with their pendulum or carry it with them no matter where they go in order to transfer their energy and personalize the tool to them. Some oracles meditate with them. Holding it while doing chakra meditation imbues the pendulum with healing powers for later healing work. But, when the oracle asks questions to the pendulum, without a board, how does the oracle know when the pendulum is giving a yes or no answer? The answer is when the oracle first gets the pendulum the oracle asks the pendulum what is a 'yes' answer and what is a 'no' answer? The pendulum will at that point move in the direction relating to the answer. The pendulum could move clockwise or counter-clockwise, or it could rock back and forth. The oracle could even ask the pendulum what is the uncertain or undetermined or ambiguous answer? The pendulum will respond to that question also. Once the oracle is clear with how the tool will answer, the oracle can then begin using the instrument for queries. There are some oracles who calibrate the pendulum to their will, meaning that they will tell the pendulum what direction is 'yes', what direction is 'no' and what movement is ambiguous.

The Ouija Board

Like most divination tools no one knows exactly where the *Ouija board* originated or where it came from. The Ouija board first hit the American toy and novelty shops in the early 1890s, according to *Smithsonian Magazine* online. Apparently, it couldn't get a patent to sell unless it was demonstrated and proven to work. Needless to say, it was proven. According to Smithsonian online, *"The Ouija board, in fact, came straight out of the American 19th century obsession with spiritualism, the belief that the dead are able to communicate with the living. Spiritualism, which had been around for years in Europe, hit America hard in 1848 with the sudden prominence of the Fox sisters of upstate New York; the Foxes claimed to receive messages from spirits who rapped on the walls in answer to questions, re-creating this feat of channeling in parlors across the state"* (McRobbie, 2013).

The Ouija board, or also called *spirit board*, is used all around the world in different languages. It is considered both a game and a medium for communication with spirits and with the spirit world. The word Ouija is said to have come from the French and German words for "yes," respectively (oui and ja). Others believe the name came from the inventors asking the spirit board what its name was, and it told them *"Ouija"*. When they asked the board what it meant it told them it meant *"Good luck"*.

The Ouija board is simplistic and basic. It consists of the board itself with letters and numbers printed on it. It also comes with a heartshaped pointing device called a *planchette*. The Planchette is about the size of a woman's or child's palm and it is designed to glide over the board to point to answers when it is queried. Ouija boards today come in many different designs and have come far from the old standard design. Some boards can be little, and some are large. Some are decorative and elaborate with the sun, moon, stars and other depictions. But what is standard on the Ouija board are the alphabets written in the middle and the numerals 1 through 0 underneath. Above the alphabets are the words "yes," and "no" and the word "goodbye" on the bottom of the board.

The Ouija board works when the oracle or querent asks the board a question. The oracle then places their fingertips on the planchette and allows the planchette to guide them to the answer on the board. The planchette also allows for more than one oracle to place their fingers on it at a time. Sometimes the answer is spelled out with the planchette, and sometimes it is merely a "yes" or "no" reply. The movement of the planchette is often called an *ideomotor response* (working through the subconscious.) Whether this response has to do with the person's true subconscious, the higher self or the actual spirit realm, has been a matter for debate and speculation. However, although I have never had the need to use the Ouija board myself, I can see how it could be used as an alternative for seeking guidance with the higher self, spirit guides and to do any needed shadow work.

In the black American spiritual community, the Ouija board is not too much of a topic of conversation in discussions about tools. This does not mean it is not used. Perhaps its use is just not spoken about. But everyone is different, and everyone has their own tool through which spirit calls upon them to use. This is the choice of the oracle.

Throwing Mediums – Bones, Dice and Cowry

We all know about dice. As children we have all played with them. We have used them for gambling, in games of chance and in board games of skill. We've played the game of *Monopoly* with them to the game of *Scrabble* with them. But dice (meaning multiple cubes) or die (meaning only one cube) have a much longer history than we can even imagine. There is evidence of dice found in Egyptian tombs dating as far back as 2,000 BC. But there are other archaeological digs that place them back even further to 6,000 BC in places like ancient Mesopotamia. Early dice were found to be knucklebones. The round ends were cut off and made to have six sides. This is why throwing dice, and other divination tools, are often referred to as *throwing bones*. Old dice made out of wood and ivory have also been found. Vast cultures from all over the world, from Africa to Asia, made use of various types of bone-throwing systems.

The throwing of the bones/dice is a very ancient divination technique where bones, stones, shells, dice, charms and even coins are thrown, and spiritual perception is given based on the arrangement of the objects and the way they fall. These patterns of each throw give insights and answers to queries. Each bone throw is as individual as snowflakes, meaning no two are the same. Meanings of each cast can be determined by various measures like how they touch each other, or how far apart they are, or the side in which they lean or fall.

While there are African Traditional Spiritualists who give classes online for bone throwing or readings, a practitioner would also do well to create their own bone-throwing system. Think about the items you wish to use. Know that every item that you throw needs to speak to you. They don't have to be dice or bones, but shells, dice, rocks or charms may be ideal. You can include things like buttons, pieces of wood, crystals or anything you wish to imagine. Once you choose the items, assign each their meaning and how they will speak to you on different throws. For example, dice have numbers on them so what will the numbers represent to you? Once you figure that out then memorize the assignments and possible outcomes.

The throwing of bones seems to be the most difficult form of divination because it seems to have too much going on to learn or interpret. However, there are others who feel it is not difficult to learn at all, and that the reward is in one's practice to learning. This helps to gain familiarity with the medium. Many believe that bone throwing, as a tool, gives a deeper understanding, builds a lot of psychic power, gives insight, connects and communicates. When you think about it, the art of one assigning meaning to the individual bones creates an act of connecting the items to the higher self, and it gives the opportunity for better psychic results. Not to mention that the art of throwing can profile a Witch as pretty hardcore and adept, and it wouldn't be a bad thing to have in one's magickal framework portfolio.

Cowry or Cowrie Shells

It is known that in some parts of the world, such as Africa and India, *cowry,* the shells of large and small sea snails, were used as money up until the 19th/20th century. Cowry shells are no longer used as currency today, but people continue to produce jewelry, ornamental costumes and headdresses for their sacred symbolism and their beautiful design.

Cowry shells, also spelled *cowrie*, are a favorite among many Africans and African American Spiritualists. According to the National Museum of American History, *"Seashells circulated as a medium of exchange in Asia, Africa, Oceania, and North America. The cowry shell, in particular, was a form of currency in West Africa during the transatlantic slave trade. West African cultures valued cowry shells from the Indian Ocean, and they became an accepted form of currency in the region"* (Smithsonian: National Museum of American History, n.d.). Perhaps this is why they are so prized and valued by African American Spiritualists today. In her book, <u>Sticks, Stones, Roots & Bones,</u> *Stephanie Rose Bird* discussed some history of the cowry. She states that the word cowry comes from the Sanskrit word *Kauri* meaning *"the yoni"* or the genitalia of the female. The cowry is the perfect image of the human vulva and is said to represent the genitalia of the divine Goddess. She writes, *"In ancient cultures, the cowry shell represented the divine vulva and the idea of rebirth."* She goes on to write that, *"Skeletons as far back as 20,000 BC have been found lavishly decorated with cowry shells, and cowries used to encourage rebirth decorated Egyptian sarcophagi"* (Bird, 2004, p. 185).

In my personal practice I lay cowry shells out on my altar when I wish to pay homage to Mama Yemaya or Mami Wata or when I wish to manifest money or when I wish to give thanks to the Universe for my many blessings. No matter what religious or traditional choice you have for cowry shells, they are charming and lovely mediums for spiritual practices. One of their popular uses is for divination. Because of their ancient history as currency for exchange, and because of their spiritual symbols of rebirth, new beginning and the divine Feminine, the cowry shell can be a potent tool for the use of charging of energy and for divination.

For a simple divination query a practitioner can use a one cowry shell toss. If the cowry shell falls to the open side, then the answer is "yes". If it falls to the closed side of a cowry, then it is "no". Another way of reading them is based on the direction of the shell. Each cowry shell has two sides. One is pointy and is considered the mouth of the shell. The opposite side is round and is considered the bottom of the shell. When the pointy side is pointing away from the oracle, after being tossed (that is pointy side up) this is considered a "yes". When the pointy side or mouth is pointed towards the oracle (this is bottom side up) this is considered a "no". When the pointy side is sideways left, this is considered an uncertainty, but odds are reduced. When the pointy side is sideways right, then this indicates uncertainty also, but chances are good. When the pointy side is caddy corner or diagonal it means the query is uncertain, ambiguous or can't be determined. It may also mean another throw may be needed or that the question needs to be rephrased for clarity.

Doing an Obi Reading

While there are many ways to read the cowry shells one of the easiest but systematic ways to read them is using the West African four shells technique called the . This is casting 4 shells after a question is placed. This divination technique gives only a "yes" or "no" answer. When the shells are thrown, they will either fall faced down (closed side) or they will fall faced up (open side). If all 4 are faced up, that means a definite "yes" and the querent will be blessed with abundance and with more than they wished. If three shells are up, it is a definite "maybe" answer to their question, and perhaps another toss should be done. If two shells are up, this means a basic "yes" or a basic affirmative to the question asked. No other toss is needed. If only one shell is up, this represents a basic "no" or negative to the answer. If all four shells are turned down it is a very strong and definitive "no". This may mean one should consult the spirit guides or Ancestors for further guidance.

Grounding Before Any Divination

When using cowry shells or any type of divination it is always good to make sure that one does not go into the divination upset, angry or in distress, if it can be helped. If one feels that they are in a cloud of negative energy it is important to do meditation, deep breathing or other calming techniques before engaging in consultation. There are two reasons for this. The first reason is that when people come to the divination tool in distress, we tend to muddle up our questions and intentions. It makes the outcome of our queries vague at best. The second reason is that distressful queries cause intense spiritual energies, and energy can cause effects. Let's say that someone was pissed off about a particular situation and they were determined to do something about it, but they decided to first consult the divination tool on if they should do it. The fact that the querent is charged by their own distress may allow for the subconscious to inadvertently alter the results to manifest to the outcome of their desire. In other words, the result one wants and not the results that one truly needs to know. We are Witches after all. Before approaching a divination medium for consultation, take a moment to relax, use fragrant oils or incense to help with a calming effect. Very low meditative music can also help. Inform the Universe or spirit guides that you are open to truth and what you need to know for your highest good and best blessed outcome. Then ask the question at least three times to be certain that the answers received are clear and concise.

Scrying

The word *scry* comes from the Old English word meaning *to descry* or *to discern* or *to make out dimly* or *to reveal.* It is said that scrying was first recorded in about the 10th Century in a Persian text called the <u>*Shahnameh*</u>, which engages the reader in poetic stories about pre-Islamic times. As Christianity rose to power, in Christian nations, scrying was outlawed and denounced as devil's work, so just as in everything else in mystical practices and divination, the art of scrying remained in the shadows to be worked by esoteric practitioners of magick. There are numerous means of scrying including cloud gazing, oil gazing, smoke gazing and wax gazing (by dropping hot wax in water).

Scrying which is also called *hydromancy* (scrying in water), *crystallomancy* (gazing with crystals or precious stones or shiny stones), *oculomancy* (scrying in the eyes of others or soul gazing), *pyromancy* (scrying with fire), *catoptromancy* (scrying into mirrors or tinted mirrors), *tasseomancy* (reading of tea leaves) are all very much popular. Crystallomancy is especially popular with those who have crystal balls. The best crystal balls for scrying should have the best clarity for the seer's spiritual vision, without hindrance, distraction or murkiness. Some crystal balls for scrying, that I have seen, are *crystal quartz, labradorite, red quartz, black obsidian* or quite frankly any crystal that speaks to the seer, and gives them good discernment, is the best gazing ball.

The art of scrying is based on analyzing images, reflections, shadows and faint visions on polished metal, semi-precious or precious stones or anything that the oracle chooses to focus or gaze upon. These practices are estimated to have been with early humans and early Shamans who sought to receive messages and visions from the spiritual realm. Scrying, a form of divination, is an art that anyone can practice or seek to practice and to enjoy. It is uniquely suited for those who are extremely visual, and like interpreting patterns or images.

Scrying, like other divination tools, helps the visionary to get in touch with the unconscious mind. While some believe it to be a medium for past, present and future evaluations, what it truly does is connect to the realm of the soul. It is a wonderful tool for finding direction and answers. This technique has been used in all cultures and it continues to be used today. Gaining the seer's ability isn't easy, however, with commitment and practice, it can be obtained. This art connects with the intuitive senses allowing us to perceive things with our third eye and or second sight.

Palm Reading

The art of *palm reading*, also called *palmistry* or *chiromancy* or *chirosophy*, is a divination of seeing various insights, interpretations and divinations of a person based on lines, waves, ripples, pliability and other characteristics on the palm of the hand. Palmistry's origins are uncertain. Various sources believe that it may have originated in ancient Northern India and spread from there. India was the original home of the *Roma*, better known by the pejorative name *Gypsies*, who read fortunes for centuries. Other lands where types of palm reading had been practiced are Persia, Mesopotamia, Greece, China and Egypt. While the form we know may have derived from India, palm reading is now one of the most common mediums of divination today, and it is used in the esoteric world as well as the secular world of pop-culture.

To reiterate, *palmistry* is the art of analyzing line features of the hands for the purpose of interpreting personality and other characteristics and or to predict future events, once referred to as *fortunes*. To a palm reader, a palm is a glance through a small window into the Universe finding insights about a particular person. When reading palms, remember that each hand of the individual has a particular dynamic. There is the *active hand* and then the other is the *passive hand* (non-dominant). The active hand is the hand one writes with and or works more often with. The passive hand is simply the hand that is less active. The passive hand indicates inherited traits and should be read as a baseline, and the dominant hand shows changes from the inherited state. If there is a major difference between passive and dominant hand this indicates that the person has worked hard towards self-improvement or change.

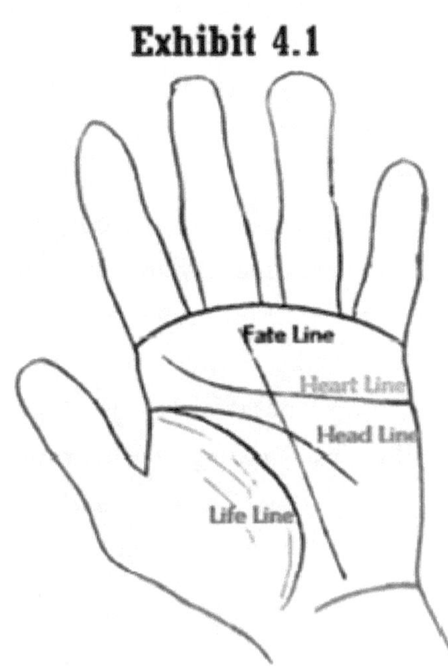

In palm reading there are many lines of the hand to interpret, but in general there are four major lines. See **Exhibit 4.1.** The first line is called the *heart line*. The heart line is the topmost line that runs horizontally across the upper part of the palm. This line represents both the physical and emotional state of one's heart. The next line of interest is called the *head line*. The head line runs horizontally across the middle of the palm and just below the heart line. This line represents the physical and emotional state of one's brain, your psyche and your mind. To continue the reading let's go to the *life line*. The life line is the curved line that begins somewhere estimated between the end of that finger and thumb which curves downward toward the bottom of the palm. Despite popular misconception this line does not indicate how long a person lives. What it represents is the various energies, strengths and vitalities a person has. It also represents an indicator of prosperity. The final line of major interest is called the *fate line*. Take note that this line is not present on everyone's hand. If a person has it then the fate line can be found tracing vertically up to the middle of the palm. This line represents one's career path and their successes.

There is so much more to learn about *palmistry*. Its art is very detailed and nuanced. Any practitioner interested in *palmistry* would do well to take the time to study its craft through books, online courses or other mediums available.

Runes

The last form of divination that will be discussed in this module is from the land of the Vikings. According to Ecyclopedia.com, runes are, "An ancient alphabet found in inscriptions on stone in Scandinavian countries. The runic alphabet belongs to the Germanic group of languages but is related to Greek and Latin alphabets. The earliest inscriptions were depicted in the hands of the goddess Idun, the keeper of the gods' magic apples of immortality. Dating from the 3rd century C.E., runic inscriptions have been found in areas between the Black Sea and the Baltic … as well as throughout Scandinavia" (Runes | Encyclopedia.Com, 2020).

Surprising to many who have watched movies of Vikings being portrayed as inexhaustible warlords, Vikings in fact left a prolific legacy of stone, wood, and metal that were all written in the alphabetic symbols known as runes. They relied on these symbols not only for writing language, but for fortune telling, casting spells, and to provide magickal protection.

The word rune refers to or means holding a secret or hidden or mystery. Runes were first developed in Early Germanic tribes of northern Europe. These were known as the Elder Futhark of 24 letters. However, much later, in approximately 700 AD the Scandinavians adopted and converted to their version called the Young Futhark with 16 letters.

While these letters were used for basic writing each letter has its own unique poetic meaning.

There is a huge debate among historians as to when Runes first came into use. <u>PBS Nova</u> writes, "Since the first objects inscribed with runes date to the second and third centuries A.D., some surmise that the runic alphabet arose no earlier than the first century A.D" (Sanderson, 2000). However, with regard to their origin, runes do have their own lore and myths. According to legend, Odin, the king of the Norse gods, impaled himself to a tree named Yggdrasil in a self-sacrificing attempt to receive rune knowledge. Odin then hung suspended from Yggdrasil nine days and nights. After the ninth night Yggdrasil bestowed the knowledge of the rune mysteries on Odin. Odin then passed on his knowledge to his people. There is great reverence and respect for the runes because of the belief that the runes have divine origin, which contributes to the belief that runes possess magical powers. According to other resources, there is also the belief that, "Rune stone divination should not be used to predict the future. That is not its function. Look at it as a tool for guidance. It allows you to work with the subconscious and focus on the questions that have been bothering you and those which you just need the answers to" (Jen, 2015). So, perhaps, in the spiritual culture, runes should be used for higher purposes rather than mere fortune telling. Runes should be used more along the lines of self-development, higher causes and spiritual growth.

When working with the runes try to memorize the meaning of each letter. See **Exhibit 4.2** for each name of each rune and their meaning. Place them in a small sachet or drawstring bag, and then clear the mind. Remember when doing divination always focus on the question and then ask the runes the question at least three times. Mix the stones in the bag with your fingers or shake them to make sure that the runes are chosen randomly or are in an unbiased manner. Pick a rune from out of the bag and read the symbol. Think of what the symbol is saying to you and what it may be telling you.

Rune pieces are made of stones, crystals or wood, and each has its own alphabet or rune letter. Many practitioners find creative ways to create their own runes out of simple materials.

Runes can be read like a daily oracle. Pick one every morning to help with the course of the day.

Runes can also be read like tarot cards, whereas one can pull multiple runes, and read their message in chorus. Runes can be used as a charm. Keep one or more in your purse or car as a charm or as an affirmation of a goal. Runes are also used for spells or rituals. Lay one on the altar that is meaningful to you.

I think of runes as high-potency alphabets that were developed by a people who conquered much of the world and passed on their language to a lot of their conquered Western world. If you think about it, plainly stated, the Vikings and Germanic people (Angles, Saxons, and Jutes) conquered Britain and gave them their language. Runes are the precursor of the English language we speak today. Because of the magickal lore of Odin hanging pierced on a tree for nine days and nights, and with the reality of all the Viking conquests, who really couldn't use some of that Viking warrior energy, from time to time, in their spiritual lives. Just saying…

The 24 Nordic Runes - Elder Futhark

Exhibit 4.2

Ansuz: *Of Odin* and God, Knowledge, Insight, Wisdom and Communication.	**Nauthiz:** *Of Needs,* Desires, Constraints, Urgency, Endurance, Obstructions, Survival, and Hope for Marriage
Berkano: *Of Freya and Goddess,* Birth, the Womb, Protection, Growth and Love.	**Othala:** *Of Heritage,* Birth, Family, Land, Legacy, Tradition, Heirlooms, Homeland and Nobility.
Kenaz: *Of the Fire or Torch,* Light, Vision, Creativity and Transformation.	**Perthro:** *Of Mysteries,* A Cup of Lots, Secrets, Unclear Meanings, The Hidden, Occult, and Mysteries of the Feminine.
Dagaz: *Of the Dawn,* Awakening, Hope, Breakthroughs, Clarity, Happiness and Embarking	**Ingwaz:** *Of the Fertility God,* Growth, Gestation, Strength, Virtues, Family, Love and Self-Actualization.
Ehwaz: *Of the Horse,* Journey, Transportation, Movement, Teamwork and Trust.	**Raidho:** *Of the Chariot:* Movement, Journey, Spiritual Paths, Inner Compass, Travel and Destiny

ᚠ	**Fehu:** *Of the Cattle,* Fertility, Initiations Luck, Creation, Prosperity, Wealth and New Beginnings.	ᛋ	**Sowilo:** *Of the Sun,* Strength, Energy, Meeting Goals, Positive Change, Accomplishments, and Good Health.
ᚷ	**Gedo:** *Of the Gifts,* Generosity, Unions, Relationships, Partnerships and Sacrifi ce.	ᛏ	**Tiwaz:** *Of Tyr,* Sky Deity Energy, Justice, Honor, Victory, Analyst, Authority, Legal Matters, and Leadership.
ᚺ	**Hagalaz:** *Of Hail,* Nature's Wrath, Air, Unrestrained Forces, Trials, Loss and Evolution.	ᚹ	**Wunjo:** *Of Joy,* Pleasure, Blessings, Harmony, Spiritual Success, Recognition, Peace and Comfort.
ᛃ	**Jera:** *Of the Year,* Fruitful Harvest, Success, Accomplishments, and Reaping What was Sown.	ᚦ	**Th urisaz:** *Of Th or,* the Th orn of Life, Confl ict, Protection, Defensive Force, Danger, Adversity, and Making Change.
ᛁ	**Isa:** *Of the Ice,* Stillness, Focus, Delay, Psychic Blocks, Challenges, Refl ection and Frustrations.	ᛇ	**Eihwaz:** *Of the Yew Tree,* Life and Death, Resilience, Reliability, Immortality, Endurance, Strength and Defense.

Laguz: *Of the Water or Lake*, Fluidity, Flow, Dreams, Healing, Fantasy and Renewal.		**Algiz:** *Of the Elk*, Warding, Protection, Shelter, Blocking, Guardian Spirits, Instinct and Shielding.	
Mannaz: *Of the Self*, Humankind, Relationships, Social Order, Ability, Cooperation, and Social Awareness.		**Uruz:** *Of the Wild Ox*, Strength of Will, Physical Strength, Magi Energy, Divine Wisdom, Power and Courage.	

Visualizations, Sympathetic and Astrological Magick & Other Magickal Workings

"When you want something, all the Universe conspires in helping you to achieve it."~ **Paulo Coelho**

Most people believe casting spells are the most important things about being a Witch. I may not totally agree, but I definitely think it is one of the top three or four. Funny thing is I never cast a true spell until I learned more about witchcraft and the way it works. As a *baby Witch* it took me a couple years before I wanted to cast my first true spell, and you know what, I never regretted that choice. Now that I look back, I believe the Universe picked up my sincerity to learn the craft first, so it helped a sister out, by sending me teachers, and it guided me to resources I needed to learn from. So, when I was ready to cast spells, I actually felt the Universe urging me on to do what I was meant to do, and I actually felt it smiled proudly like it was watching its child take its first steps, or watch me graduate into a new level in life.

Some people believe that spell casting is easy. A wave of the hand, a few words and a lit candle, and the spell is on its way. Believe it or not sometimes that is all it takes. There have been times that I have just talked to my altar not thinking that it was actually listening and *bam!* things strangely happened for me, and I had to remind myself that I had a talk with the Universe the other day. However, spells don't always work that easily. At least not when we are first starting out, and sometimes there are complex issues that will take at least some moderate effort. Sometimes spells don't work the first time and we have to do another magickal run. After years of theorizing why this is, I have come up with some logical actions for casting effective spells that I will get into on separate modules of advanced magick, but for now just know that if it were easy everyone would be able to do it. Know that for now you are learning the basic methods of the game of magick, and how to play it.

In my experience in casting spells, I found that there are certain techniques that help with successful spell casting. Those techniques are:

1) *Visualization* for *Spellcasting* through *Meditation practices*,
2) *Sympathetic Magick*,
3) *Using Crystals, Herbs, Oils, Charms, Talismans and Amulets*,
4) *Numerology*,
5) *Magickal Astrology* for Casting Spells.

DEVELOPING VISUAL SPELL CASTING THROUGH MEDITATION

"Magick is the projection of natural energies to produce needed effects."
~ Scott Cunningham -Wicca: A Guide for the Solitary Practitioner

As was stated in the previous lesson, it is my humble opinion that if a Witch has no other technique in their framework, skillful meditation would be all that they would need to become an adept Witch and Conjurer. Scott *Cunningham* wrote, *"The art of using our brains to 'see' what is not physically present is a powerful magical tool used in many Wiccan rituals"* (Cunningham, 1996, pp. 82).

Over half of spell casting consists of using visualization to cast a spell. For example, if you desire to point a wand, or your hand, at something to cast a spell upon, you would need to visualize energy coming from the wand and direct it to your chosen object. As discussed previously, meditation and visualization can help you focus and direct that energy. If you know your intention for the spell, it would be more beneficial to lie down, breathe and relax, and then imagine the spell you wish to perform. Go through the steps, one by one, and if there will be direction of energy then visualize that energy flowing. What color will the energy be? Will it look like water, ice, fire or light? Imagine what the outcome of the spell will be. Then perform the spell by visualizing the energy as you execute.

Visualization through meditation, before a spell, can also be inspirational on what to use in a spell. Sometimes spirit will give ideas on the best way to formulate one's spell. Often, I get ideas of various tools to use, herbs, crystals and incantations to say during meditation.

Also, meditating before a spell can help the organizing of one's energy. Many times, we are often keyed up about performing rituals. Many times I have found myself over-wound before casting a spell. This is often because I rushed to collect everything I needed, or I was just apprehensive about the spell. As a result, I became stressed in the process. Needless to say, most of the time the outcome of the spell fizzled out or was not as successful as it could have been. Taking the time to meditate before the spell directs and calms the energies and helps with the concentration needed for a more successful outcome. Also do not rush a spell to get it over with. The spell will most likely not work. The Universe looks for sincerity and authenticity, that is for the practitioner to be their most authentic self when one is spellcasting.

SYMPATHETIC MAGICK

While anyone can practice magick without the use of *Sympathetic* techniques, unless it is the most basic of spells, Sympathetic Magick is vital in receiving a desirable outcome. We touched on Sympathetic magick in previous modules, but here we will tie it all together with the description of basic magick. According to *Merriam-Webster Dictionary*, Sympathetic magick is *"magic based on the assumption that a person or thing can be supernaturally affected through its name or an object representing it"* (Merriam-Webster, 2020).

Well, that is kinda right, but I would like to think of it as much more philosophical. *Sympathetic* magick is intuitive and metaphorical. In fact, I would really prefer the term of *Metaphorical magick*. It is much more poetic. Pun intended. I think *Dictionary.com* had a much better definition for Sympathetic magick when they defined the word "metaphor". It stated, *"a thing regarded as representative or symbolic of something else, especially something abstract."*

Sympathetic magick works with the *Law of Correspondence* that we discussed before – *"as above so below"*. It could also be said that it works with the idea of associating. For example, when we want more money; add the color green to our spell. When we seek more wisdom; add a depiction of an owl on our altar. When we want to dedicate an altar to Yemaya; place seashells between two candles. When we want to heal someone through magick or want to start a healing altar, we can use *Valerian* or *Ginseng* or *Goldenseal* or *Feverfew* or *Garlic*. I think you have the idea. It is all about associating one thing with another.

So why does Sympathetic magick work? Again, it works because based on the *Law of Correspondence*, which means that everything is connected. Secondly, it works because of one more principle called *The Law of Mentalism,* meaning the Universe is one big brain sending and receiving thought waves. When declaring our intention during a spell, and associating objects to one's desired outcome, because it is representative of the spell, it makes it easier to transmit the spell into the universal frequencies.

GATHERING YOUR MAGICK ITEMS: CRYSTALS, HERBS, OILS, CHARMS, TALISMANS AND AMULETS

As established Witches we tend to have certain items handy and awaiting our spiritual use. Even before we became Witches certain items may have come to us naturally, because we were spiritually drawn or inclined to them. We made teas out of *herbs*. We took baths with *crystals* to balance us. We studied our own horoscopes or the horoscopes of our friends and family. We may have kept an old *charm* for good luck. Yet we may not have, considered ourselves to be a type of *paramagician* at the time. It just seemed natural to us.

When deciding about how a spell will be cast there are a wealth of basic items that Witches may use in addition to their basic altar tools. Some of these items are *Crystals, Herbs, Oils, Incense, Sigils, Charms, Talismans* and *Amulets*. The best way to choose the items we want for our spell is to again visualize what our intention is and then find the item that best fits to create a spell of sympathetic magick. Below are some items and their basic definitions.

Crystals

The best definition I found was from Judy Hall, who wrote, <u>The Crystal Bible</u>. In the book she wrote, "Crystals are efficient absorbers and transmitters of energy. One of their functions is to cleanse and transmute negative energies" (Hall, 2003, pp. 13). Crystals are gemstones, formed within the Earth. They are considered the essence, life blood and some of the beauties of Mother Earth. Crystals are used by people to be the aspirators and respirators of magickal energy. They are often used to absorb, to be charged with, to give off positive energies, and to bind energy. When charged with positive energy they are often used to make or accompany charms, talismans as types of batteries. When used for protection crystals are utilized to create shields or they are placed in parameters or grids to protect areas. When used for any energy work crystals should be cleansed for a period with one or more of the natural elements like salt, water, earth soil, sage, or air. Once they are cleansed it is important to charge and imbue them with our own energy, or the energy of our choosing. You can dance with them, sleep with them, expose them to your favorite music. You can coat them with your favorite essential oils. You can even talk to them and let them know your intentions for them. Once they are charged then they are ready for your magickal use.

Each type of crystal has its own characteristic, and the color of each crystal gives off a certain type of energy. One common crystal is the Rose Quarts, which is pink and is often used for love or attracting people or relationships. Another is the Agate, which comes in a variety of colors, and is used to stabilize auras and emotions. Another good crystal, for example, is the Obsidian, which is an igneous rock filled with Ogun type energy. This stone is used for protection, shielding and to build strength. If a practitioner feels a crystal is warranted then finding the right one can be effective and it can give fortification to a spell through its vibrational attributes.

Herbs

Performing a spell with *herbs*, for me, is one of the most wholesome parts about being a Witch. Especially since I am an *Herbal* and *Green Witch*. I could spend all day online checking out different herbs or spend all day at a quaint witchy herbal store. There are more herbs in the world than anyone could count, and each of them have their own healing properties which are also, more often, their own magickal attributes. These magickal attributes are how a Witch selects the herb they desire for their spell. They may use *rose hips* for a love spell, since roses are the flowers of love. They may use *basil* for luck. They may use *angelica root* to invoke an Ancestral spirit. They may use *lavender* for deeper and lucid dreaming, or they may use *patchouli* to enhance sexual desire. When it comes to herbs, the world is our total oyster. We can plant them in our home or garden, or we can forage for them in the parks or forests. We can even buy the dry or fresh at the supermarket.

Herbs are a spiritual journey all by themselves. Herbs can be placed in a pillowcase for bedtime. They can be made into a tea for spellcasting, relaxation or healing. Herbs can be burned in a censer or prepared for spiritual baths. Many people keep them in *sachets* or *mojo bags*—which is a bag of power and considered to be a *Talisman* of sorts, with small magickal items within it. For many Witches working with herbs is pretty much the be-all of being a Witch.

Essential Oils

Essential oils are compounds extracted from plants, roots, flowers, bark, fruit or leaves through different methods like distillation or cold pressing. In these processes the oils keep the natural scent, flavor and the essence of the source plant. Essential oils are considered *a gift from the Earth* and are used for aromatherapy, body fragrance, food flavorings, spiritual charging or cleansing, and magick. Essential oils can be diluted with vegetable or mineral oils which are then called carrier oils. Many people place these oils in their *sacred* or *spiritual baths*. Most oils can be applied directly on the skin for healing or for their pleasant aroma.

According to *WebMD.com, "Simple smells such as lavender, chamomile, and rosewater may help keep you calm. You can breathe in or rub diluted versions of these oils on your skin. Scientists think they work by sending chemical messages to parts of the brain that affect mood and emotion. Although these scents alone may not take all your stress away, the aroma may help you relax"* (Gardner, MD, 2020). This part of the brain, which is mentioned here, I suspect, may also be the part of the brain that facilitates the magick to manifest, while in meditation, or prior to casting spells. I use essential oils to anoint myself before spells or rituals, and or to anoint my magickal petitions. Some use it to rub on mojo bags or charms. The most popular uses for oils are to *dress candles*, which is to rub the candles with essential oils, herbs or to carve sigils or runes into them before casting a spell. I have found though that soy candles don't do very well with oils anointed on them, because it does not allow for the candles to burn very well. Beeswax, on the other hand, burns just fine with these oils, although nowadays beeswax candles are hard to find.

The Difference Between Amulets, Charms and Talismans

Amulets

For thousands of years *amulets* were articles that have the power to *ward off negative energy, evil spirits, and to be an agent of protection.* They are magickally imbued with power to repel negative energies and influences. An amulet can be any item, but traditionally it is worn around the neck to be carried by the person of its charge. Today a few Afro-Witches, and Hoodooists, carry chicken feet as amulets. This member is dried, painted and then preserved in some way. A chicken foot could be used as an amulet to ward off curses, hexes, crossings, bad situations, bad luck etc. It is said that the chicken foot's magick is to claw away bad energy.

Charms

A *charm* can be any object from the size of a button to the size of a horse shoe. Charms are items that one can carry but are imbued with *good luck* to attract good fortune. When I was a kid the popular luck charm was a rabbit's foot that many of us carried around on a keychain. While I personally wouldn't use it now as a charm it was a common belief, in those days, that it was very lucky.

Talisman

Talismans and amulets are words that are often used interchangeably as the same type of magickal charm, but to be precise they shouldn't be. As a matter of fact, a talisman is the total opposite of an amulet, and the talisman has energies more similar to a magickal charm. Talismans are charms that are magickally imbued with energy that enhances, magnifies or gives a strength and or power to the person for whom it has a charge. So, in short, a talisman is many times stronger than a charm. A Talisman is usually charged and consecrated and given assignment for its intended use. Talismans can be worn or carried. Talismans are usually carved with symbols, runes, sigils or words to increase their power. The best talismans are made with crystals, stones or any type of natural material.

NUMEROLOGY AND ASTROLOGICAL MAGICK

Numerology

Now let's continue with *numerology*. Numerology is the ancient occult study wherein numbers hold cosmic and mystical connections which relay divine meaning. They provide information and messages which are important to us in our daily lives. This information is used for divination, life purpose, guidance and gives us insight about our inner selves. These numbers either come to us through synchronicity, coinciding events or our own calculations. Those who study numerology believe that each number not only holds numeric value but has a related cosmic vibration. Numbers that come in combinations tell a story, give a message or hold explicit meaning. Experts in numerology use numbers to determine the best time for major activities and important life decisions like when to invest, when to travel, relocations, career decisions or the best time to get married. The study of numerology has multiple arts. The ones we will touch on in this module are the *Basics of Numerology, Guardian Numbers* (most often called *Angel Numbers*) and *Life Path Numbers*.

Basic Numerology

"If you want to find the secrets of the Universe, think in terms of energy, frequency, and vibration." ~ **Nikola Tesla**

Many would like to give credit for the study of numerology to the Greek Philosopher and Mathematician, *Pythagoras*, who is known as the father of Western Numerology, and who lived between 500 and 400 B.C. But, to others, numerology goes back further than that. Its arts are believed to have been first practiced in ancient Mesopotamia and Sumerian civilizations.

It is through numbers that the Universe speaks to us. I am a firm believer in this because one of my very first spiritual awakenings was through departed family members visiting me in a vibrant otherworldly dream, and they handed me numbers which helped me to confirm later that I was a child of 9s. This made me recognize and ponder the fact that the number *nine* has followed me all through my life. It was there from my birth year (it has two nines in it), to the month my daughter was born (September), and to the actual time she was born (it added up to 9). It was in my first living address and the first house I purchased. Even the goddess who first called to me on my true spiritual path, the goddess *Oya*, Her favorite number is nine. Even my first name has the word "nine" spelled out in it. When doing research on this number I discovered that the number was inexplicably me, down to every personality, desire, energy and every detail. To make things more dramatic the number "9" I found out to be my *Life Path Number*. With this I could only come to one conclusion and that is my transitioned family members wanted me to know that there was no end to spirit, and only transition. And, this was my very first realization that numbers are the true language of the Universe and that we are all connected to the Universe.

Please find **Exhibit 5.1**, which gives a description of each number based on its vibrational energy and meaning. You will find that basic numerology corresponds, to a great extent, with tarot card divination and their numeric values. While different resources may vary in some vibrational meanings, I have presented what appears to be most common, average and sensible in meaning on this chart.

Exhibit 5.1

Basic Numerology Meanings	
0	*Symbol of the Universe. The Mother and the Womb. God. Before the Beginning.* connecting to Source, void, alpha and omega, clean slate, before the journey, dark moon energy, infinity, darkness, pure Spirit
1	*Primal. Genesis. Manifesting. Divine Energy.* originator, initiate, independent, leader, innovator, individual, beginning, leadership, new moon energy, successful, to embark, beginning the journey, newness, naivety, optimism, trusting, manifestation, transform, liberty, change agent

2	*Divine Love. Intuition. Kundalini. Divine Gender. Divine Union.* diplomatic, romantic, non-confrontation, duality, insightful, graceful, sensitivity, balance, harmony, planner, coupling, supportive, peace maker, kind
3	*Creation. Divine Gift. Sacred Trinity.* artistic, imaginative, communications, self-expression, team player, Spring, creativity, spiritual pursuits, fruitfulness, new birth, opportunity, team work
4	*Universal Protection and Strength. Guardian Spirits Assistance, Grounding.* dependability, pragmatism, assistance, order, achievement, foundation, financial reward, organizer, planner, security, problem solver, discipline, fertile soil, worker
5	*Free Spirit. Walker between Worlds. Universal Expansion.* transformative, dynamic, energetic, change, growth, progressive, action, innovative, intelligent, creative, adventure
6	*Flower of Life. Ethereal Presence. Ancestral Call. The Magnificence of Creation.* flowers in bloom, prosperity, family, motherhood, sacrifice, teaching, compassion, nurturing, protection, responsible
7	*Spiritual Awareness. Divine Faith. Universal Inner Growth. Twin Flame. Soul Mate.* counseling, shadow work, marriage, autonomy, spirituality, perfectionist, prudence, tolerance, study, seclusion, determination, truth seeker, hermetic, self-awareness
8	*Karma. Infinity. Divine Prosperity. Earthly World.* materialistic, wisdom, foresight, balance, fortune, career, greed, business, striving, authoritative, assertiveness, developing, realistic, achievement, compromise

9	*Divine Judgment. Transition of Cycle. Divine Consciousness. Humanitarianism.* humanities, fairness, open-minded, tolerance, idealistic, death, arrogance, political, sympathetic, sentimental, confidence, termination cycle, judgmental

Guardian Numbers or Angel Numbers

What Are Guardian Numbers?

Do you have periods in your life in which you keep seeing 111 or 1111 or 333 or 777 or any repetitive or sequential number on clocks, watches, cellphones, license plates, street signs or etc.? If you have then you are not alone. As I have mentioned before the Universe communicates to us through frequency and vibration, and often the results are what I call *Guardian Numbers,* but most commonly known as *Angel Numbers.* I call them Guardian Numbers, because the word *Angel* is a Christian term. Pagans, Afro-American Pagans specifically, more often refer to celestial beings as either *Ancestor Spirits* or *Guardian Spirits.* But whatever the term you feel more comfortable with, guardian numbers refer to duplicate or sequential numbers that carry spiritual guidance, with each number having a specific numerological meaning. This guidance is believed to be given by celestial beings who guide us as their charges.

In numerology, the occult science of numbers, it is understood that each number carries with it a specific vibrational meaning that goes beyond their basic value. Their vibrational frequencies are similar in nature to the number's frequencies at which celestial beings resonate. We see these repeating numbers when guardians want to get our attention or send us a particular message. They will often send us these sequences of numbers which will repetitively appear in our life experiences. This repetition of numbers can easily cause many to get the impulse to do research to find out their meanings wherever one can.

Guardian numbers work through *meaningful coincidences* or *synchronicity*. Synchronicity, as was mentioned before, is the belief that our minds are connected to a Universal frequency, that works on *The Law of Mentalism*, which is that we are all connected to the *Universal Mind*, and that there is a single *Universal Consciousness*. Some call it the *Collective Unconscious* and some call it an *Unified field of Consciousness*. The physicists, *David Bohm*, said to have been the founder of quantum physics, said, *"The universe and everything in it – including us – may, in fact, be part of a grand cosmic pattern where all portions are evenly shared by every other…"* (TMhome, 2013). This means we are connected without realizing it on a conscious level. This connection is why we are able to vibrate and why the guardians are able to transmit to us. We think of these synchronicities as mystical nudges from some unseen guiding force sending messages from the spiritual realm. So, we may wake up at 3:33am for no particular reason and during the same period we may go to the grocery store and get a receipt for \$3.33. That same afternoon while driving home we may get stopped at the light, and see a license plate ahead of us with the number '333' on it. And so, it goes.

Guardian Number Meanings

Interpretation of the Guardian Numbers are often hit or miss depending on the receiver. Some just interpret the sight of the numbers as encouragement by the guardians that they are on the right track, and to continue. Others become so adept in deciphering the numbers that they chart their steps by the interpretive translation. In *Doreen Virtue's* book, <u>*Angel Numbers 101: The Meaning of 111, 123, 444, and Other Number Sequences,*</u> she wrote, *"Your angels often communicate messages to you by showing you sequences of numbers."* She continues to say that, *"they subtly whisper in your ear so you'll look up in time to notice the clock's time or a phone number on a billboard"* (Virtue, 2008).

People who see guardian numbers are usually *"spiritually awakened,"* at some level. This means that they became cognizant of a new spiritual reality outside of conventional constructs of thought. Also, seeing these numbers not only means that the guardians are encouraging you and cheering for you, but it is also their way of letting you know that they are there in the first place. It is often a good idea to affirm to them that you are seeing the numbers and thank them in a verbal manner. Then ask them to help you make things happen. They will immediately get to work to help and they will continue to set things up, and line up good things for you. They are on your side working with you, and for you, to make things happen. See **Exhibit 5.2** for information or interpretation of guardian numbers.

Guardian Number Interpreter Exhibit 5.2	
111 or 1111	A portal of opportunity has opened, and a new journey has begun. Keep positive thoughts in this time of new beginnings. Eliminate all doubt. Step into your role as a creative Sage and manifest your goals. Connect with Higher Self.
222	That which you seek is coming into focus and is on its way to manifest for you. Make sure that you stay balanced in health, relationships and harmony. Keep the faith and stay positive
333	You are in a blessed and prosperous period. Your body, mind and spirit are open to expand for knowledge of humanities. Your positive qualities are heightened. Develop your soul mission. Your Ascended Master has been summoned for you.

444	All the Earth's elements are laid for your foundation. Your Ascended Master and your guardians are now with you and will guide you to success. Be open to your intuition and inner wisdom and trust them. Continue your path.
555	You have graduated to a new level and a time of transition. Your guardians are with you and will see you through. The Universe is clearing a path for you. This change is not negative or positive. It is a step towards a life lesson and evolution.
666	It is time to consider self-care. There may be an imbalance and you may need to spend more time in the spiritual world and less time with the physical, emotional, material and financial issues. Find harmony by seeking a deeper loving connection.
777	This is a sacred time for you. You are leaving the darkness. You are evolving spiritually. Embrace your gifts. Your spiritual guides are calling you. You are surrounded with love and light. Celebrate, do rituals and give thanks.
888	There is light for you at the end of the tunnel. You have put in the work and your guardians are sending you a message that increased abundance and achievement is coming your way. Remember karma and the universal law of cause and effect.
999	You are being called by the Universe to tie up loose ends and participate in healing oneself and others. Many lessons were learned. A cycle is ending and a new one is about to begin. Use your lightwork, humanitarianism and higher perspective.
000	This is a message that you are one and in tune with Source. All things are possible, so do not allow excuses to keep things from happening. Take risks. All things have come full circle, so don't be afraid to embark. The Universe is here to guide you.

Life Path Number

The *Life Path Number* is a practice in numerology that has been used for thousands of years. It is the sum of the birth date. This number represents who we are at birth and the innate traits that we will carry with through our lives. The most important number that will be discussed here is the Life Path number. The Life Path describes the nature of this journey through life and determines our possible life direction.

To calculate your Life Path Number, you must first add your birth month and day and year together to get a total. So, for example let's calculate *Erykah Badu's* birthday. Sistar Badu was born on February 26, 1971. That breaks down to:

2 +2+6+1+9+7+1 = 28 ~ break 28 down further to :

(2+8 = 10) break it down again to

(1+0 = 1)

This means Erykah Badu's Life's Path Number is a "1".

Another way to think about it is this: Let's now use the birth date of *April 12, 1954.*

Take the month: April is the 4th month of the year. 4 reduces to 4.

Day: The date of birth is the 12th. 12 reduces to 3. (1 + 2 = 3) Year: The year of birth is 1954. This year reduces to 1. (1 + 9 + 5+ 4 = 19 , then 1 + 9 = 10 and finally 1 + 0 = 1).

The Life Path number for this birthdate is 8. (4 + 3+ 1= 8)

Depending on your birth date, you might end up with another double-digit number after these initial steps. Just keep reducing the digits until you arrive at a single-digit number, or unless you calculate to *Master*

Numbers. Master Numbers are *11, 22* or *33*. If this is the case then you don't have to reduce them any further and perhaps you may first wish to consider the *Master Number* level message. You can always reduce it later for the single digit *Life Path Number*.

So, when you arrive at your single digit Life Path Number what do you do with it? You then use that number to find your *Life Path* attributes. Find your Life Path attributes on **Exhibit 5.1**. If your Life Path number is a Master number, you can find the *Master Life Path attributes* described below in **Exhibit 5.3**

<table>
<tr><td colspan="2" align="center">Master Life Path Attributes
Exhibit 5.3</td></tr>
<tr><td>11: Intuitive Old Soul</td><td>Gifted with intuition, spiritual insight, empathy and natural intelligence. Also gifted with immense power, charisma, leadership, inspiration, inborn duality or dynamism.
Negatives: inner conflict, anxiety, shyness and stressed energy.</td></tr>
<tr><td>22: Master Builder</td><td>Has the ability for spiritual understanding, high self-esteem, natural intelligence, leadership, visionary, ambitious, manifesting, idealism, Earthy and pragmatic.
Negatives: A strong need for overachieving and placing too high a standard on oneself.</td></tr>
</table>

33: Master Teacher	Embodies creativity, joy and excitement. They are spiritually involved and educate others. They are quick to volunteer. They are influential and have a great amount of sincerity and devotion. They are highly knowledgeable, communicative and engender harmony with others. *Negatives: overly ambitious.*

Astrological Magick

Now we are here at *Astrological Magick*. If you google astrological magick you would most likely get anything between *Magickal Zodiac* or the practice of using *Mansions of the Moon*. Each of them in their own way refers to the art of *instrumental magickal timing*. But, at this time, let us discuss the part of astrological magick in which we use fundamental astrological timing. That is using some basic astrological events to plan magickal workings. We use these events to plan for rituals, ceremonial invocations, spells etc. Here we will discuss the fundamental astrological events that are more common, are on our calendars, or are often in the news without the need to chart for them. These basic astrological events are planetary movements, lunar phases, and other celestial factors. While the lunar phases show the relationship between the Sun and the Moon when viewed from Earth (New Moon, Full Moon or Dark Moon etc.), planetary movements and celestial events view planets and the stars from the Earth's orbit.

The origins of astrological magick are lost in the annals of prehistory, but as astrology studies developed from astral omens and esoteric celestial religions, so too did astrological magick stem from the veneration of the planets, stars and other celestial factors. Astrology is the study of the positions of celestial bodies, (planets, stars, constellations, asteroids etc.)

and how they influence human behavior, human affairs and both the material and the natural world. Astrology can help us to know just the right time for our practical magick based on our spiritual needs. As the Earth, Moon and other planets move through the heavens, they create patterns of energy that can be either beneficial or adverse to magickal intentions.

So, in essence, the purpose of astrological magick is to assist with synchronizing or getting in harmony with the Moon, the planets and the Earth's orbit in order to aid with workings of healing, knowledge, protection, love, success and prosperity. But, when you think about it, magickal astrology is also good to keep in mind when making decisions, like when is the best day to get a haircut, when to start a business, what day should one start a diet, or when we should just sit tight and let a period pass before starting any engaging projects. This is not to say that astrological magick should run a person's entire life, like what time should I eat dinner? That is a bit overboard to say the least, but it can be helpful during some mundane or important events. This module will give just a few abbreviated definitions of some celestial events, and will discuss their energies that are conducive to magickal works. The events for discussion are *Planetary Days, Lunar Events, Planet Retrogrades, Meteor Showers, Planetary Alignments and Lion's Gate Portal.*

Planetary Days of the Week

We all know the names of the days of the week, but very few know how they got their names. Our weekly calendar has seven days, and each is given a planetary reference and or is named after a deity. We can use their characteristics and planetary reference designation to plan spells, rituals or devotions. Orisha correspondences are also provided.

See **Exhibit 5.4** below. Their correspondences are as follows:

Day of the Week	Name Correspondence	Greek/Roman Correspondence	Orisha/Loa Correspondence
Sunday	Sun's Day	God Masculine Magick	Obatala
Monday	Moon's Day	Goddess Feminine Magick	Yemaya
Tuesday	Tyr's Day	Aries/Mars	Ogun
Wednesday	Woden's/Odin's Day	Hermes/Mercury	Oya/Papa Legba
Thursday	Thor's Day	Jupiter	Shango
Friday	Freya's Day	Venus/ Aphrodite Muses	Oshun
Saturday	Saturn's Day	Cronos	Oduduwa

Exhibit 5.4

Sunday

Sunday is the day of Earthly *illumination* and *evaluation*. It is a day to reflect on successes of the previous week and to bathe oneself in the satisfaction of conquest and accomplishment. The *sacred Masculine* rules here. Sunday is a time to know that we control our own destiny. It is the time of the big "I AM." It is a time of devotion to ourselves and to the Universe.

Monday

Monday is the day of the *Moon*. Its light is that of *clarity* and *intuitive reflection*. The *sacred Feminine* rules this day. You have given birth to your goals and this is the day of *creative action* and *initiation*. The full potential of one's power is realized here.

Tuesday

Tuesday is the day celebrated in memorial of all of the gods of War. Therefore, it is the day of the *Warrior*. It is a day of *full-on engagement* with the *gods of the craftsmen*. On Tuesdays we are in full spiritual armor taking on the week ahead of us. We have our goals for work, family, self-improvement, and all other tasks ahead.

Wednesday

Wednesday is also called hump day. There is a reason for that. It is the day we come to the middle of our weekly journey. Wednesday is the time in which we either stand on top of the mountain that we climbed, or we come to our spiritual crossroads. All *gods of the Crossroads* meet there. Either way we look back at our travels from Monday and then we turn forward to look ahead. On Wednesdays we make a determination as to which direction we will go from there. Wednesday is a good day to work with divination, spirit guides and advisors for one's next measures. This is also a day of testing one's powers and skills, because the *trickster* and *inquisitor* gods rule here from the *otherworld*, and it is easy to make the wrong choices.

Thursday

Thursday is the day of the renaissance. It is a time of *seeing the light at the end of the tunnel* and putting on that final sprint to the finish line or a period of rest. We tend to get our second wind on this day. Our inner craftsman is at play. We fully engage with our tools like axes and hammers to complete the tasks that we have started during the week. This is a good day to call upon the *Warrior* spirits for encouragement.

Friday

Friday is the time of knowing that the week of toil is at end. It is a time of nurturing oneself with the TLC that is deserving, and taking a breather. It is the time of celebration, for the *goddesses of beauty, arts, muse, and love* rules here. This is not a time for regret or remorse. It is a time for *loving oneself* for the effort and performance during the past week. This is a good day to *pay tribute* to goddesses like *Oshun*.

Saturday

Saturday is the day of taking charge of one's own autonomy, knowing self and doing what one chooses. It is a time of *Saturnalia* and *Bacchanalia*. It is a time of gathering family and planning outings. Saturday is the day of well-earned receipts. Sit back and enjoy all that you survey. It is also a good time to pay homage to *the spirits of providence*.

LUNAR EVENTS

The Moon goes through one complete cycle in roughly between 27 and 30 days. The Moon has *feminine energy* because of its synchronized correlation with a woman's menstrual cycle and other factors. While in its cycle it goes through two stages. These stages are called the *Waxing stage*, when the Moon grows from *New Moon* to *Full Moon*, and the *Waning stage*, when the Moon begins to decrease in size and shrinks to a *Dark Moon*.

The Waxing Moon

The Waxing Moon is the period during which the Moon grows from New Moon into Full Moon. This Moon has magickal attributes of pushing outwards, growing, overtaking, engulfing, abundance, free-flowing energy, surging force, rising, ascension, soaring, time of maturating, fertility, expansion, prospering, intensification, inward tidal flow (what you want to come in from the tide), growth, achievement, returns, advancement and boosting.

The Full Moon

To Witches and Pagans, the *Full Moon* is usually considered to be a very powerful time to do almost anything spiritual. It is considered the period of the harvest. It is the reaping time, a time of claiming and reclaiming. It is also a time of being present, it is the big *"I Am"* which is why it is a good time for meditation or journeying or communing with Spirit. It is a wonderful time for divination work since its light's energy illuminates from the darkness and sings its ancient timeless tales. The magickal attributes of the Full Moon are *goddess energy, feminine energy, claiming, declaration, illumination, inheritance, foundation, Ancestor magick, full maturation, power source, partnership, insight, self-awareness, involution, romance, spiral dance, clarity, other worldly, conjuring, invocations, evocations, ultimate harvest, power of the mother, menstrual energy, folic, vigor, divination, blood energy, full ascension, balance, full circle energy, full potency, love, and stability.*

The Waning Moon

The *Waning Moon* is the time period when the Full Moon starts the transition from fullness to diminishing, moment by moment. This is the time period that energies begin to release and reduce. It is not the best time to start a new, lucrative project. *The magick of this Moon is aligned with inward reflection and elimination of negative energies or that which no longer serves. The predominant goals and attributes of this energy are overcoming obstacles, resolving conflicts, termination, removal, cleansing, tidal flow (what you want to send out with the tide), eradication of illness, purging, the breaking of bad habits, ending of bad relationships or partnerships, cutting, stopping, binding, and banishing.*

The Dark Moon

The Dark Moon is a Moon I never hear any Witches discuss much, if at all, and this is unfortunate because I personally think of this Moon as a very blessed period during the month. The Dark Moon is a Moon that only lasts for approximately 23.5 hours and less than one day. It is a time when the Moon is not visible to the naked eye and it sits between the Waning Moon and the New Moon. That alone is magickal.

As I have stated before, it is the Dark Moon in which Hecate called to me, guided me and taught me the disciplines of dedication to witchcraft while I was a new baby Witch. It was during this Moon that I purged my old thoughts, beliefs and misconceptions and was born anew. I used this time for going inward and mapping my spiritual direction. I did this by cleaning my house and then I would dedicate an altar to goddess Hecate every Dark Moon for roughly about two years. It was like bootcamp for me, but this Moon trained me as a witchling, and it nurtured me like a sapling before I began to stretch out my roots to begin my spiritual journey.

Much of the characteristics of this Moon runs similar to the Waning Moon, however, what is distinct is that it goes further than just eliminating from the surface. It is an old-fashioned deep cleaning. The best way to explain the difference is that the Waning Moon is like the sweeping and cleaning up the dirt off one's floor, and the Dark Moon is like the stripping and mopping the floor with ammonia, bleach, or *Florida Water*. The Dark Moon is like your grandma disinfecting.

This Moon is especially blessed if one is beginning at square one or starting at zero and or wanting to make sure they are straight before the embark. This Moon is dark but latent with bright beautiful stars on the darkest backdrop. Its silence sings a low, slow jam that is conducive to meditation and shadow work. *The characteristics of this Moon are exorcism, chakra cleansing, disinfecting, eradication, karmic work, removal, void, meditation, atoning, gestation, solitary or hermit energy, attuning, inner world travel, finding justice, new beginning preparation, power of the crone, past life regression, development, introspection, contemplation, smudging energy and purification.*

The New Moon

Next to the Full Moon the *New Moon* is considered popular among Witches. This Moon comes a day after the Dark Moon. This Moon is the very beginning of the lunar cycle, so it is a good time for contemplating what one wishes to create or manifest in one's life if it was not done so during the Dark Moon. Typically, this is a favorable time for *initiating new projects and ventures* and it is good for anything that involves *increasing, attracting or manifesting what one wishes in their life.* The New Moon has similar attributes as a Waxing Moon, but it has the distinction of being the embodiment of new beginning energy. *The attributes for the New Moon are new beginnings, fresh starts, visionary, manifesting, prosperity, initiation, sowing seeds, new ventures, dreams, journeying, attracting, new relationships, inspiration, the maiden aspect, fresh engagement, goal setting and air magick.*

Blue Moon

We have discussed the *Blue Moon* in a previous lesson. Here it is important to repeat the definition again in the context of astrological magick. Once again, there is usually one Full Moon per month, except for the one month out of the year having two Full Moons. The second Moon in that month is often called a *Blue Moon*. However, according to the <u>*Farmer's Almanac*</u>, an older yet more confusing definition was asserted, over 80 years ago, stating that there are *"normally three Full Moons for each season of the year* (Yankee Publishing, Inc., 2022). *But when a particular season ends up containing four Full Moons, then the third of that season is called a Blue Moon!"* So basically, a Blue Moon was based on a season according to them. At any rate, the second Full Moon of any month is a rare Moon, and it is considered a very potent Moon. When placed in context any rare astrological event is considered a magickal time portal and is a good vehicle for the use of strong magickal ambitions, and it fortifies any magickal spell. The Blue Moon *is a good event for repurposing a spell that did not have a successful outcome in the past, aiding with difficult circumstances, performing portal magick, and or helping with shieldings and protections.*

Super Moons

A *supermoon* is when either a New Moon or a Full Moon comes to its closest point to Earth within its orbit. This is when a Full Moon or New moon comes within 90% or more of its closest approach to Earth which is measured to the center of the Moon. This is why the Full Moon appears brighter and larger than normal. For magickal purposes this Moon magnifies the magickal potency of a regular Full Moon and brings an added effectiveness to Full Moon spells and rituals.

Moon in Void of Course (VOC)

Every two to three days, the Moon moves from one *astrological* sign into another. During the transition, when the Moon is not in any particular sign, the Moon is considered to be *Void of Course* or VOC. Commonly, this is said to be a bad period to do magick. Since the Moon rules our feelings and emotions, the Moon is said to be unstable during the void since it is somewhat *homeless*. If one is planning to do any ritual, it is always good to have a *void of course* calendar or app to avoid those periods for working. A period of a void can range anywhere from 30 mins to 24 hours or even longer.

Eclipses

Eclipses are thought of as sacred periods of time and they have the dynamics that take on the same energy as Waning Moons. There are two categories of eclipses: they are *lunar eclipses* and *solar eclipses*. Let us start with the lunar eclipses.

Lunar Eclipse:

During a *lunar eclipse*, Earth comes between the Sun and the Moon, blocking the sunlight reflecting on the Moon. There are two types of lunar eclipses—either a *total lunar eclipse* or a *partial lunar eclipse*. A total lunar eclipse occurs when both the Moon and the Sun are on exact opposite sides of Earth and the Moon enters the Earth's shadow. The Moon will appear in total darkness with exception of some possible outline. A lunar eclipse occurs when the Moon is full. A *partial lunar eclipse*, on the other hand, happens when only part of Earth's shadow covers the Moon, because the Moon and the Sun are not quite opposite for each other, so some sunlight has partial reflection on the Moon. Lunar eclipses can be used for *spiritual change or new beginnings*.

Solar Eclipse:

A *solar eclipse* occurs during the New Moon, and it occurs when the Moon sits between both the Earth and the Sun with the Moon casting a shadow over the view of the Sun for a few minutes. A *partial solar eclipse* occurs when the Moon, the Sun and Earth are not completely in alignment. Magickal uses for solar eclipses are often for *significant or serious material goals, and or personal self-improvement.* Use for *intentions of elimination, banishing* or even *to begin a clean slate for new beginnings.*

Planetary Retrogrades

The word *retrograde* has its origin from the Latin word *"retrogradi."* This term means "backward steps" or "to go backwards" or "to reverse movement" or "to revert." When a planet is in retrograde this is when a planet appears to be going backwards or in a reverse orbit. While the planet is not actually reversing, its orbit viewed from Earth gives it an apparent illusion that its motion is going backwards. This illusion happens when the Earth passes a planet in their orbit around the Sun. Since outside planets are slower than the Earth's orbit around the Sun, as the Earth passes these planets (Mercury, Mars and Pluto for example), they appear to be going backwards.

The quandary with retrogrades is that spiritualists and astrologers believe that all celestial bodies can affect human existence on Earth. Since each planet has its own attribute or characteristic, a planet going backwards would change that functional characteristic of what humans are accustomed to. Mercury in retrograde, for example, is the most dreaded, and perhaps that is because it rules over technology, mechanics and communications. When Mercury goes retrograde it is believed that all that it rules has an opportunity to fail, and chaos ensues. Venus, in another example, is the planet of love, relationships, sex, beauty, and fertility. When Venus is in retrograde many dread interruptions or the negative effects in all types of relationships, such as business, casual communications, partnerships and affairs of the heart. Many people believe that when a planet goes into retrograde, like Mercury or Venus, magickal workings should be placed on a back burner and more meditation should be practiced for healthier harmony. While all practitioners do not practice magickal abstinence during these events, a planet in retrograde is definitely something to take in consideration when planning magickal workings or basic life events.

Meteor Showers

A *meteor shower* is a group of space rocks called *meteoroids*. Meteoroids enter Earth's atmosphere and fall towards our planet. The force of gravity and resistance when entering Earth's atmosphere causes the rocks to become extremely hot and fiery. These fiery rocks we see whirling across the dark sky are what we refer to as *shooting stars* or meteor showers, although most of them become nothing more than fiery gases by the time they approach Earth. Some meteor showers like *"Lyrids"* or the *"Perseids"* are celestial events that happen every year. Many people believe that the fiery dust of the meteors is akin to *magic dust* and if one can see them shooting, while contemplating dreams or intentions, magick can happen. This magickal event is very conducive to *wishing spells*. Sitting out in your yard or on your porch while watching meteor showers can be very beneficial for manifesting one's desires.

Planetary Alignment

Planetary Alignments or *Conjunctions* are when two or more planets in our solar system line up in such a precise row that you can draw a straight line through each of their middle points. Sometimes this alignment points directly to the Sun. Sometimes the alignment is not pointed to the Sun but can be viewed from Earth as a straight configuration across the night sky. Some alignments are rare, and some are more common. One common alignment is when the Sun, Moon and Earth line together to cause a solar or lunar eclipse. This alignment is called a *Syzygy*.

Using periods of planetary alignments is conducive in rituals, spells and intentions. For example, in the middle of April 2020 Jupiter, Saturn and Mars aligned in conjunction with one another and straight across the night sky. Jupiter is considered the counselor and wise man aspect with characteristics of health and prosperity. Saturn's aspect is considered the father figure, the authority and the governor. The planet Mars has all the aspects of a warrior. When they line up, in such a way their vibrations begin to merge together. A conjunction like this would be a dream for someone who is looking for a portal of time for magickal workings in finding justice, winning court cases, and working towards positive outcomes in any litigation. To give another example, let's look at a conjunction with Venus, Mars and Saturn. This would aid in the magick for someone who is looking for a commitment for a long-term relationship or to get married.

Lion's Gate Portal

The *Lion's Gate* Portal opens on *August 8th*, but its spiritual period, for the purpose of magick can last from *July 26th to August 12th*, and it is believed that this period resonates high vibrational energies to planet Earth. The reason for this is because of the star *Sirius* which is known as our *Spiritual Sun*. Sirius is the second brightest star in the sky for us, the first, of course, being our Sun. It is believed that Sirius emits a spiritual energy for us, and its light helps in the process of spiritual awakenings, healing, magick and has a connection for us towards spiritual ascension. During the end of July, Sirius moves towards alignment with Orion's Belt on August 8th (8/8). This is the heart of the Lion's Gate, and its energy peaks allowing for magickal workings and spiritual consciousness. This is a good time-portal for *seeking spiritual awakenings, exploring past lives, engaging in spiritual journeying, seeking truths and self-exploration. It is also a good time for divinations and other magickal workings.*

LESSON SIX

The Basics of Creating and Casting Spells

When we were children in Philadelphia my mother used to do a routine with us. We had a huge bay window in my bedroom looking out into the main street, and on occasions my mother would look out of that window to see the Full Moon that managed to peep out between, or above, the tall city buildings. My mother would then call us all to the window to view how beautiful it was. Then my mother, with all her Christian upbringing, would have us all recite two prayers. One would be, *"I see the Moon and the Moon sees me. God bless the Moon and God bless me."* The other poem was, *"Star light, star bright, first star I see tonight. I wish I may, I wish I might, have the wish I wish tonight."*

These are very old verses, and I would bet you have heard at least one before. Those were magickal times for me, because you see, unbeknownst to my mother or myself then, those prayers (or spells) we recited activated a deep-seated spirit within me which grew with me all through my life. You see, my mother did not think of it as reciting spells. She thought of it as passing down what she was taught, *the old ways* or reciting old nursery rhymes. But the quaintness is that some spells are hidden in nursery rhymes, old prayers, and traditions. One tradition my mother always had was to only trim our hair during the New Moon. I never understood why that was until I became a Witch, and then it all became clear that your hair should always grow with the energy of the Moon, and not against it for best results. Another tradition, and one that we have all done, is to light candles on the birthday cake and then make a wish before blowing them out. Why would we continue these traditions? Quite simply, we love practicing *spellcasting* and *wishing magick* on birthdays. Or how about when you were a child and you wanted to go out, but it was raining, and you couldn't go out to play? Did you ever recite, *"Rain, rain, go away, come back next time another day?"* This was a *climate spell.* Or have you ever played jump rope with your friends and counted, "…how many boyfriends (or girlfriends) will you have…" and counted them off before your jumping ends. This was a child's practice of what is called a *divination spell.* I was so bad at Double-Dutch I never really counted off many boyfriends, and now that I stop to think about it, that divination came true…LoL!

So, for the sake of getting started, what is *spellcasting?* I can put it simply in one sentence. *Spellcasting is a practical act of communicating to the Universe one's hopes, ambitions, dreams, needs and desires for the goal of them coming to fruition.* Let's just face it, most spells are indeed self-serving. Some are to help others, and some are strictly devotional in nature as a way of *paying homage* or *dedicating oneself* in spiritual alignment with the Universe. While prayers may have similar goals to spellcasting, there is a real difference between the two. *Prayers* approach the Universe at a position of weakness, subordination, vulnerability, subservience, and imploring. The origin of the word *'pray'* itself is from the old English word for *"I beg"* or *"to plea."* In old Shakespearian plays, for example, you may often hear someone say, *"I pray thee kind sir"* or I pray thee my king." This approach to the Universe or God is to plead a case for one's desires to be met and then to place the outcome in the hands of God.

The *Spellcasting* approach to the Universe is totally opposite in nature. The spellcasting approach to the Universe is in a position of power, strength, co-manifestor, or co-creator, and from an *"I AM the Universe"* viewpoint. This sends a message to the ether that one is a part of the divine energy as opposed to approaching the Divine as an untouchable outside entity. This is important, because in the belief of those who manifest, what you relay to the Universe is what you are. If one says for example, that *'I can't seem to learn anything'* or *'No one loves me'*, the Universe will continue to make it happen. So, presenting oneself as *lowly,* or less than, relays to the Universe that they want no power. Spellcasting works best when a practitioner presents personal power along with goals, while acknowledging oneself as a part of the *Universe, Source* or as part of *God/dess.*

So, what are the attributes of practicing good spellcasting? I have listed a few of my methods through the years:

1) Discern what you truly want to get accomplished and write it out.
2) Write your *Incantations* in *rhyme* if at all possible and to the best of your ability.
3) *Cleanse* and *Consecrate* your tools.
4) Apply *Sympathetic Magick* to your spells when at all possible.
5) Find the best *Astrological* and or *Chronological* time period to perform the spell.
6) Dress for *Magickal Success.* Even your birthday suit (*skyclad*) can work well.
7) Casting a circle before the spell can help in many ways.
8) Raise a *Cone of Power or Energy.*
9) Using *Visualization* and *Meditation* helps to direct energy.
10) After the spell *imagine your spell manifesting* to your desired outcome.
11) Give the Universe *a way for you to receive what you want manifested--As Above ~ So Below..*

CREATING YOUR SPELL

So, you decided to cast a spell, but you are having trouble deciding how to start. I have always started from the beginning. As stated in the beginning of the lesson, spellcasting is a way of communicating with the Universe and relaying a desired *goal* and *intention* in order for that intention to be clearly proclaimed and for it to be actualized.

WRITE OUT YOUR OUTCOME

So, the first step in creating a spell is to write what you want to manifest, and if it is something in a series of steps write that out too, even if it is just in an outline. For example, say you want to get a promotion. You then write what you would like to see happen. You write out that you went into work and your supervisor calls you into the office. The supervisor has a big smile on their face, and they tell you that you got the promotion. They also tell you about the pay increase of an additional $20,000 per year. You then go out with your friends, coworkers and your spouse to celebrate. Believe it or not, just writing out your goal sets in motion your spell before you even light a candle. Everything we create, physically or spiritually begins with a dream or conception. Writing out your dream begins your communication with the Universe. What you have written can also be used as a petition when you begin your spell. After writing your goals and intentions then begin writing what you wish to say to the Universe, in order *to speak it into existence.* This is your *incantations.*

RHYMING YOUR SPELL OR INCANTATIONS

I have noticed where many seasoned Pagan writers and fellow Witches, write that a spell does not have to be done in rhyme. To a great extent that is true. But, perhaps, they write that because they find rhyming not that easy or not very easy for many of their readers. For sure, arranging a spell in rhyme can be a difficult task for most of us. Many of us do not have that right-brain creativity or even the patience to take the time to place it in rhyme. But if you can challenge yourself at all to create a spell in rhyme, I would highly suggest that you do so, and for four reasons. The *first reason* is that the ancient Witches created spells in rhythmic patterns long before recorded history. When you think about it, they didn't do it just for fun. Well, maybe they did, but I am sure that they also did it because they found it more effective. Something that is so venerable, and continually done from time immemorial, has to be paid attention to. The *second reason* is because spells in rhyme are easier to remember. Rhyming makes memory patterns in the brain that can be more easily accessed for recall when needed for repeat spells. The *third reason* is that it informs the Universe that you are willing to go the extra step to reach your goal. That in itself is an act of reinforcing a spell. The *fourth, and most important reason* is that the Universe works on frequency that enacts vibrations. All types. Poetic rhymes have distinctive rhythmic frequencies like ABAB schemes and stanzas and other numerous vibrations the Universe runs on. Since frequency patterns are the language of the Universe it would make sense that we would want to create a more magickal environment to improve our chances for a more favorable outcome. It is like speaking the birth tongue of someone you want to impress. Sure, they may speak plain English but think of how you would influence them by speaking your ideas in their native African or French language. There are even some schools of thought that believe spells are best stated in *Latin* since Latin is an ancient language. But that should be saved for another discussion. While it is not always possible to put our spells in rhyme, especially when casting in a pinch, and may not always be necessary to do so, it is always more advantageous and more favorable when we can.

CLEANSING AND CONSECRATING TOOLS

Cleansing the Tool

When we receive new tools for our spiritual practices it is always beneficial to cleanse the tools before using them. The reason for this is because no matter where we get our tools or who we get them from, there is always a chance that the tools were exposed to energy that is not conducive for our magick. Even if the tool came from a store, or was given to us from a loving friend, or if we found it at a Witch's swop, it is to our benefit to make sure that the tool is free of energy contamination. Energy contaminates can adversely affect our magick.

There are many ways to spiritually cleanse a tool. Most find that the best way to cleanse their tools is working through the elements: *Air, Fire, Water* and *Earth*. I have left out the Element of Spirit here because I personally use the element of Spirit for Consecrating. Below find in **Exhibit 6.1** a few suggestions for cleansing tools, but there are many other ways.

<table>
<tr><td colspan="2">Cleansing Tools by Element
Exhibit 6.1</td></tr>
<tr><td>Air</td><td>1) Place the tool outside during a windstorm or hefty breeze.
2) Smudge with frankincense, myrrh, rosemary, rose petals, lavender, sage or any other purification incense.</td></tr>
<tr><td>Fire</td><td>1) Pass the tool above burning candle or open fire and recite words or incantation for cleansing.
2) In meditation, visualize Witch's fire burning all negative energies from the tool.
3) Place the tool in direct warm sunlight and allow the tool to bathe in the sunrays for purification.</td></tr>
</table>

Water	1) Dip the tool in river or ocean water and allow negative energies to be released from the tool. 2) Briefly dip the tool in water with a pinch of sea, kosher, table or black salt. 3) Place the tool under an open faucet and visualize the running water washing away black or dark negative energies down the drain.
Earth	1) Bury the tool in the earth and allow the soil to absorb negative energies and purify. 2) Bury the tool in the sand and allow the soil to absorb negative energies and purify. 3) Lay the tool in a flower garden or patch of green herbs so as to neutralize the tool. 4) Place the tool in a container and cover it with table, black, kosher or any variety of salt.

It is best to also use discretion when choosing cleansing techniques. Choose the technique that is best for the tool. Techniques with salt can be corrosive and rust certain metals. Crystals that are water soluble can be damaged in water. Some people place their tools in the elements for only a few minutes, and some leave them in the elements for many days. This is totally at the discretion of the practitioner.

Consecrating the Tool

The purpose of *consecrating tools* is simply to make the tool sacred for one's use. It is for informing the Universe of one's intentions for its use, and to inform the tool itself of its purpose. Unlike spiritual cleansing of the Wiccan tools, many Pagans don't believe in the necessity of consecrating tools. Many believe that a tool is assigned its purpose and made sacred upon its first use by the practitioner, thereby imbuing the energy during the first spell or ritual. Others feel the act of consecrating a tool is vital for the spiritual relationship between the article and the practitioner. It is like having a hand-fasting with one's tool. Any magickal workings the magician does afterwards would only empower the tool even more.

For consecrating a tool, feel free to cast a circle first. Then say incantations that speak to the tool or do one's own declaration.

MORE ABOUT SYMPATHETIC MAGICK

Sympathetic Magick has been discussed in this entire study in great detail and possibly even ad nauseum, but if you don't get anything else out of this study you are sure to get the Sympathetic Magick part down. At the risk of beating a dead unicorn, however, Sympathetic Magick is *Metaphorical Magick* that works with the *Law* or *Principle of Correspondence*—like attracting like. To many practitioners Sympathetic Magick brings a lot of value to a spell because it uses symbolism to harmonize a spell with one's desired outcome. Thus, you are using synchronizing energy patterns to relay one's spellcasting. What does this all mean? A spell's outcome, I find, works better when the magician is in what I call *spiritual vibration mode*. If the practitioner is not *feeling it* then a spell has little chance to give a good outcome. Sympathetic Magick helps the practitioner get into the *zone* to evoke magick and to manifest. It is visual and/or aroma meditation for synchronization. For more detail, please review Sympathetic Magick in the previous lessons.

Some of the best items to use for Sympathetic magick are *colors* and *herbs.* Use the following for candle magick and other items:

Colors and Magickal Properties

|**Red**| Passion, courage, energy, root chakra, strength, power, blood healing, Mother goddess, menstrual, warrior magick or willpower.

|**Yellow**| Intellect, inspiration, imagination, knowledge, divination, solar chakra, empowerment, masculine energy, clarity, positivity or Sun energy.

|**Pink**| Love romance, newness, child, or baby magick, emotional healing, affection, lover or friendship or inner peace.

|**Green**| Prosperity, employment, money, fertility, heart chakra, health, good luck, money, healing, abundance, Earth or productivity.

|**Purple or Indigo**| Royalty, ascension, meditation, third eye magick, connecting with Divinity, wisdom, leadership, Crone magick, the sacred or high mysticism.

|**Orange**| Insight energy, attraction, vitality, stimulation, wellness, creativity, sacral chakra, Sun magick, curative energy or positivity.

|**Blue**| Serenity, peace, truth, wisdom, protection, tolerance, inspiration, communication, justice, harmony, throat chakra, therapy or healing.

|**Black**| Banishing, releasing negative energies, transformation, blocking, shielding, enlightenment, invoking power, baseline, involution, shadow work, drawing or invoking energy.

|**White**| Cleansing, clarity, new beginning, spiritual growth, understanding, hope, purification, openness, or a substitute for any other colored candles.

|**Brown**| Grounding, Earth magick, balance, to calm, animal magick, home magick, foundation, stability, security, root magick, stabilization or to anchor.

|**Gray**| The in-between, time of contemplation, neutrality, without judgment, reserve, binding magick, uncertainty, unseen or between worlds.

Herbs

Herbal Magick or herbal workings is the art of using herbs in spells, potions, and rituals. If a Witch is like me, they also use them as a way of life in gardening, sacred baths, healing and drinking in teas.

For spells, all herbs have their own characteristics as in color magick. So, based on the need of a spell the herb is chosen to be used by the practitioner. When selecting herbs for magick do research on which one is best for you. Below are just a sample of a few herbs I have used and their magickal properties:

Herbal and Their Magickal Properties

- |**Angelica Root** – **teas, potions, baths, incense and magickal uses~**| *Magick:* Enhances female power, protects the home, wards off evil, protects children and for guardian call. *Health:* for heartburn, flatulence, plague, loss of appetite, arthritis, circulation, nervousness, and insomnia.

- |**Anise - teas, potions, baths, incense and magickal uses~**| *Magick:* Afro-American rootwork, exorcism, shielding, releasing, eliminating, and mojo bags. *Health:* for digestion, cramps, nausea, bloating, gas, and constipation.

- |**Chamomile Flower** – **teas, potions, baths, incense and magickal uses~**| *Magick:* meditation, luck, money, warding, out of body experiences, solar magick, purification, threshold cleaner, and masculine energy. *Health:* for potassium, digestion, diabetes, cancer, relaxation, anxiety, sleep, skin treatment, menstrual and cramps.

- |**Cherry Bark** – **teas, potions, baths incense and magickal uses~**| *Magick:* love, divination, sex, charm builder, both feminine and masculine aspects for manifesting. *Health:* for coughs, colds, diarrhea, stress, asthma, stomach upset, cardiac issues, digestion, and cramps.

|**Cinnamon – teas, potions, baths, incense and magickal uses~**| *Magick:* healing, spiritual power, love, protection, attraction, prosperity, and high spiritual vibration. *Health:* for antiinflammatory, lowers blood sugar, anti-diabetic, heart health, cancer fighting, and lowers the blood pressure.

|**Dragon's Blood – used mostly in topical potions, baths, incense, pomace, and magickal uses~**| *Magick:* power, purification, protection, fire, love, consecrations, meditation, and invoking guardian. *Health:* mostly topical use—anti-inflammatory, woundhealing, antiviral and topical ulcers.

|**Damiana – teas, potions, baths, incense and magickal uses~**| *Magick:* luck, love, aphrodisiac, conjugal relations, magickal energy, clairvoyance, divination, and spell enhancement. *Health:* for antispasmodic, menstrual cramps, helps nervous system, anti-depressive, insomnia, asthma, diuretic, and constipation.

|**Devil's Shoe String** (*Hobble Bush or Vibrunum Alnifolium*) **– teas, potions, baths, incense and magickal uses~**| *Magick:* Hoodoo uses, breaking curses, good luck, finding jobs, tying, binding, money, success, mojo bag, and protection to trip up harmful enemies. *Health:* for anti-spasmodic and promotes intestinal cleansing as a mild stimulant or tonic.

|**Elderberry – teas, potions, baths, and magickal uses~**| *Magick:* goddess magick, protection, faery magick, home security, exorcism, blessings, and Crone and guardian magick. *Health:* for vitamins A, B, C, immunities, headaches, stress, kidney issues, fever, preventative for cold and flu.

|**Jasmine Flowers – teas, potions, baths, incense and magickal uses~**|*Magick:* sensual, spiritual, love, moon

magick, clairvoyance, sacred feminine, meditation, and money. *Health:* for immunities, brain tonic, cancer fighter, diabetes, heart, energy, stress, and good for the skin.

|**High John the Conqueror Root Flowers – baths, incense, oils and other magickal uses~**| *Magick:* Hoodoo magick, luck, success, personal power, money, prosperity, libido, door openings, and mojo bag protection. *Health:* its primary use is for magickal workings and is not recommended for human consumption.

|**Lavender Flowers – teas, potions, baths, incense and magickal uses~**| *Magick:* attraction, banishing, finding joy, psychic dreaming, purification, love, smudging, and protection. *Health:* for anxiety, depression, insomnia, stress, and dementia.

|**Lemon Grass – teas, potions, baths, incense and magickal uses~**| *Magick:* cleansing, purifying, aura cleansing, positive energy, clarity, exorcism, shapeshifting, and divination. *Health:* for digestion, metabolism, cold or flu, hypertension, diuretic, abdominal pain, and antibiotic.

|**Life Everlasting – teas, potions, baths, incense and magickal uses~**| *Magick:* Gullah Low Country magick, promotes long life, immortality, spiritual growth, health, vigor, and adds potency to any ingredients of a spell. *Health:* for anti-inflammatory, sedative, astringent, digestion, gallbladder issues, water retention, and rheumatism.

|**Mugwort – teas, potions, baths, incense and magickal uses~**| *Magick:* feminine energy, spirit guide magick, Moon magick, divination, psychic world, dreams, finding balance, purification, and protection. *Health:* for diarrhea, constipation, indigestion, worms, helps the liver, energy booster, helps anxiety, and depression.

|**Pine Needles – teas, potions, baths, incense and magickal uses~**| *Magick:* spiritual cleanser, attracts money, exorcism, immortality, masculine energy, and floor wash magick. *Health:* for colds, vitamin A for eyesight, mental clarity, improves hair and skin, purifies the blood, flu, expectorant for coughs, congestion, and sore throats.

|**Polo Santo – teas, smudge stick, oils, potions, baths, incense and magickal uses~**| *Magick:* smudging, cleansing energy, divinity, calm, emotional, and spiritual clarity, enhances healing, instilling blessings, well-being, promotes spiritual endeavors. *Health:* for relieving colds and flu symptoms, stress, anxiety, is antiviral and antibiotic.

|**Red Chili Pepper – teas, potions, baths, incense and magickal uses~**| *Magick:* exorcism, vanquishing evil, masculine energy of Mars and Shango, spicing up one's life, aura cleansing, strengthening, and breaking curses. *Health:* for vitamins A, C, and B6, weight loss, pain reliever, antibiotic, helps stomach ulcers, reduction of cholesterol and diabetes.

|**Roses – teas, smudge stick, oils, potions, baths, incense and magickal uses~**| *Magick:* Wiccan magick, finding love, feminine energy, luck, intuition, satchel magick, good health, healing, protection, and spiritual devotion. *Health:* for vitamin C, antioxidants, headaches asthma, anti-inflammatory, exorcism, mood enhancer, and helps digestion.

|**Rosemary – teas, smudge stick, oils, potions, baths, incense and magickal uses~**| *Magick:* Both male and female energy, brings luck in marriage and weddings, cleansing, house magick, good health, exorcism, smudging, charm and satchel magick. *Health:* for iron, calcium, vitamin B-6, memory and brain, immune system, healthy hair, and digestion.

|**Rue:** *Take caution, using this in excess may cause liver damage* - **teas, oils, potions, baths, incense and magickal uses~**| *Magick:* exorcism, herb of warriors to stop enemies, charm magick, clears third eye blockage, purification, warding, and vanishing. *Health:* for digestion problems, respiratory system, artery conditions, antiinflammatory, arthritis, and toothache.

|**Sage – teas, smudge stick, oils, potions, baths, incense and magickal uses~**| *Magick:* sacred to Pagans, protection, purification, Crone magick, consecrating, healing, wisdom, prosperity, manifesting, spell booster, and for good luck. *Health:* for antiinflammatory, antioxidant, oral health, anti-carcinogens, diabetes, heart health, and skin health.

|**Skullcap – teas, smudge stick, oils, potions, baths, incense and magickal uses~**| *Magick:* Hoodoo magick, exorcism, spiritual cleansing, mojo bag magick, money, good dreams, or good luck. *Health:* for sedative, muscle relaxer, seizure, anxiety, nightmares, healing, insomnia, schizophrenia, menstrual cramps, depression, cancer treatment, sore throat, headaches, and fibromyalgia.

|**Solomon's Seal:** *Take Caution, only the roots and tender young shoots can be consumed safely in excess.* **– teas, pomace, oils, potions, incense and magickal uses**| *Magick:* exorcism, charm/ satchel magick, purification, binding evil, Sage magick or wisdom, healing, sore muscles, inflammation, and smudge or pomace to seal. *Health:* for lung disorders, as diuretic, hemorrhoids, bruises, rashes, ulcers, boils, anti-inflammatory, diabetes, and astringent.

|**Willow Bark – teas, smudge stick, oils, potions, baths, incense and magickal uses~**| *Magick:* Wiccan magick, dreams, scrying, divination, guardian spirit, prophecy, healing, and cleansing.

Health: for acne, gout, eliminating pain, swelling, cramps, colds, arthritis, flu, headaches, and anti-inflammatory.

|**Witches Grass:** *Take caution, not recommended for internal use, and may have unknown side effects* – **smudge stick, oils, potions, baths, incense and magickal uses~**| *Magick:* happiness, good luck, lust, overcoming obstacles, unhexing or uncrossing, exorcism, finding love, eliminating melancholy, spell booster, or charm bag magick.

Health: recommended for an external anti-inflammatory only.

|**Yarrow – teas, smudge stick, oils, potions, baths, incense and magickal uses~** | *Magick:* Warrior herb, healing, enhances power, aura cleanser and healer, keeps enemies away, draws love ones and allies, increases psychic powers and divination. *Health:* for suppression of wound bleeding, menstrual issues, lowering high blood pressure, better circulation, rashes, anti-bacterial, sinus congestion and lowers fever.

CHRONOLOGICAL TIME PERIODS OR WITCHING HOURS

To recap from a previous lesson, *Astrological Magick* are etheric time periods, or events, used to plan magickal workings. This is planning magick based on the stars, planets and time periods. However, we can also use events like birthdays, anniversaries, esbats, sabbats, holidays, etc. We use these events to plan for rituals, ceremonial invocations, spells etc. Some people use *Guardian Number* time periods like *1:11am* or *11:11pm*. Some may use the old school magickal *witching hour* of *12:00am* (the exact time between night and morning.) Some may use the *spirit hour* or what is now called the *new witching hours* of between *3:00am* and *6:00am*. This time period is said to be the time that the *pineal gland* is the most active, and when spirits or Ancestor energies can be highly sensed. Some may believe casting a spell on the time and day of their birth facilitates the release of unawaken energy. Whichever the time that is chosen, it is important that it corresponds to the purpose and the intention of your magickal workings, and the symbolism of whatever the time means to you.

DRESS TO IMPRESS FOR MAGICKAL SUCCESS

A magickal practitioner getting in the mood, or zone or groove to cast a spell is very important. The spells that were the most successful for me were the spells I was feeling. When I felt *witchy*, when I felt the connection, when I felt *sensual*, when I felt *in the groove*, and when I felt that I was a part of the spell itself, were the times when the spells were the most successful. This is why dressing-for-casting can be very important. While we can't always have the opportunity to dress in our favorite garbs to do our best ritual in a pinch, it really helps when we can wear the black silky robes, our most sexy witchy outfits or to just go full out or half-skyclad. It is often the outfit that ignites the vibrations one cast, and it really doesn't hurt to make an effort to impress the universal spirits either.

CASTING A CIRCLE BEFORE THE SPELL

Casting a circle before the spell is key in many ways for a practitioner. Many of us know about the protection given in a safe space in order to practice magick, but it offers much more than that. Casting a circle:

1) defines a sacred space,
2) gives a circumference of magickal protection for a group or an individual to work inside of,
3) signals to the Universe and the guardian spirits that a casting or ritual is about to begin, and,
4) it places the practitioner into a different realm in the spiritual world that can be felt by the magician.

Full directions on casting a circle and closing a circle will be discussed in a following lesson.

RAISING A CONE OF POWER/ENERGY

The Universe is made of energy. It is a constant moving and never static force. It is swirling, flowing, fluid and spiraling energy. When this energy is directed it can build, give birth, create, manifest and can sometimes cause destruction. Because this power exists, often Wiccans and other practitioners conjure the energy within and without when casting spells. They do this by visualization, meditation, singing, chanting, repeating of incantations, dancing, beating drums and playing other instruments like shakers or singing bowls. The Pagan writer Starhawk used the phrase for the universal whirling energy as *"The Spiral Dance"* in her book by the same name (Starhawk, 1999). It is believed that our magickal source of this energy is the *Root Chakra,* which is located at the base of the spine, and it is one of a group of seven, commonly known, energy centers of the human body. The Root Chakra is believed to be the tinder that sparks the energy needed for the *Cone of Power*. This power then rises upwards to the top of the head where the *Crown Chakra* is housed. This energy then forms to a point at the head- thus the name *"Cone of Power"*. The Crown Chakra is our communication point with Spirit or the Divine.

When Wiccans create a Cone of Power during ritual or spells, they use this cone to conjured psychic energy, and to manifest their intentions. This is done by creating it and sending it out into the Universe.

VISUALIZATION AND MEDITATION DIRECTING ENERGY

During the spell, say your incantations and visualize the spell in action. First, do meditation and envision direct energy of light flowing freely from your hands or wand. Visualize light energy flowing from them to carry out your desires. See the light change into what you want it to, and enact what you want to be enacted.

AFTER THE SPELL IMAGINE YOUR SPELL MANIFESTING

After the casting, see your spell, see your intentions and see your desires coming into fruition. Visualize them before it happens and know that it is because of the direct result of your actions. Believe it to be a done deal.

Then thank the Universe for giving your spell that positive outcome.

Give the Universe an Avenue for Delivery

Let's discuss the story of a lady who was sailing her yacht alone and found herself caught in a storm. The storm became a typhoon, and while she landed on a deserted island safe and well, her ship crashed into shreds. Fortunately for her though, she had been a devoted Hedge Witch for many years, so she was close to the Earth and was able to survive. However, her hope was that she would be rescued and taken back to her home. She decided to create an altar, used some natural tools she found, and cast a spell so that she would be rescued. Unfortunately, she was thousands of miles from civilization on an unknown Pacific Island, so her chances of being rescued was next to zero. Our Witch was not deterred. She cast the spell anyway. Months went by and our Hedge Witch never even saw a plane go by. The Witch decided to cast another spell, but this time she decided to increase her odds for a positive outcome. In addition to casting another spell she decided to do two additional things. She had some plastic water bottles so she wrote three notes with her story and her coordinates and placed them in three bottles. Then she threw all three of the bottles into the ocean hoping that the current would take them to civilization. She knew it was a long shot for someone to find any of the bottles, but she figured that it was better than not sending them out at all. The other thing she did was to make a large bonfire and keep it burning so that a passing plane would spot it, and she would have a better chance of being found.

Around one month later a plane spotted her bonfire and landed to find her. The pilot of the plane introduced himself as a scientist working on a nearby island. He said ordinarily he would have gone back home to the states a month ago, and not return for 4 months, but oddly his research took him to a positive breakthrough causing him to want to stay a little longer. He explained that on that day he was working on the beach collecting science samples and he watched a bottle come to shore with paper in it. He read the note and decided to attempt the rescue. He admitted that he might have never found her if it weren't for the fire that she built.

What this Hedge Witch did was to give the Universe a conduit or avenue in which to deliver her desires, even though they were longshots. Would she have been rescued if she had not dropped the bread crumbs for her rescuer to follow? It is possible. But what she did was increase her chances for a successful spell. She made it easier for the Universe to deliver to her, and to expedite the process. She told the Universe what she wanted and she put in the work to get it. Many of us do things like cast spells for a new boyfriend. Then we sit at home and wait for him to knock on the door. Sure, it is possible that the new boyfriend could turn out to be the pizza delivery guy. But one's odds are increased by going out to family events, taking trips, going to spiritual meetups, or even practicing some safe dating board activities. Don't just do a money spell. Rich dead uncles with a will are extremely rare. Give the Universe a way to deliver the money. Start a business or invest. It is like the old adage says: *The Universe helps those who help themselves.*

Ritual, Offerings, Invoking Deity, Casting the Circle and Releasing the Circle

What is a Ritual?

Spellcasting is a practical and symbolic act of communicating one's hopes, ambitions, dreams, needs and desires with the Universe, with the goal of them manifesting or coming to fruition. In contrast, a *ritual* may include a spellcasting, but not always. It is a ceremony with various degrees of magickal pomp and circumstance that one may include with the spellcasting. This may comprise of music, chanting, meditation, spiritual bath, tool consecration, tool cleansing, prayer, dancing, pouring of libations, deity or Ancestor invocation, giving of offerings, initiations and self-initiations, spiritual devotion, healing practices, journeying, divination, the celebration of sabbats, holy days and esbats, the sharing of food and drinks etc. Spells are sometimes cast without rituals, but for the most part many practitioners plan some sort of rites with their casting. Rites can be as substantial as performing a hand-fasting (marriage), performing an initiation, devotional, or even a rite of passage ceremony. On the other hand, rites can be as simple as giving an offering and pouring libations.

Magickal rituals are, more often than not, very important to Pagans and Witches. It is through rituals Pagans attune themselves with the rhythms of divine frequency, Nature and or communion with others. It is through ritual that a Pagan's practice evolves and connects to that which gives them growth, power and change. For many Wiccans rituals are often done on sabbats and esbats. But they can also be done at any time or day. They can be performed by a single solitary practitioner or by a group of Witches and or Pagans. Some Pagans dedicate one day a week to do a devotion ritual. Some rituals are well planned, some are given a standard ritual, some are scripted and some are performed with utter and complete spontaneity.

Wiccan rituals include altars with the basic tools like chalices, pentacles, wands, incense, crystals, athames, cauldrons etc. Wiccans wear street clothes, Pagan robes or go skyclad.

Some of the basic practices of a Wiccan ritual include:

1) Casting of the Circle,
2) Calling of the Watchtowers or Spirits,
3) Giving of Offering,
4) Purpose, Intentions or Goals,
5) Spellcasting,
6) Food and Drink Sacrament,
7) Showing Gratitude and Paying Farewell to the Spirits and

8) Releasing the Circle.

While these are the basic sequences of framework, as stated above, a ritual can include other ceremonial practices.

CASTING OF THE CIRCLE

The act of casting a circle is the drawing of a spiritual line between the area of magick and the mortal plane. It defines where magick and ritual will take place and where it ends. It defines that space which is *sacred* (sacred space). It also alerts the Universe that magick or magickal workings are about to begin.

There are many ways to cast a circle. One way in which I have cast a circle is with an athame or a besom/broom or a wand. First determine how big you wish to have a circle for your magickal workings. Make sure that it is big enough to accommodate all attendees and all the tools needed for your ritual. Once you decide the width that your circle will be, then point one of the tools downward to draw the circle in a clockwise or *deosil* motion. In your mind's eye, visualize a blue light drawing a circle defining your sacred space. I usually trace the circle three times in order to make sure the circle is reinforced. It is best to make sure your tools and altar are within the circle you cast, and make sure you have everything you need within the circle you cast. Believe me it is an awkward experience, to say the least, forgetting a tool you needed and having to step outside the circle to get it.

The other technique I have been using lately is to draw a circle with a burning sage wand. I use the smoke of my sage to outline my circle as I repeat the words, "I create the circle." When I have smudged the outline of my circle 3 times with the wand, I then know that my circle has been completed. The final way I have seen people cast a circle is to simply walk around 3 times the perimeter to where they want their circle. Visualize creating a force field as you walk the perimeter of your created circle. Walk the perimeter 3 times clockwise to reinforce it. Think happy thoughts when creating the circle, especially when you are walking the circle. Again, regardless of what technique is used to cast a circle *deosil or clockwise is the direction* when doing so.

CALLING OF THE WATCHTOWERS OR SPIRITS

Once your circle is cast the next step is to know what direction is *north, south, east* and *west* in the circle. A compass would help here. If you don't have a compass just memorize where the sun rises (east) and sets (west). Next, be prepared to call upon the protectors, the guardians or what Wiccans call the *Watchtowers* or the *Four Quarters* or the *Quarter Masters* within your circle. Watchtowers are *the elemental* and *directional spirits* that are invoked to protect you as you perform your ritual. These directions are the elements and characteristics as shown below:

Some practitioners also honor the *Spirits Above the Earth* and the *Spirits Below the Earth.* Which are hailed last. The hail to the spirits can be elaborate or simple. The hails can be long or short. For now, I will offer some simple hails to use. See **Exhibit 7.1** for the corresponding directions, elements, Orisha energy and the spiritual energy of the directions that you might want to use.

Exhibit 7.1			
Direction	**Element**	**Orisha Energy**	**Spiritual Energy**
East	Air	Oya	Intellect
South	Fire	Shango	Motivation/Movement
West	Water	Oshun	Emotion/Drive
North	Earth	Yemaya/Ogun	Knowledge/Creation/Nurture

Giving Hail

I call upon you, the Ancient Watchtowers (or the Elements or the Guardians if you prefer), to protect as I perform magickal workings.

Face the East, then say,

Guardian of the East—Intellectual Spirit of Air, I call upon you and ask that you be with me (or us) *now. I need your inspiration and your protection.*

Now envision either a blueish mist, or a spirit guardian, or a column of light, or anything you wish the Watchtowers to be for this element. I have on occasions called to Oya as an air guardian within a community circle.

Face the South, then say,

Guardian of the South—Manifestational Spirit of Fire, I call upon you and ask that you be with both now. I need your vitality and your protection.

Envision a wall of fire or a fire guardian appearing. Here you can call to Shango if you prefer.

Then turn to West and say,

Guardian of the West—Emotional Spirit of Water, I call upon you and ask that you be with both now. I need your motivation and your protection.

Envision your water guardian materializing. Here you can call to Oshun as guardian if you prefer.

Finally, turn to the North and say,

Guardian of the North—Nurturing Spirit of Earth, I call upon you and pray that you be with both now. I need your wisdom and your protection.

Visualize the last spirit coming towards you in your desired image. Visualize a mountain, a rock Spirit or a tree Spirit. Here you can call to Yemaya or Ogun as your Earth guardian if you prefer.

At this point you may want to look up and call to the *Ether Spirits* above, and then look down and call to the *Nether Spirits* below, and then asked them to also be with you. Then verbally declare that the circle has been cast. You have now completed the casting of your circle.

Blessed Be~

GIVING OF OFFERINGS

It is customary to give an *offering* to deity or the Universe after the circle has been cast. This is a courtesy, like bringing flowers to someone you are having dinner with. It is basically an act of showing devotion, appreciation or a small symbol of love and respect. The act of giving an offering is an act of placing energy into the ritual, which is the energy of giving.

Articles given for offerings are up to the practitioner. Some offer the favorites of a particular deity. For example, when paying devotion, Oya is partial to eggplants, plums and tobacco, and Oshun loves pineapples, honey and oranges served on gold or brass mirrors. Papa Legba loves rum and cigars. Study the deity you wish to pay tribute to. Some practitioners prefer to give based on the theme of the spell or ritual. For example, for a love spell apples or pomegranates are among the best suited. For a money spell many would consider giving avocados, green apples or leafy greens and herbs. Such themes contribute to sympathetic magick. For Afrocentric sensibilities or the African Diaspora perhaps foods from the homeland or island would be best such as jackfruit, okra, coconuts, plantains, or yams. Most certainly foods or offerings in which we make, grow and or cook, can make for the best favor to the patrons and the spirits, because of the energy we placed in them.

Sacrifices

Sacrifices are a little different than basic altar offerings. In some other spiritual communities, a sacrifice may be offering live animals during ritual. In Wicca, sacrifice is a *personal* expense and not that of another sentient being. To Wiccans, sacrifice is giving up something at a light hardship to *oneself.* For example, if someone gives their last dollar, for the week, to someone else, knowing it would be some time before getting paid again, this to Wiccans would be considered a sacrifice. Eating a sandwich because you are hungry but sharing half of it to a hungry dog or another human being, knowing you won't be full with half, is a sacrifice. Even giving up part of a favorite food for an altar offering that your aunt made for you is a sacrifice *(especially if she is a good cook)*, because it is something that is hard to replace. Some Witches even believe that *fasting* before a ritual is a sacrifice of giving up food. Not only does it prove a dedication, but that it allows one to enter the spiritual realm easier, since eating food tends to ground. Sacrifices don't have to be that big of a hardship, but it is a giving of oneself in earnest. Giving sacrifices before ritual is an energy of giving that will resonate within one's magickal circle, and it is a *karmic* act that extends into one's everyday life.

Universal Offerings

Universal offerings are offerings of charity. They can be thought of as *paying something forward.* It can be random acts of kindness, a donation to the homeless, feeding birds in the park or just an act of giving to those in need. It doesn't have to be a hardship offering. It could be the act of volunteering one's time for a worthy cause. It doesn't have to be too big an act, but it can bank up on karma. As an example, when my daughter was about to graduate from college, she really needed an internship. She had an interview at school to intern as a buyer for a very well-known theme park. They only needed 3 or 4 interns and my daughter was a minority in a majority school. Everyone wanted that job. I decided to help my daughter out and give her an edge. I let her know I was lighting a candle for her. I was doing a ritual anyway so I decided to also do a petition for her. Before the ritual I stopped by the store for some green offerings. At the counter I was asked to give to a charity. I decided to do it. I normally give anyway, but I made sure to do it that time as a universal offering. Needless to say, my daughter was hired for the internship and was the only person of color to get the job. While my daughter is pretty persuasive and shrewd, doing the petition and the universal offering gave me that extra peace of mind

In the *Ifa spirituality*, both the *sacrifices* and *universal offerings,* demonstrated above, would be referred to as, *"giving Ebo"*. In the Ifa tradition the principle of Ebo is, *in order to get something, you must give something.* This is the energy of giving and taking. All of these types of offerings work on the *Law of Cause and Effect,* for with the Universe, what you put out, echoes back with universal vibrations.

ANNOUNCING INTENTION, PURPOSE AND GOALS

The next step after the offering is to clearly state one's intention and purpose for the ritual. Having the attitude of, *"This is why I am here and I am badass about it too",* gives a confidence that the spell will be successful. Stating one's intention starts the sequence of vibration to put one's goals into action. The Universe then rides with it. Write your intentions clearly and speak them clearly. I normally ring a bell before I give my intentions and I ring the bell after I have finished the announcement.

SPELLCASTING

Please see the previous lesson for extensive info on spellcasting. Spellcasting is usually performed sometime after the intention. It could be after meditation or after building a cone of power.

FOOD AND DRINK SACRAMENTS

Food and drink sacraments are often practiced in rituals with multiple participants, although it may also be practiced by solitary practitioners in private rituals. The purpose of this sacrament is to pay hail to the *Lady* and *Lord* (God and Goddess) and to honor them. In a group ritual it is also a way of bonding in *fellowship*. It is almost certain to be done in sabbat circles. Food and drink sacraments are a way of spreading blessings to the circle members, much like the Christian communion that many of us have attended on certain Sundays of the month. This ceremony is usually the last thing that is done before releasing the circle.

The food sacraments are usually cake, cookies, freshly-baked breads, wine, ale or non-alcoholic drinks. The food is usually set aside during the rite, and is covered with special cloth. When the ritual is almost complete the food and drink is placed on the altar and uncovered. At this point, some circle leaders, Priestesses or Priests, may lead a food blessing within the circle. It is then that each person is given a baked good and drink. One circle I frequent would offer different types of drinks and would ask if you preferred *leaded* (alcoholic) or *unleaded* (non-alcoholic). Sometimes they would give you your own cup. In Heathen or Norse circles, that I have attended, they were pretty big on sharing, and drinking from the same cup or bottle. Everyone in the circle would be instructed to take a bite of the baked goods. As you bite into the food the leader would say, *"may you never hunger"*. Then the leader would instruct you to take a sip of drink. Then the leader would say, *"may you never thirst"*. If the members of the circle are sharing the same cup or bottle then the bottle is then offered person by person, and each person is given the blessing of *never thirsting* as they drank. There are a few ways to do the food and drink sacrament, but the *"never hunger or never thirst"* blessing is usually stated.

SHOWING GRATITUDE

The energy of showing gratitude to the Spirits being present for ritual, casts its own spell. Be sure to thank deity and the Universe for their attention within your ritual. Thank the Watchtowers for being witnesses and for their protection and energy, then dismiss or release the Watchtowers. To dismiss the Watchtowers, you do as you greeted them but in reverse. Start by facing the North and say:

Guardian of the North—Nurturing Spirit of Earth. I thank you for your wisdom and your protection. For your presence here I am grateful now. May you go in peace to where you dwell, and with a heartfelt kiss I bid you farewell.

Then turn to West and say:

Guardian of the West—Emotional Spirit of Water, I thank you for your motivation and your protection. For your presence here I am grateful now. May you go in peace to where you dwell, and with a heartfelt kiss I bid you farewell.

Then turn South and say:

Guardian of the South—Manifestational Spirit of Fire, I thank you for your vitality and your protection. For your presence here I am grateful now.

May you go in peace to where you dwell, and with a heartfelt kiss I bid you farewell.

Then turn East and say:

Guardian of the East—Intellectual Spirit of Air, I thank you for your inspiration and your protection. For your presence here I am grateful now. May you go in peace to where you dwell, and with a heartfelt kiss I bid you farewell.

If you called upon a god, goddess, Loa or Orisha, in your hail, be sure to also call their names in the farewells. At this point if you had invoked the ancient *Ether Spirits* above, and called to the ancient *Nether Spirits* below, then show them gratitude also and release them. Never leave a Guardian Spirit hanging. While you don't have to recite the *hails* and the *farewells*, to the Watchtowers, the way they are written above, allow them to be a guideline for creating your own. Your hail can be as simple as saying, *"Guardian of the East be with me now for protection"*, and saying, *"Guardian of the East I release you. I am grateful for your attendance and your watchful protection."*

RELEASING THE CIRCLE

You will find that many Pagans use the terms *"opening a circle"* and *"closing a circle."* This always confused the heck out of me when I was a baby Witchling, because it seems to run counter to what it was meant to mean. I use the terms *casting the circle* and *releasing the circle*. Casting the circle means creating the circle, so releasing the circle is done when the ritual is at end. So, since there is no more purpose for the circle you release it, so that it ceases to be. Closing it, to me, sounds like it is made a permanent fixture. Whether you call it closing a circle or releasing a circle, at the end of a ritual you will want to make sure the circle no longer exists. To do this the practitioner reverses the way they created it. If sage was used to smudge the circle and create the perimeter then it is best to do the same thing to erase the circle, but do it counterclockwise or *widdershins*. If the circle was reinforced three times it is a good practice to remove it at least three times to be assured the circle is released. As you walk to remove it keep saying,

"I release the circle." Visualize it dissipating. Once it is done then announce that the circle is now released.

Just before leaving, circle members either sing or recite these parting lines together:

"May the circle be open, but unbroken. May the peace of the Goddess be ever in your heart. Merry Meet, Merry Part, and Merry Meet Again!"

Ethics of Wicca

Ethics of Wicca

As stated in *lesson three*, the difference between Wicca, and *many* other witchcrafts, is that Wicca is a religion. It is a religion because, among other factors, those who practice it are called to *observe* some *ethical guidelines*. Many other practitioners are self-directed and keep their own counsel. How they practice is left to their own discretion and autonomy. While some Witches may disagree and believe that their eclectic practice is a religion, then I would agree and say, a Witch's practice is what a Witch *knows* it to be. *Starhawk's Reclaiming and Goddess Worshiping* movement, for example, is a religion. On the other hand, many Witches take pride in that their personal practice is not a religion, and may think of their practice as a spiritual journey.

It has been my experience that Wiccan guidelines are basically of two categories. I call these guideline categories *"Direct Wiccan Principles"* and *"Self-chosen Ethical Principles."* Self-chosen Ethical Principles can also be called *"North Star Principles."* This is why Wicca is a calling. The very nature of witchcraft is the freedom to be. For thousands of years the practice of witchcraft has been suppressed all over the planet by the patriarchal religions, so it stands to reason that the majority of Witches believe that they should no longer have any restraints in their magick, ethical or otherwise. This is so very understandable.

For those of us who choose to follow the Wiccan religion, and its ethical observances or principles, it is not a choice, it is a calling. It is a calling because we are drawn to *ethical missions, redes and creeds.* Like the *Knights of the Round Table,* or the *Dora Milaje Warriors of Wakanda,* we wield our magickal swords, seeking certain principles, which is selfsatisfying. This is not to say that only Wiccans follow *positive principles,* because that would never be true. Many eclectic Witches, for example, are Lightworkers. But since this study is mainly about Wiccan practices, only Wiccan ethical principles will be discussed here.

The word *observance,* in our principles, is used very loosely here. Its meaning is to *witness, pay respect to,* and to *educate oneself* on the meanings of the ethical context of our principles. It does not mean that they should be strictly abided by or adhered to under all circumstances. It does mean that Wiccan practitioners acknowledge them as frameworks to be used as references. How much to use and how little is entirely up to the judgment of the Wiccan, but as Wiccans, our practice calls for the weighing of our principles when we are at a fork in our journey. In all of witchcraft, sovereignty is what gives a Witch their power. But all Witches, their lifestyles, beliefs and their circumstances are definitely not the same. Therefore, it is up to the judgment of the Wiccan as to what degree they wish to use, or follow through on these principles.

DIRECT WICCAN PRINCIPLES

Direct Wiccan Principles are guides that are commonly known to be Wiccan, such as the *Wiccan Rede* and the *Charge of the Goddess.* These principles were written by Wiccans for Wiccans. This does not mean that other Pagans and Witches do not use them, because many Witches do.

SELF-CHOSEN NORTH STAR ETHICAL PRINCIPLES

Self-chosen Ethical Principles may be known to be for Witches, Spiritualists, Magi or Pagans, but not contributed as official guides or principles of Wicca. They may also be moral or ethical guidelines or teachings that a practitioner wrote for themselves, received from a mentor, was passed down in a family *Book of Shadows*, or from a family member, or received from other practices or religions like Buddhist affirmations.

Some Direct Wiccan Principles:

1) The Wiccan Rede.

2) The Charge of the Goddess *(The Most Contemporary Version is credited to Doreen Valiente).*

3) Thirteen Goals of a Witch: As found in Scott Cunningham's Book, <u>*Wicca: A Guide for the Solitary Practitioner.*</u>

Examples of What is Often Used for Self-Chosen North Star Principles:

1) The 42 Laws of Ma'at.

2) The Witches Pyramid – *"To Know, To Dare, To Will and To Keep Silent" (Written by Eliphas Levi in 1854).*

3) The Buddhist Gongyo.

4) The Nine Insights of the Celestine Prophecy.

5) EBO - Ethical Principles of Sacrifice (from African Tradition of Ifa).

6) Self-written Principles, Affirmations, or Old Family Principles.

In this lesson we will discuss Direct Wiccan Principles and two of the aforementioned possible North Star Principles.

EXAMINING SOME WICCAN PRINCIPLES

The Wiccan Rede

The *Wiccan Rede* is a type of spiritual *"Golden Rule"* for Wiccans/ Witches. While some credit is given to teachers *Aleister Crowley* and/or *Gerald Gardner* for creating the Wiccan Rede, the truth about its origins is murky at best. According to Mankey (2013), the only contribution found of the Rede, by Gerald Gardner, is what he wrote in his book, <u>The Meaning of Witchcraft</u>, which was published in 1959, and which stated, *"Do what you like as long as you harm no one"*. And even to this point, he contributed the line to an author of other literature.

One of the most used versions of the Wiccan Rede was published by *Doreen Valiente*, who was Gerald Gardener's student, and which was written in the early 1960s. Another popular version was published by *Green Egg E-Magazine* in 1975, called the *"Rede of the Wiccae"* by "Lady Gwen". There are various versions of the Rede now posted throughout the Internet. While the wording changes to different degrees, the heart of the meaning remains. The word *"rede"* is an old English word meaning *"advice" or "counsel"*. Most people think of the Wiccan Rede as just one line, *"and if ye harm none do what thou wilt."* This is unfortunate, because the long or full version of the Wiccan Rede has much more content, and it has wonderful lines of jewels and delightful witchy Crone wisdom in its text.

Below is a rendition of the long version of the Wiccan Rede that was first published by *The African American Wiccan Society's* website in 1999. It was written to have a little more clarity for today's Witch, and it was adapted for the black cultural Spiritualists.

AFRICAN AMERICAN WICCAN SOCIETY'S WICCAN REDE:

With Perfect Love and Perfect Trust

1. Observe the Wiccan spiritual law, and in your endeavors, there'll be less flaw...
2. Love and happiness the Universe bequeaths, the more you give the more you'll receive.
3. Cast your circle and cast it thrice, else spirits will enter ~ pay the price.
4. Fortify your spell and every time, say it that it will rhyme.
5. The Universe speaks but not many hear, so be reverent in all things and it will come clear.
6. As the Lady Moon approaches full, use Her blood as divining tool.
7. As the Lady Moon begins to fade, in your sorrow ask for aid.
8. When the Lady Moon is new, fresh endeavors you pursue.
9. When the Lady is full and ripe, passions are true, so find your type.
10. Give respect to Oya when She works Her broom, for when the dust settles, new flowers will bloom.
11. When energy enters from the east, prepare for adventure and set the feast.
12. When energy enters from the south, be not discouraged, success will out.
13. When energy enters from the west, take it slow, hope for the best.
14. When energy enters from the north, heed its message, bring truth forth.
15. Elder is the Lady's tree, burn other woods, leave Elder be.
16. Turn wheel, wheel turn, on Beltane the fires burn.
17. Wheel turn, turn wheel, light the log when it is Yule.
18. When Winter snow comes out the blue, remember that the *Horned One* rules.

19. Respect all of Nature, bird and tree, for by Our Lady blessed you'll be.

20. Respect the Lady and Lord you must, with perfect love and perfect trust.

21. If you have a dire need, avoid the temptation of immoral deeds.

22. Be careful with whom you lay and sleep for you are judged by the company you keep.

23. Open your door for those in need, friendship and charity plants fertile seed.

24. Bad or good deeds, the threefold law, three times bounce from off its wall.

25. When negative spirits beset you, remember the star and the color blue.

26. Be true to love pound for pound, for what goes about, comes back around.

27. Do these eight words if no others you fulfill: …*and if ye harm none do what thou wilt.*

A different version closer to the original Rede can be found on the *Massachusetts Institute of Technology website* (Witches Rede, 2022).

The Charge of the Goddess

The credit for the creation of *The Charge of the Goddess* is given to both *Gerald Gardner* and *Doreen Valiente*. You can find a copy of Valiente's *Charge of the Goddess* on The Official Doreen Valiente website (Doreen Valiente Foundation, n.d.).

The Charge of the Goddess is an inspirational passage that depicts the universal Goddess speaking to those in the aspects of devotion to Her. It describes who the universal Goddess is to Witches and how Her devotees see Her.

About the Thirteen Goals of a Witch

The Thirteen Goals of a Witch was written by Scott Cunningham in his book: <u>Wicca: A Guide for the Solitary Practitioner</u> (Cunningham, 1996 , p. 151).

The Goals were written to encourage Wiccans to develop a healthy mind, body and spirit, as well as a better magickal practice. The goals are pretty straightforward and comprehensible.

Thirteen Goals of a Witch

1) *Know yourself*
2) *Know your craft* (Wicca)
3) *Learn*
4) *Apply knowledge with wisdom*
5) *Achieve balance*
6) *Keep your words in good order*
7) *Keep your thoughts in good order*
8) *Celebrate life*
9) *Attune with the cycles of the Earth*
10) *Breathe and eat correctly*
11) *Exercise the body*
12) *Meditate*
13) *Honor the Goddess and the God*

If I could add a *14th Principle* I would add, '*Keep an open mind.*' Many of us come into this craft carrying the same old mental processes, skepticisms, cynicisms, negative thoughts and non-disciplines. Freeing the mind of biases, prejudices and putting one's feet in other people's shoes opens *sacred channels*, and helps to free up a channel of free-flowing energy. It clears blockages and gives the *3rd Eye* more clarity. To gain the keys to a kingdom one must escape the mental conditioning and ideas of the oppressor, or the maladies of the oppressor's society. As the actor *Alan Alda* is quoted to have said, "*Your assumptions are your windows on the world. Scrub them off every once in a while, or the light won't come in.*" I always tell my students before you begin your practice try looking into *Shadow Work*. Shadow work helps one to get in touch with the self, and gives a clarity that a Wiccan needs to begin her/his journey into magick.

EXAMPLES OF SOME NORTH STAR PRINCIPLES: SELF-GUIDED PRINCIPLES THAT CAN BE CHOSEN FOR AN INDIVIDUAL'S PRACTICE

About the 42 Laws of Ma'at

Found in the *Egyptian Book of the Dead,* is what is called, "*The 42 Negative Confessions*". They are better known today as the "*42 Laws of Ma'at*". They were called "Negative Confessions" because, in their translation, each principle would start off as, "I have not," as in, "*I have not stolen*" or "*I have not told lies.*" As people began to rewrite them for easier meditations the negative phrases were removed to make more positive affirmations such as, "*I do good*" or "*I keep the waters pure.*" Many people utilize '*The 42 Laws*' for morning or nightly prayer or meditation. Below is a version adapted for *The African American Wiccan Society.* While some words have been changed, the positive intentions remained the same.

42 Laws of Ma'at

1. I honor and practice virtue.
2. I benefit with gratitude and obligation.
3. I am peaceful and I teach peace.
4. I respect the property of others.
5. I affirm that all life is sacred.
6. I give offerings that are genuine.
7. I live by truth.
8. I regard and respect all altars as sacred.
9. I live in the pursuit of truth.
10. I consume only my fair share.
11. I offer words of good intent.
12. I relate in understanding.
13. I honor animals with reverence.
14. I am worthy of trust.
15. I care for Mother Earth.
16. I keep my own council.
17. I speak positive of others.
18. I remain in balance with my emotions.
19. I am trusted in relationships.
20. I seek life's essence.
21. I light my world with beauty.
22. I do the best I can.
23. I communicate with openness.
24. I listen to all viewpoints.
25. I create harmony.
26. I invoke laughter.

27. I am open to love in various forms.

28. I am forgiving.

29. I am kind.

30. I act respectfully towards others.

31. I do not judge others.

32. I follow my inner guidance.

33. I converse with awareness.

34. I do good.

35. I give of myself to others.

36. I keep the waters pure.

37. I learn daily.

38. I honor the Goddess and the God.

39. I am humble.

40. I achieve with integrity.

41. I advance through my own abilities.

42. I embrace the All.

About The Witch's Pyramid

What is now called *The Witch's Pyramid* was first written by a French Transcendental Occult magician named *Eliphas Levi* (1810-1875). These principles were later called The Witch's Pyramid sometime after his death. They are now considered by many to be good foundational guidelines for Witches and Magi to follow. The principles are provided below. Along with them I have written some short interpretations of their meanings in my own view, but they are subject to the interpretation of the individual practitioner's own standpoint.

The Witch's Pyramid

1) TO KNOW ~ *To be a continuous lifelong student of the universal mysteries through continuous study and practical magick, for the purpose of continuous learning.*

2) TO DARE ~ *To go outside of societal norms, work alone, think differently, seek your spiritual truth, and face that which will be revealed to you by the Universe.*

3) TO WILL ~ *To be confident and adept when conjuring, invoking and manifesting. Showing the big "I Am" in one's practice.*

4) TO KEEP SILENCE ~ *To listen and learn, and not to speak of that which the Universe chose only to grant privy to you. Do not tell those who are unworthy of knowing, and especially about any personal sacred and spiritual work one does.*

If you find that the Wiccan tradition is right for you, consider creating a *Book of Shadows* and add Direct Wiccan Principles and/or North Star Principles for yourself. You can also create your own North Star Ethical Principles, or find some that speak to you. Remember that basic Ethical North Star Principles can be principles your grandmother once told you, principles from your coven or circle, or they could even be your favorite bible verses. The choice is up to you.

The Book of Shadows

Congrats to you reader! You have learned the basics of other traditions and Wicca. You have studied the basics of magick and how and when to perform them. You have learned the ethics of Wicca and witchcraft. Now comes what many have awaited thus far: spells and such. But before we get into spells, let's talk about the origins of the word *spell* itself. There is a little bit more on record about the origins of the word "spell" then there is for the words Witch or Wicca. The word spell has roots in the old Germanic languages, such as *"spel"*, meaning to recite, speak, tell stories, talk or even to have discourse. It could also mean to speak slowly or to enunciate. Another older word that is derived from *spel* is *godspel*, meaning telling good stories, giving god's message or giving a good sermon, which is how the church music got the name *gospel* music.

Eventually the word spell began being understood as an *undetermined period of time* in which, I would imagine, stemmed from the old folks asking people to *sit for a spell*, this referring to sitting for a conversation, talk, or for good storytelling. It was also used for periods of working or shift work. They would state that *he is working for a spell in the fields*. It also referred to people going through a time of trouble or sickness like, *she is going through a coughing spell*. I would imagine that, in that context, people would conflate the term as meaning a time of being crossed or cursed with illness. Today we know the word *spell* is a casting of magick that is called from our most inner spirit and sent out to the Universe in order to receive our desires. In other words, a spell is *speaking the word(s)*. This can be in silent meditation or in speaking the spell out loud.

Many people come to witchcraft for the magick of *spellcasting*. But when creating or receiving spells, one wants to have a place to store them for later or future use. This is where a *"Book of Shadows"* comes in. But what is a *Book of Shadows* (or BoS) in the first place?

A *Book of Shadows*, which is also called a *"Grimoire"* or a *"Shadow Diary,"* is a journal of spells, lore, ceremonies, ritual instructions, chants, prayers, herbal lore, potions, recipes, personal records, wise tales, poems or diary entries of thoughts, and/or of dreams. Nowadays it could be an actual book with page entries, but the modern Witch today would most likely have it on a *Disk of Shadows* or a computer *File of Shadows*.

When I first started studying the craft, just short of 30 years ago, I read a lot of interesting yet tragic lore pertaining to where the name, *Book of Shadows* originated. Much of my reading then discussed the *Inquisitions* starting from the 1400s in Europe, and into the early North American colonies, and when witchcraft went into hiding. This period is called by today's Witches, *"The Burning Times"*. It was the time when predominantly women were accused of being Witches and executed and massacred. It is said that, with the fear of prosecution, many of the spell books were hidden in the darkness of old wells, under the foundations of houses, within floors and in old cellars—thus, why they were called *The Book of Shadows*. Most inform that *Gerald Gardner* introduced this term to modern Witches, but the tales of where the name originated is not often told as it used to be.

In this Lesson, *Book of Shadows,* you will be exposed to just a minute taste of what is in a *BoS*. Included will be a few spells, poetry, affirmations, and some wise information. Know that the most effective spell is the one you write yourself. The second most effective spell is the one you find that speaks to your heart. If you find a spell or create a spell that you are not feeling, hold off on using it and find one that does. Spells are like lovers. If you are not feeling it, then it will most likely not work. Feel free to tweak the spells in this lesson, and make them your own. Like any other spell you find, you don't have to use the spell word for word. You can use other herbs and oils with similar attributes that resonate with you. Rewrite the spell for your taste and your deepest desire. As long as the true purpose and intention of the spell remains, it should work well.

Anointing Candles for Spells

Before performing almost any spell, many practitioners prefer to anoint or dress the candle first before using it. Since candles are considered the focus of the spell, and one of the main conduits in which one's main stream of magick flows, then dressing the candle is a way of putting energy in it or assigning your energy to the candle. Many practitioners carve symbols or sigils on the candle with a boline or other tools. Many people also rub oils onto the candles. As I stated previously, I have found that most soy candles do not burn well if too much oil is applied, but beeswax candles do burn well with essential oils. Some Witches dress them up with glitter and magickal herbs and carve purposes, intentions or affirmations on their candles. Some rub the candles to apply their own energy on them. Some Witches even talk to their candle and tell them their will. Remember that, as you dress the candle, you are instilling energy into it as a way of consecration. While you are anointing the candle, or once the candle is dressed, say these words before spellcasting:

Candle of energy, element of fire, bring fruition to this spell as I desire, Spirit be with me until this spell is done, and as always, I ask thee to harm none.

Spell for Consecrating a Tool

As stated in a previous Lesson, *cleansing* a tool is a way of eliminating poor, negative or adverse energy. *Consecrating* a tool is a way of assigning the tool, or spiritually connecting a tool to a practitioner. For the most effective results, I find it best to cleanse a tool on the Full or Waxing Moon, and consecrate the tool on a New Moon. Once the tool is cleansed, cast a circle for consecration. You can also consecrate the tool just before casting a spell. Feel free to anoint the tool with your chosen herbs or essential oil as you recite:

Instrument (or Athame, Cauldron, Besom etc.) of my desire. I speak to you.
I transfer my energy; I flow through you. To work my magick, I do instill,
The power to manifest, do my will.
So, Mote it Be.

You can repeat the incantations three times or as many times as you like until you feel it is done.

Wind Chime Spell for House Protection

It is believed that the sound of bells and chimes ward off negative spirits while producing good karmic energy around them. This may be the reason why so many churches keep bells in their steeples or in their courtyards. It may be the reason that Buddhist monks ring bells or bowls before chanting. The sound of chimes or bells, most often, signals the ringing in of something good or magickal. Wind chimes around the home, on the porch or hanging near the front door can bring good luck, protection and prosperity. On a Waxing or Full Moon hang up a wind chime and say these words:

Chime of beauty, Chime of sound,
Upon this house, spread luck (or love) around,
Guard these doors and windows too,
Keep negative energy from entering through.
So, Mote it Be.

You may wish to anoint the chime while reciting incantations, with a protective element like rose oil, lavender oil, peppermint oil, clove oil or frankincense oil. It would also be a good idea to sage your home before the chime spell.

New Moon Wealth Ritual

Do this ritual on a Dark or New Moon

For this you will need:

- 1 Green candle to burn during ritual.
- Angelica Root to burn and summon the spirits of *Prosperity*.
- A little bit of dried oats to signal wealth and foundation.
- A green herb for prosperity. You can either use dried rosemary, patchouli or basil.
- Self-initiating charcoal and censer for burning.

1) Take a green herbal salt bath (optional)

2) Dress your candle (optional)

3) Cast your circle

4) Light the candle

5) Light the charcoal

6) Sprinkle some of the Angelica Root on the coals when hot, then sprinkle some of the dried green herbs.

7)   Meditate on the good things to come for you.

8)   When you are done meditating say:

To the Mother and Sire,
Let the Universe Conspire,
To Manifest My Desire,
Let My Energies Control My Destiny,
My Path is to a Wonderful Job, and Prosperity,
Spirits of Fortune I Summon Thee,
That All Roads and Doors are Open for Me,
Love and Money Will Come Freely.
AS I Will It, NOW It SHALL BE!

Now sprinkle the rest of the oats and green dried herbs on the charcoal and say:

Ase Create, Ase Manifest, Ase Do No Harm!!!

9)   Thank the Spirits and Release the Circle

10) If you can, throw the cold ashes outside and around your front door so that *Fortune* will know what door to enter through.

Wishing Spell

Some wishing spells are petitioned by a practitioner through one of the elements. They are either blown away into the air, floated away on water, buried into the earth, or burned into fire. One of the most magickal of them are the *wishing spells of air*, because of what the element itself naturally does for the senses and the spirit. I am sure that most of us can remember finding a feathery bristled dandelion, plucking it and making a wish before taking a breath and blowing its pappus into the wind. Little did we all know this was one of the most perfect spells of air, because when blowing its pappus we were, in effect, blowing the fertile seeds of our desires.

The best time for wishing air spells is in Autumn, when leaves are just starting to fall and the air is really breezy. The best wishing spells are the simplest ones, like blowing out candles on a birthday cake. The following *air wishing spell* is a very uncomplicated one. Try to do this during a Full, New or Waxing Moon, but any time is good fun.

Leaf Wishing Spell

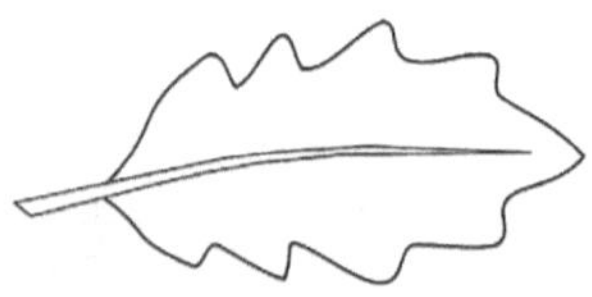

This spell is best done in the Autumn. On a very windy day, find a nice wide leaf that has fallen and is dry enough to write on, but has a little green on it for prosperity or luck. Get a marker. It could be black or dark green or dark blue. Write your wish on it. Then go to the highest place you can find, like a window, or balcony, or hill. If you can't find a high place, anywhere there is a good wind to carry it is fine. Sprinkle a pinch of cinnamon over the leaf. Wait for the next good breeze and say:

Leave leaf, go, blow away.
Make my wish come back true, very soon someday.
And harm none. It is done.

Then release the leaf and allow it to blow away into the wind and know that your message will be received by the universal forces. This spell can also be done by floating it away in a river or stream. You would just say instead, *"Leave leaf, float away."* A bay leaf is also a good substitute for an Autumn leaf.

Inspirational Divination Jar

 Many mornings we may wake up not knowing what is ahead of us. That feeling of insecurity when beginning the day may be alleviated by just reading a daily affirmation. A universal message from an elder sage, a spoken word, or prophet always helps. Creating your own inspirational divination jar is easy, and is a good way of seeking insights from Elders, Sages or Ancestors like: *Buddha, Alice Walker, Confucius, Sonia Sanchez, Tupac Shakur, Iyanla Vanzant, Common, Nipsey Hussle, Toni Morrison, Martin L. King, Les Brown, Luisah Teish, Mahatma Gandhi, Ida B. Wells, Dick Gregory, HH the Dalai Lama, Cornel West, Chief Seattle, Maya Angelou, Nikki Giovanni, Socrates, Pluto, Langston Hughes, Malcolm X, Gloria Steinem, and Wayne Dyer* are just a few who come to mind. You can even use an old saying, or an inspirational gem that your mother or family member may have passed on to you.

This jar can be placed on your altar, beside your bed, or in any sacred space that is accessible to you in the mornings. It can be an instrumental spark of inspiration every morning to start you on your way. To create this jar, you will need:

1) A 1-quart or a 2-quarts jar or canister that is decorative or can be decorated. Attempt to get one that is not plastic. It can be glass, wooden, metal or clay. It is best to get one with an opening that is big enough for your hand to fit through comfortably and freely. I do recommend that you get one with a lid to keep its contents secure.

2) Cut slips of paper 3 inches x 4 inches or at least big enough to write a sentence or two, and that can be folded. There should be at least 30 of these in order to have one for each day of a month. 3) Tools and material for decorating the jar (optional).

This project will take a little research and perhaps a little time, but once it is done, it will be very much worth it. If you do not buy your jar decorated, please decorate it yourself. In fact, the jar, or any tool, that is imbued with your energy, spirit and creativity will work far better. You can do any number of things like paint it or glue beads and other material to it. You can also paint runes, Ghanaian *adinkras*, sigils, pentacles or Egyptian hieroglyphics if you wish.

The next step is to make a list of your favorite poets, philosophers, thinkers, writers or prophets. Then go online and look for their famous quotes. If you happen not to know of any writers or prophets, you can just google famous quotes or inspirational quotes. Then print or write out the ones you like onto the 3 x 4 cards or paper, and then add them into your jar. Try to make sure there are not any duplicate quotes, and that each one is meaningful to you. When the jar has thirty or more slips of quotes in it, consecrate it on the next New Moon. It will then be your inspirational tool for your morning divinations.

How to Use:

Just before starting your day or going off to work, place your *hand of power* on or over the jar. This is any hand that you feel has the most energy. Then say:

Goddess of Inspiration, Goddess of Love,
Send to me your messenger dove,
To enlighten me as I travel on my way,
Through my sacred journey this day.

Place your hand of energy inside the jar and pull out a random slip of divination. Read the quote until you understand its meaning. Take heed, this is a message that the Universe wants you to know for that day's journey. At this point you can either remove the quote from the jar, so you won't pull it again, or fold it back up and place the slip back into the jar so that you can reread for another day. The method is totally up to you. When replacing, shake the jar up or mix it with your fingers. You can now go on your way feeling prepared and more selfassured. Do this once every morning before starting your day or when there is a need for inspiration. The jar can be replenished with more quotes whenever the feeling strikes you to do so.

Daily Cleansing Spell

If you are like me, you may have a collection of daily washcloths of all types and colors. Years ago, after I began practicing witchcraft, I realized the value of having multiple-colored washcloths, so in the morning when I am about to start my day, I determine what type of day I am having. If I am going to have a day that involves business transactions or need some prosperity, I grab a *dark green washcloth*. If I am going on a date, and I want it to be romantic and successful, I grab a *red one*. If I need concentration for a day full of complexity, I grab an *orange one*. If I want a day of fun, sun and healthy activity I grab a *yellow washcloth*. If I am not feeling well or out of sorts, I grab a *light green cloth* for healing. If I feel the need to be empowered, I use a *purple cloth*. If I am feeling the need for grounding or the need to eliminate negative energies, I use a *brown or black cloth*. I do this regardless if I am taking a bath or taking a shower. I have even been known to do it when I do birdbaths.

This spell uses the element of water to power your energy. As you rub soap on the cloth, visualize the power of your energy flowing through your arm and down into your hand, penetrating the soap as the soap soaks through your wash cloth or *colored wash sponge*. Then apply it to your body, visualizing that energy soaking through you as you say:

Now visualize the energy that is the color of the wash cloth flowing on you with the soap. Feel its energy on you, and assuring you that your desires will be fulfilled. When you rinse, feel, the residue of energy that will be carried with you all through the day. For reinforcing energy use a suitable essential oil along with your soap.

A Quick Spell for Spring or Early Summer

Get, 1 tbsp. of lavender flowers, 1 tbsp. of seeds (any seeds will do like poppy, sesame, coriander, dill or any seeds you don't plan on planting) and a small amount of crushed or powdered eggshells.

Mix the seeds, shells and lavender flowers all together. Lavender for spiritual power, seeds are for sowing prosperity and powdered eggshells are for their magickal congruence. On a Spring morning or evening go outside and toss the ingredients on the soil and say:

Ostara Prosperity Spell

The time of Ostara is a very blessed time. It is a time for growth, newness and a fresh start. It is also thought to be a beginning period of fertility, which makes it an excellent time for a prosperity spell. This prosperity spell is pretty simple, and it also helps one engage in the spiritual season of spring. For best results perform this spell between March 20th – 25th (on or around Ostara.) Here is what you will need:

1) 1 Hard cooked egg by boiling it with a little basil, rosemary, green dye, and a star anise (to represent the goddess Ostara).
2) 1 Green candle (anointing is optional).
3) 1 Marker any color (with a fine point,) or pencil that is dark enough to write across the egg.
4) 1 Bell or gong or rattle.
5) 1 Pinch of cinnamon.

How to Perform the Spell

*Anoint the candle using the anointing spell given previously.
*Light the candle.
*Ring the bell or gong or rattle.
*Now write the following on your green egg in very small print so it will fit:

Magick Egg with Prosperity Light,
Bring Prosperity within My Sight,
Let Money and Wealth Come to Me,
As Rain is this Season,
Let Prosperity Flow Freely.
And Harm None.
It is Done.

It helps if you read the words as you write them. If you don't have enough room on the egg to write every line you can get a small brown bag, write the words on the bag, and place the egg in the bag. Alternatively, you could write the words on a piece of biodegradable paper, and then wrap the egg in the paper.

*Sprinkle cinnamon on the egg, then ring the bell again.
*Go out to bury your egg. It is best to bury it near a tree or bush, but burying it outside y our doorway is a good spot too. *When you bury the Egg say:

Universal Spirit—Fertilize My Home.
Let Prosperity and Abundance Grow, from What I have Sown.
So, Mote it Be.

Qingniao Messenger Spell

In the spirit of the messenger gods like *Anubis, Hermes, Eshu, Th oth,* and *Mercury,* one could dedicate a spell in which a messenger delivers one's desires to the Universe. I have a spell that I have been using for a while. I now call it the *Qingniao* (king-yow) *Messenger Spell.* I named it after I read the lore about beautiful messenger birds called *Qingniao* who delivered messages, to and from a Chinese goddess of Fortune named *Xi Wangmu* (shee wang-mu). The birds were said to be beautiful and colored in either blue, green or black. In some lore they were called crows. I thought the name was appropriate since the spell I use requires a Chinese fortune cookie. This is another simple spell that anyone can do. You will just need:

1) a green, or blue, or black pen, or a pencil will do.

2) a fortune cookie.

3) tweezers (optional).

The first step is to very gently pull out the paper fortune inside the cookie without breaking the cookie. You may need the assistance of tweezers for this. In some attempts you might break the cookie so it is a good idea to have at least 2 cookies on hand. Next you take the fortune and write your desires (money, love, good job, successful business, etc.). I normally read the fortune first. Sometimes the fortune will give you a type of response or commentary to the message you are sending. Just recently I received one that said, *"Your wish is about to come true."* Don't feel awkward that you are writing on top of the fortune. It is all good. You don't have much room to write so make it short, maybe two to three words tops. On the other side of the fortune write the name of your patron to whom you are sending the message. If you don't have a patron to send it to, you can just address it *"to the Universe"*.

The next step is to gently re-insert the fortune back into the cookie. This is not as hard as it sounds. It does go back in without too much trouble. Now your cookie is the envelope of your message and it is all ready to send out to the goddess *Xi Wangmu* or the love goddess *Oshun* or the prosperity god *Ganesh* or *the Universe* or whomever you addressed it to. Take your message and lay it under a tree so that the *Qingniao* (in the guise of a crow or squirrel or etc.) will take it and deliver the message. Then say this incantation:

Qingniao (king-yow), *hear my call,*

Receive this message by beak or paw.

Take this message through time and space.
Deliver it to Divinity's place.
As the Universe sees so shall it be.

Walk away knowing that the message will be delivered and received by the Universe, because the *Qingniao* received the offering or payment of the cookie. Don't feel uneasy about the messenger digesting the message. They will break open the cookie and remove the message.

Three Penny Luck Charm Mojo Bag

 Carry this bag with you to keep luck and fortune. This charmed mojo bag is for bringing money, jobs and prosperity.

You will need:

1) Rose Oil or a Money Oil

2) Sprig of fresh Rosemary

3) Rose Petals

4) Green Candle

5) 3 Pennies

6) Small Satchel Bag for carrying

7. Rose Quartz (or Pyrite or Aventurine or Citrine or Jade) Crystal

This charmed mojo bag is for bringing luck, money, jobs and/or prosperity.

Instructions:

On the day/night before the Full Moon light your candle. Lay all of your articles in front of you. Anoint each penny and your crystal with rose oil and carefully place them inside the bag. Then place the other items into the bag as well. Now anoint the bag with a drop or two of your oil, and as you anoint it say these words:

I anoint thee bag of penny three.
I anoint thee to bring luck to me.
I anoint thee to bring to me, money and prosperity.
So, Mote it Be — It is done.

Say the incantation three times for best results. Next place your mojo bag outside under the moonlight, or place it on your windowsill where the Moon can shine its light to it. Let it remain under the moonlight at least overnight, and through the day of the Full Moon. Remove it the following afternoon, if you wish. Your charm is now ready to carry with you. It is great for carrying in your purse, pants pocket or any carry bag. Rub it between your palms when you need extra luck. Whenever you feel the charm needs to be recharged, add a fresh sprig of rosemary, a few drops of oil and place it under the Full Moon again. This will give it a fresh charge. The more you recharge it the more potent the magick of the mojo bag becomes.

Imbolc Simmering Pot Spell

Here I offer my version of a spell called *the simmering pot* or *simmer pot*. This is a simple spell that will help clear out the old energies of the home, and replace them with new positive energies. It can also bring luck into the home. The season of Imbolc is a time to begin renewal. This is not only a great time for evaluation or changes of the self, but it is also a good time for cleansing the home of the stale shut-in remnants of the Winter season. This spell can also be used any time of year that you feel the need to clear out stale energies, bring in positive energies or feel luck is needed in the home.

To perform this spell on or around Imbolc you will need:

1) One large pot (any large pot will do, but of course the favorite is cast iron.)
2) Water
3) Cinnamon (sticks or powder will do)
4) At least 3 of the following of your choice:
    a) Cloves
    b) Lemon grass
    c) Some drops of your favorite essential oil
    d) Sliced citrus fruit or peels (either lemon or orange or both)
    e) Allspice
    f) An apple sliced
    g) Bay leaves
    h) Lavender
    i) Rosemary
    j) Mint
    k) Basil

To begin fill your pot full with water, place on your stove and allow the water to boil. Once it boils, turn down the heat to allow it to simmer, then add the cinnamon and your chosen 3 or more ingredients. Then visualize the pot radiating with the light of the Sun. Stir the pot clockwise with a spoon and say:

I stir you pot,
You good and hot,
Bring positive energies for this time of renew,
Block unwanted energies from getting through.
And so, it is….

You can also write a wish or intention on a bay leaf and add it in before saying your spell. Make sure your pot has a slow simmer, and allow it to simmer for as many hours as you wish. If the water runs low, feel free to add more water until you feel your spell is done. Take in and enjoy the smells and aromas of this pot as it circulates within the home. Allow it to cool before disposing. I strain mine of the fruit, and then I pour it outside of both my front and back doors for extra good energies.

AFFIRMATIONS AND CHANTS

Wildlife Universal Offering Prayer

One of the ways I give back to the Universe for the blessings I have received, is to feed wildlife. I follow the old saying, *"to whom much is given much is required"*, or as Peter Parker said in Spiderman, *"with great power comes great responsibility."* Being able to eat every day is a powerful thing that many of us take for granted. Many beings and humans may go days without eating on end. Anything that I can offer is my way of giving back to the Universe as it feeds me, physically and spiritually. I feed the wildlife in my backyard at least 3 times a week, in addition to my bird feeder. There I have squirrels, small birds, crows, turtles, rabbits, raccoons, possums, crows, etc. When I give my offering, it is usually at night when the moon is high. That way the night-crawlers can eat too. As I give my offering of food, I say this verse:

> *"Under universal sight, I give my offering tonight, under the moonlight.*
> *May your beings feed, and may the Universe be pleased. Blessed Be."*

Instead of *moonlight,* if you feed during the day, you can say, *sunlight, morning light, daylight* or *twilight.* If there is no Moon you can say, *starlight* or *the sight of night.* Make the prayer your own. The food is normally gone with the morning light. If you live in an urban area and don't have access to wildlife you can take bread, meat or bird seed to a park or green area, and say the prayer there.

AFFIRMATION TO THE MYSTICAL UNIVERSE
This is an affirmation to recite during times of personal spiritual devotion.

Mystical Universe

Let Me Be Who I am Meant to Be.

Open All Doors to Prosperity for Me.

Grant Me the Will to Stand Up When I Stumble and Fall.

Give Me the Endurance to Succeed in My Goals.

Give Me the Strength to Aid Others Along My Journey.

Grant Me the Sight to See that Which I am Meant to See.

Allow Me to Be the Priestess (or Priest) of My Journey,
Laid Before Me.

So, Mote it Be.

A PRAYER TO THE ANCESTORS
I Light a Candle for Thee

Spirits of the Ancestors I call upon thee.

Your life forces are far beyond what we can see.

You are the Ancestors, my Guardians, and my
blood still pumps with thee.

Rest assured you are not forgotten, because you live inside of me.

May your spirits be at peace, and your energy pure light.

Do not concern yourself with the struggle, for it is now
my time to fight.

I only ask that in your protection, you guide me on my way, Keep
me on the straight and narrow, and do not let me stray.

Watch over those who gave me life, and protect
those who depend on me.

Oh, Spirits of the Ancestors, I light a candle for thee.

A CALL TO OYA

Oya, blow your wind our way,

We need Your air and knowledge this day.

Oya, blow Your rain our way,

We thirst for Your passion for life today.

Oya, blow the soil our way,

We need the nurture of Mother-Earth this day.

Oya, blow Your thunder away,

But bring us the comfort of Your arms this day.

Cross Roads Three Sonnet

Many years ago, too many years for me to remember, I was awoken by a spirit. I knew who it was immediately. It was *Papa Legba*. I could almost hear him say, *"Git out of bed gal! There is work ta do."* I immediately arose from my bed and went to my computer. All of a sudden, my fingers began to type. By the time I was done I had created this narrative. To this day I 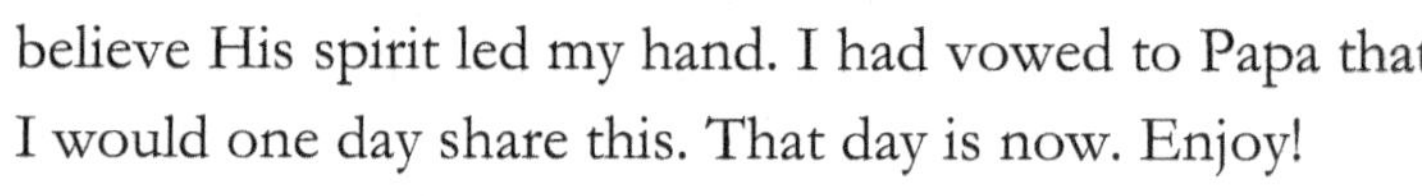 believe His spirit led my hand. I had vowed to Papa that I would one day share this. That day is now. Enjoy!

The Crossroads Three

Three coins I threw beyond my knee, to the crossroads that held the number three. Is it you that I am meant to see—right here and now— at Crossroads Three?

"My you are a feisty gal." Took off his derby and gave a bow.

Nod he did—this ancient Loa, distinctively dressed from head to toe-ah.

"You know spirits like us —we are meant to dance." Put on his hat—he began to prance.

The Midnight hour was more than near. Ancient rhythms I began to hear.

"Come on gal, dance with me, here and now at Crossroads Three."

He wiggled and danced—he was smooth as stealth. I laughed and grinned despite myself.

"That's the spirit-- feel the beat. Dis the reason that we meet." Before I knew it, I lost my pride.

"That's right gal—I need to ride."

We danced below the silver Moon. My heart beat fast, and I began to swoon.

No… no Papa, I pretend aloof, I bring you here to speak the truth.

"So, you want what is in me. Let me see what we can see."

A portal opened within the roads. I peered within its foggy nodes. *"That's right gal—be you be. Look to see what you can see."*

My heart went faint—I swooned again. I feared that I would fall within.

"Stand up gal. Be what you is. You come too far—to succumb to diz."

He pulled out his pipe and began to smoke. My heart beating loud— I began to choke.

I stood up tall—and looked within.

"That's it gal! It's not a sin!"

It told my story— all of me, all my lives and history.

Just when I thought my story was done, my future made a bigger run.

Laugh I did, and then I cried.

Happy I felt, and then I sighed.

Emotions churned deep inside me.

Papa, I asked, is this to be? What I saw — and what I see?

"Be careful what you wish for child. For when you get it—it speaks real loud."

Beside the crossroads, my offering was rum. He picked it up and drank him some.

"Well, my gal, — I wanya ta know. It's nearing time for me ta go."

With that he danced—then made a bow. Tipped his hat—and made a smile.

Papa, I asked, do you have to go?

"Com'on child, you otta know. Keep your eye up to the star, and know you's Papa's never far."

He looked at me and gave a wink. He disappeared within my blink.

I picked up the bottle of leftover rum, pulled out the cork, and drank me some.

I looked into the midnight sky, threw Papa a kiss and said goodbye.

~Goodbye Papa Legba~

RECIPE

Lil' Sis Hacked Sweet Pie

When I was a child in Philly, we had a neighbor named Miss. Johnson. She lived in a house directly in front of my family's row house. Miss. Johnson was a beautiful, dark-skinned, middle-aged to older woman who wore her hair tied back in a bun. I don't completely remember what she looked like. I only remember her from head to shoulders because the only time we ever saw her was when she was sticking her head out of the first-floor window. Miss. Johnson was our unofficial community-watch person. Nothing ever happened, in our neighborhood that Miss. Johnson was not aware of. Day or night, Miss. Johnson was on duty, looking out the window. On Halloween she would even hand out candy and fruit through her first-floor window. The thing that I really remembered about her was her sweet potato pies. Miss. Johnson sold them to anyone for one dollar a pie and they were good. She sold them in two flavors: cinnamon on top or nutmeg on top. She would just shout out the window to let us know that they were ready. I would run across the street with my two dollars to buy two pies, one cinnamon and one nutmeg. She would wrap them with wax paper and hand them to us out of her magickal portal. I remember the paper being steamed with the warmth of the pie as I carried them back to my house where my whole family was waiting for them. My younger sister has been practicing for years trying to imitate the taste of Miss. Johnson's pies, and she has managed to capture the taste of Miss. Johnson's pies. My sister's pies are delicious, and we couldn't even dream of having a family gathering without her bringing some of her pies to it. The following is the recipe for my sister's pie, and I hope you enjoy it as much as my family does.

Sweet Potato Pie Recipe

In a large bowl mix together the following ingredients:
- 3 large cooked and mashed yams or sweet potatoes
- 1 /2 cup of melted butter or preferred shortening
- 2 large eggs
- 1 /2 cup of sugar
- 1 /2 cup of brown sugar
- 1 /2 cup of sweetened condensed milk

- 1 3/4 oz package of vanilla instant pudding
- 1 1/2 teaspoon of nutmeg
- 1 1/2 teaspoon of cinnamon
- 1 tablespoon lemon juice
- 1 tablespoon of vanilla
- 1 tablespoon of Kahlua liqueur (optional)

Mix eggs, sugars and yams together, then mix all other ingredients until they are well blended. Add mixed ingredients into 2 deep-dish pie crusts. Sprinkle your choice of spices on top. Bake at 325 degrees for 20 to 35 minutes or until your fork comes out dry when poking it.

May you find what you are looking for in your journey, and may the Universe Bless ~ ASe'

READINGS

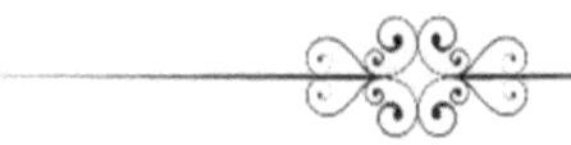

Bird, S. R. (2004). *Sticks, Stones, Roots & Bones: Hoodoo, Mojo & Conjuring with Herbs.* (Illustrated ed.). Llewellyn Publications.

Bunning, J. (1998). *Learning the Tarot: A Tarot Book for Beginners.* (Illustrated ed.). Weiser Books.

Campbell, J. (2008). *The Hero with a Thousand Faces (The Collected Works of Joseph Campbell.)* (Third ed.). New World Library.

Coelho, P. (2014). *The Alchemist, 25th Anniversary: A Fable About Following Your Dream.* (25th ed.). HarperOne.

Cunningham, S. (1996). *Wicca: A Guide for the Solitary Practitioner.* (1st ed.). Llewellyn Publications.

Dorsey, L. (2020). *Orishas, Goddesses, and Voodoo Queens: The Divine Feminine in the African Religious Traditions.* Weiser Books.

Franklin, J. H., & Moss, A. A. (2000). *From Slavery to Freedom: A History of African Americans.* (8th ed.). Knopf.

Gardner, G. B. (2004a). *The Meaning of Witchcraft.* RedWheel /Weiser.

Gardner, G. B. (2004b). *Witchcraft Today.* (Illustrated ed.). Citadel Trade.

Hall, J. (2003). *The Crystal Bible.* Walking Stick Press.

Hazzard-Donald, K. (2012). *Mojo Workin': The Old African American Hoodoo System.* (1st ed.). University of Illinois Press.

Initiates, T. (2018). *The Kybalion: Centenary Edition.* (Centennial ed.). TarcherPerigee.

Kumari, A. (2020). *Isese Spirituality Workbook: The Ancestral Wisdom of the Ifa Orisa Tradition.* Independently published.

Mbiti, J. S. (1990). *African Religions & Philosophy*. (2nd Revised & enlarged ed.). Heinemann.

Neimark, P. J. (1993). *The Way of Orisa: Empowering Your Life Through the Ancient African Religion of Ifa*. (1st ed.). HarperOne.

Smith, P. C. (2006). *Annancy Stories by Pamela Colman Smith*. *Amsterdam University Press*.

Starhawk, S. (1999). *The Spiral Dance: A Rebirth of the Ancient Religion of the Goddess: 20th Anniversary Edition*. (20th Anniversary ed.). HarperOne.

Virtue, D. (2008). *Angel Numbers 101: The Meaning of 111, 123, 444, and Other Number Sequences*. (5/13/08 ed.). Hay House Inc.

LINKS

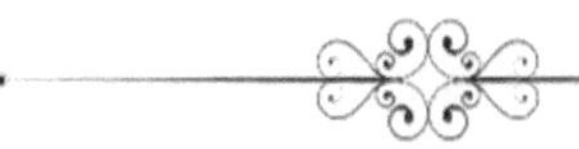

Cox, K. (2021, March 22). Nine-in-ten Black 'nones' believe in God, but fewer pray or attend services. Pew Research Center. https://www.pewresearch.org/fact-tank/2021/03/17/nine-in-tenblack-nones-believe-in-god-but-fewer-pray-or-attend-services/

Doreen Valiente Foundation. (n.d.). The Official Doreen Valiente Website - Doreen Valiente - Doreen Valiente Poetry. Retrieved 2022, from https://www.doreenvaliente.com/Doreen-Valiente-Doreen_Valiente_Poetry-11.php#sthash.3j863uEI.dpbs Charge of the Goddess

dowsing. (2020). Retrieved October 6, 2020, from https://www.oxfordreference.com/view/10.1093/oi/authority.20110803095729590

Fearnow, B. (2018, November 18). Number Of Witches Rises Dramatically Across U.S. As Millennials Reject Christianity. Retrieved September 17, 2020, from https://www.newsweek.com/witchcraft-wiccans-mysticism-astrology-witchesmillennials-pagans-religion-1221019

Gardner, MD, S. (2020). Slideshow: Dos and Don'ts of Essential Oils. Retrieved October 8, 2020, from https://www.webmd.com/skin-problems-and-treatments/ss/slideshow-essential-oils

Hart, T. (2009). Wicca. Retrieved September 22, 2020, from https://www.mtsu.edu/first-amendment/article/1379/wicca

History.com Editors. (2018, August 21). Wicca. Retrieved September 22, 2020, from https://www.history.com/topics/religion/wicca

Hobgood, K. (n.d.). Pythagoras and the Mystery of Numbers.

Retrieved October 6, 2020, from http://jwilson.coe.uga.edu/
EMAT6680Fa06/Hobgood/Pythagoras.html

Lewis, D. (2015, November 24). Lucy the Australopithecus Turns 41
(Plus 3.2 Million Years). Smithsonian Magazine. https://
www.smithsonianmag.com/smart-news/lucy-
australopithecusturns-41-180957384/

Liew, J. (2020, September 28). Venus Figurine. Retrieved September 28,
2020, from https://www.ancient.eu/Venus_Figurine/

MABE, C. (1989, November 18). *Sun Sentinel* - South Florida - Sun
Sentinel. Retrieved May 7, 2022, from
https://www.tribpub.com/gdpr/sun-sentinel.com/

Mankey, J. (2013, October 3). The Rede of the Wicca. Retrieved
December 17, 2020, from https://www.patheos.com/blogs/
panmankey/2013/10/redeofthewicca/

Magi | Encyclopedia.com. (2020, September 10). Retrieved September
21, 2020, from https://www.encyclopedia.com/philosophyand-
religion/ancient-religions/ancient-religion/magi

McRobbie, L. R. (2013, October 27). The Strange and Mysterious
History of the Ouija Board. Retrieved October 7, 2020, from
https://www.smithsonianmag.com/history/the-strange-
andmysterious-history-of-the-ouija-board-5860627/

Melyn. (2014, December 27). What does the Latin Word 'oraculum'
mean? Retrieved October 6, 2020, from http://latinmeaning.
com/what-does-the-latin-word-oraculum-mean/

Merriam-Webster. (2020). sympathetic magic. Retrieved October 7,
2020, from https://www.merriam-webster.com/dictionary/
sympathetic%20magic

Rhabdomancy. (2020). Retrieved October 6, 2020, from https:// occult-
world.com/rhabdomancy/

Runes | Encyclopedia.com. (2020, September 31). Retrieved October 7, 2020, from https://www.encyclopedia.com/literature-andarts/language-linguistics-and-literary-terms/language-andlinguistics/runes.

Sanderson, N. (2000, May 9). Viking Runes Through Time. Retrieved October 7, 2020, from https://www.pbs.org/wgbh/nova/article/viking-runes-through-time/

The American Society of Dowsers. (2020, August 3). Dowsing History. Retrieved October 7, 2020, from https://dowsers.org/ dowsing-history/

Witches' Rede. (2022). Massachusetts Institute of Technology. Retrieved March 1, 2022, from http://web.mit.edu/pipa/ www/rede.html

TMhome. (2013, July 15). Unified field of consciousness backed up by modern science. Retrieved October 8, 2020, from https://tmhome.com/news-events/unified-field-of-consciousness-onemany/

Vernor, E. (2011, November 1). Warlock Corvis Nocturnum on The Lexi Show "The Church of Satan".mp4. YouTube. https://www.youtube.com/watch?v=Yjnqd9Ut74c&feature=youtu.be

What Is Witchcraft? | Wicca. (2013, September 22). [Video file]. Retrieved from https://www.youtube.com/watch?v=jPSwnit_vr4

Wigington, P. (2019, February 9). Celebrate the Full Moon with an Esbat Ritual. Retrieved September 21, 2020, from https://www.learnreligions.com/esbat-rite-celebrate-the-fullmoon-2562864

Wyard, A. (2011). Glossary Definition: Metaphysical. Retrieved September 21, 2020, from https://www.pbs.org/faithandreason/ gengloss/metaph-body.html

Yankee Publishing, Inc., (2022). *Blue Moons: When Is the Next Blue Moon? Almanac.Com.* https://www.almanac.com/what- blue-moon

RESOURCES

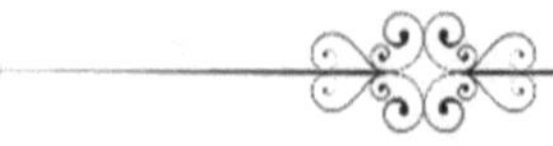

African American Magickal Books

Finding Soul on the Path of
Orisa: A West African
Spiritual Tradition
By Tobe Melora Correal

Isese Spirituality Workbook:
The Ancestral Wisdom of
the Ifa Orisa Tradition
By Ayele Kumari, PhD

Mojo Workin': The Old
African American Hoodoo
System
By Katrina Hazzard-Donald

Orishas, Goddesses, and
Voodoo Queens:
The Divine Feminine in the
African Religious Traditions
By Lilith Dorsey

Paschal Beverly Randolph:
A Nineteenth-Century

Rootwork: Using the folk
Magick of Black America for
Love, Money and Success
By Tayannah Lee McQuillar

Hoodoo Medicine: Gullah
Herbal Remedies
By Faith Mitchell

Jambalaya: The Natural
Woman's Book
By Luisah Teish

Of Water and Spirit: Ritual,
Magic, and Initiation in the Life
of an African Shaman
By Malidoma Patrice Some

African American Wiccan Society
Online School:

Black American Spiritualist,
Rosicrucian, and Sex
Magician
By John Patrick Deveney

Sticks, Stones, Roots and
Bones:
Hoodoo, Mojo & Conjuring
with Herbs
By Stephanie Rose Bird

The Way of the Elders: West
African Spirituality &
Tradition
*By Adama & Naomi Doumbia
Ph.D.*

*Portal of Light Extensive Study
Online.* www.aawiccan.org

The Way of the Orisa:
Empowering Your Life
Through the Ancient African
Religion of Ifa
By Philip John Neimark

Metu Neter: The Oracle of Tehuti
and the Egyptian System of
Spiritual Cultivation
By RA Un Nefer Amen

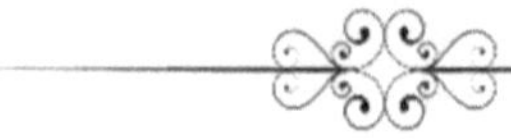

OTHER RESOURCES

The Hero with a Thousand Faces *By Joseph Campbell*	Learning the Tarot: A Tarot Book for Beginners *By Joan Bunning*
Living Wicca: A Further Guide for the Solitary Practitioner *By Scott Cunningham*	The Meaning of Witchcraft *By Gerald Gardner*
The Witches Qabala: The Pagan Path and the Tree of Life *By Ellen Cannnon Reed*	The Spiral Dance: A Rebirth of the Ancient Religion of the Great Goddess *By Starkawk*
Sacred Contract: Awakening Your Divine Potential *By Caroline Myss*	Witch School (First, Second and Third Degree) *By Lewis-Highcorrell*
The Power of the Witch: The Earth, The Moon, and the Magical Path to Enlightenment *By Laurie Cabot w/Tom Cowan*	Wicca: A Guide for the Solitary Practitioner *By Scott Cunningham*
Wicca Made Easy: Awaken the Divine Magic Within You *By Phyllis Curott*	Witchcraft Today *By Gerald Gardner*

GLOSSARY

Adinkras: Ghanian symbols representing concepts, popular proverbs or aphorisms. While they are often seen on tradition Akan cloth these symbols can be found on fences, homes, furniture, pottery and even made into tattoos.

Aku-Aba: This is a disk-head shaped fertility figure from Ghana, and its nearby areas. It is said to both bless for prosperity and to promote pregnancy. In Ghana they are consecrated by Priests and taken to women who wish to conceive a child.

As Above So Below: A paraphrase of a statement found in *The Emerald Tablet*, credited to be written by Tehuti Trismegistus (Thrice great) meaning, *all things on Earth are merely reflections of each other and of the Universe.*

ASe: It is often written as *Ashe'* and it is pronounced *Ah-Shay.* It is from the Yoruba language and is used as a strong word of affirmation. *ASe* means the divine life force or the life energy that resonates in all things. ASe is our power to make things happen. In Yoruba culture it is believed that the power of ASe is passed down to them from their spiritual Ancestors. The word ASe is used during, spell work, at the end of a prayer or even shouted out in affirmations similar to the word *Amen.* Ancestors: Either of blood line or beloved guardian spirits, Ancestors are those who dwell in the spirit realm and oversee and protect us. While mostly invisible they can make contact through dreams, meditation, divination or very often synchronicities.

Animism: The belief that all which is animate and inanimate has a soul and/or spirit, which proves the connected relationship between human beings and all things.

Archetypes: Are individual images, human models and patterns of behavior which can be unconscious symbols collectively inherited and recognized by the human psyche.

Ascension: Reaching a higher state of spiritual awareness. Connecting more with the Higher Self. Knowledge base increases. Reaching a higher level in the direction toward Source.

Astral Projection: A term used to describe an intentional out-of-body experience (OBE) where a person consciously wills the astral body to leave the physical body and travel through what is called the astral plane. The astral body can then consciously observe from a lucid and detached perspective while flying to desired locations.

Deosil: It is of Scottish-Gaelic language, meaning to walk or go in the same direction as with the hands of a clock or the Sun. Clockwise. For the purpose of magick this direction is said to help in gaining or adding or receiving.

Earthing: refers to the act of walking barefoot on the Earth's surface of grass, sand, rocks or dirt for the purpose of connecting to the Earth's natural healing energies and electrons in order to bring about healing, grounding and spiritual well-being.

Ebo: Meaning *"sacrifice"*, it is a practice within the Ifa religion with the theory that in order to receive something one must give something in sacrifice. It is about give and take. While some sacrifices may be in offerings, others may be of volunteer service or making personal changes within their lives.

Eclectic Witch: People who follow this witchcraft utilize different cultures, paths, traditions and beliefs, in order to incorporate and design their own practices. Eclectic Witches do not follow a path of religion or structure, but believes in the evolution of their practices.

Ether or Ethereal: When Pagans refer to the Ether (especially in paying hail) they are referring to the upper regions and all realms of the Universe, all multiverses and all planes of existence as well as out into space.

Feminism: Feminism: Is a social movement aimed to establish justice and equality, not only between the genders, but all other issues relating, but not limited to politics, social justice, economics, LGBTQ and spirituality. Feminism seeks to find balance between both the male and the female points of view.

Handfasting: An ancient Celtic wedding or partnership ceremony that dates back as far as 7000 BC. The ceremony consists of joining the couple's hands together and a Priestess or Priest tying them with cord or ribbon. This ceremony is used for many Pagan marriages today.

Inanna: Is the ancient Mesopotamian Sumerian primordial goddess who was worshipped as far back as 5000 years BCE. She was a goddess of sex, love and war. She was the precursor for many other goddesses like Venus, Aphrodite, Astarte and Ishtar. She was the first *goddess of the morning star* we now call Venus.

Gaia: In Greek mythos, She is the Greek goddess of Earth and Mother of all life. In Pagan and environmentalists' circles, Gaia is also the other name for Mother Earth when Earth is thought of as a living, breathing, ecological organism spreading blessings to all the life She nurtures and sustains.

Gullah: People of the Gullah-Geechee are Africans who were enslaved on the rice, indigo and cotton plantations of the lower Atlantic coast. They settled in the low, country regions of Georgia, Florida, South Carolina and North Carolina. The GullahGeechee have a rich culture, with some of their people still practicing root magick or root medicine.

Goddess-centered Spirituality: This spirituality is the practice of experiencing the divine female energies within the Universe. While it was predominately practiced from the Paleolithic Age with our early human Ancestors in Africa, it was suppressed with the predominance of organized religions. Goddess-centered spirituality is making a resurgence throughout the world where the Great Mother is worship by both men and women.

Green Man: He is the fertility aspect of the Pagan god. He is commonly hailed during the Spring and Summer months because He represents the cycle of the green seasons. Like the Maiden aspect He heralds in Spring and the burgeoning of fresh green growth. The Green Man is depicted with green leaves surrounding His face and body.

Lightworker: Is anyone who feels that they are here to bring light into the world for the purposes of peace, harmony and/or healing. While it is said that they are often people who have experienced hardship in their lives, it is not necessarily the case. Lightworkers are often people who are born for this cause.

Mojo Bags: These are magickal bags of power created to hold stones, crystals, herbs, charms, potions and more. These bags are usually created to imbue strong magick in order to receive luck, love, money or prosperity.

Nature: A nurturing feminine energy, also known as *Mother Nature*. Nature is connected to the Divine, and is a regulatory power which controls our environment in order to sustain us and all life.

Nether world: For the purpose of paying hail, the Nether world is all of that which is beneath our feet. It is often referred to as a place of the dead.

Neo-Paganism: An Earth-based movement in which practitioners have reconciled the old and ancient ways of paganism (such as polytheism) with ideas of contemporary times, and have adapted a practice similar to those of the ancient ways.

Ori: Term used in Ifa practices. It means *"the head"* and is the soul essence of a person's spirit and the spark of human consciousness. Ori is the divine self which is directly connected to Orisha energies.

Paganism: An umbrella term for the many Earth-based spiritualities and religions that are not Islam, Christian or Judaism. Examples of Pagan religions are Druidism, Hoodoo, Witchcraft, Wicca, Asatru, Celtic, Kemetism, Eclectic Pagan, etc.

Patriarchy: An oppressive systemic social structure of inequality, in which men dominate all aspects of society over women and minorities in areas of government, business, religion and financial systems. Wherein giving men privileges, social status and capital, that women and minorities have less access to.

Poppet: This term comes from old English root word *popet*, meaning doll. Poppets are usually people-shaped dolls and is used by Pagans for sympathetic magick.

Primordial: Being there from the beginning. Existing when matter and time was created.

Priestess/Priest: In Wicca, Priest and Priestess are the roles of the man or woman leading group rituals and deliberating over the initiations, study and degrees of others. Many solitary practitioners choose the path of self-initiation after studying

for a year or more. Often, the title of High Priestess and High Priest is given by Elders and mentors.

Purple Haze: Time of awakening characterized by euphoria, ambiguity, nebulousness and intense inspiration during a third-eye activation.

Reclaiming: In spirituality it is the recovery, retrieval and repossession of a spiritual culture or heritage which was prohibited, persecuted, lost, or faded from existence.

Sacrament: A Wiccan sacrament is the eating of food and drinks, which is usually cake, cookies and wine, while receiving blessings during ritual ceremony.

Sage Wand: An ancient tribal medium first used by some Native American nations. It consists of sage tied into a wand stick and burned, which is also called smudging. It is believed to have spiritual and cleansing properties.

Seven Hermetic Principles (Laws): The 7 Hermetic (Kemetic) Principles are an ancient set of guidelines said to have been written by Tehuti Trismegistus (Thrice great) the teacher of Ancient Mystery Schools in Kemet. People use these principles so to empower themselves. These laws are of *1) Mentalism, 2) Correspondence, 3) Vibration, 4) Polarity, 5) Gender, 6) Rhythm and 7) Cause & Effect.*

Shadow Work: Developed by the famous psychiatrist Carl Jung, shadow work is a form of healing by therapeutically exploring one's own unconscious self to find the part of the personalities and emotions that have been suppressed, be it positive or negative in order to reconcile with that self and bring it into the light.

Sumerians: Dating back 6000 years ago, the Sumerians created one of the first great civilizations in human history, known as *the cradle of civilization*. Sumerians were among the first to abandon their nomadic way of life and created cities, infrastructure and culture. Their homeland was Sumer in Mesopotamia, and they lived near the floodplains between the Tigris and Euphrates rivers, which is now present-day Iraq and Syria. Known as one of the earliest civilizations on Earth, Sumerians introduced their practices of farming techniques, spirituality, writing, mathematics and astronomy to the world.

Synchronicity: The term was first coined by psychiatrist Carl Jung, meaning the occurrences of mysterious and significant events in the form of meaningful coincidences like sequential or repeating numbers, words and symbols. It is believed that these events are messages from guardians, spirit guides or even the Universe connecting or giving a wink that one is on the right path or track in their lives.

Tehuti: This teacher of science, mathematics, philosophy, astronomy and magick was also known as Thoth or Hermes Trismegistus (thrice great). Thoth and Hermes were names given by the Greeks. Tehuti is given credit for writing the Emerald Tablets, being the head of the ancient Egyptian Mystery Schools and writing the 7 Hermetic Laws. He was later deified as an Kemetic god.

The Horned God: For Wiccans, the Horned god is viewed as the personification of Nature, and the energies of animals in the wild. He is also known as the god of Hunt from the time of ancient Europe. The Horned god is viewed as the divine mate, being both equal and opposite to the Goddess. Because he bares the antlers of deer and elk, the Christian church used His image to create their image of Satan and portrayed Him as evil. However, Neo-Pagans venerate him today as a powerful Nature spirit.

Trickster gods: These gods are in every cultural spiritual myth throughout the world. They usually hold a prominent role because they have purpose behind their tricks and troublemaking. Operating outside the framework of right and wrong, tricksters do not recognize the rules of society because of their degree of intellect or secret knowledge. They can pose as humans or animals and are often shapeshifters. In reality, trickster gods are teachers and inquisitors who teach lessons, and are valuable in life's journey, and are often the ones who give rewards to those who learn those lessons.

Universe: Is a term used (spiritually) to refer to, Source, the Divine, the Most High, the Divinity of God(dess) or *The ALL*.

Widdershins: A word of Scottish Gaelic origin, meaning to walk or go in the opposite direction to the hands of a clock, or the Sun, counter-clockwise. For the purpose of magick this direction is said to help in reducing or removing or eliminating.

Yin and Yang: This ancient Chinese symbol is well over 2000 years old. Yin and Yang is of Chinese philosophy and constitutes the concept in which the Universe contains polarities or dualities, and while each pole is totally opposite from the other, they are connected, in harmony, interdependence, and are complementary, interrelated and interactive. Yin represents the female aspect of the Universe and Yang represents the male aspect of the Universe. This philosophy is similar to the *Law of Gender* and the *Law of Polarities* (Dualities).

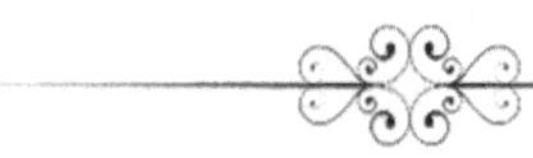

INDEX

Past life regression, 211
Patriarchy, 63, 86
Patrons, 104, 242
Pendulum, 161, 166, 168, 169
Pentacle, 86, 122, 123, 135
Perfect love and perfect trust, 254
Persephone, 104, 107
Petition, 124, 221, 244
Pineal gland, 23, 154, 232
Planetary Alignments, 205, 215
Poppet, 76
Portable altar, 127, 129
Poseidon, 111
Potions, 66, 67, 68, 71, 147, 227, 228, 229, 230, 231, 232, 261, 296
Priest, 2, 15, 35, 59, 71, 160, 161, 278, 295, 297
Priestess, iii, x, 2, 19, 20, 25, 35, 61, 75, 76, 102, 103, 107, 161, 278, 295, 297, 298
Primordial, 31, 36, 73, 75, 120, 295
Prophetic Dreams, 152, 154
Prosperity, 20, 94, 127, 131, 146, 158, 179, 197, 205, 211, 216, 228, 229, 231, 263, 264, 266, 269, 270, 271, 273, 274, 275, 293, 296
Purple haze, 22, 23
Pythagoras, 122, 195, 287, 288
Quarter days, 44
Rabdomancy, 166
Recipe, 283
Reclaiming, 74, 209
Reiki, 77
Releasing the circle, 245, 247
Religion, 4, 6, 9, 10, 12, 13, 14, 29, 33, 34, 46, 50, 57, 58, 63, 70, 75, 86, 87, 89, 249, 250, 287, 288, 294, 295, 297

Retrograde, 214
Rituals, 2, 3, 24, 32, 39, 40, 42, 43, 53, 55, 66, 70, 74, 81, 85, 88, 98, 103, 106, 114, 115, 118, 119, 121, 122, 123, 140, 147, 182, 188, 193, 201, 204, 205, 212, 216, 227, 232, 237, 238, 245, 297
Roman Church, 33
Root Doctor, 68
Runes, 161, 180, 181, 182, 183, 289
Sabbats, 4, 33, 43, 44, 46, 52, 63, 66, 129, 232, 237, 238
Sacraments, 245
Sacred Feminine, 24, 207
Sacred Geometry, 77
Sacred Masculine, 206
Sacrifices, 243
Sage, 16, 57, 121, 135, 191, 223, 239, 247, 264, 267, 298
Sage wand, 121, 239
Salves, 67
Samhain, 41, 50, 51, 58, 96, 97, 98, 99, 109, 117
Sangoma, 73
Santería, 59
Satanists, 80
Saturn, 46, 111, 206, 216
Saturnalia, 46, 208
Scrying, 54, 161, 176, 177, 231
Seasons, 4, 20, 28, 31, 32, 33, 42, 43, 44, 46, 50, 129, 296
Sekhmet, 104, 109, 114
Set, 111
Seven Universal Laws, 144
Shadow work, 53, 150, 154, 171, 197, 211, 226, 298
Shakti, 104